Research on China's Market Economy Development

Wei Liu

Research on China's Market Economy Development

Market-Oriented Reform Process and Economic Growth with a Structural Evolution

Translated by Chi Wei Su, Yannong Xie

中国财经出版传媒集团
经济科学出版社
Economic Science Press

Springer

Wei Liu
Renmin University of China
Beijing, China

ISBN 978-981-97-1400-1 ISBN 978-981-97-1398-1 (eBook)
https://doi.org/10.1007/978-981-97-1398-1

Jointly published with Economic Science Press
The print edition is not for sale in the Mainland of China. Customers from the Mainland of China please order the print book from: Economic Science Press

This Springer imprint is published by the registered company Springer Nature Singapore Pte Ltd.
The registered company address is: 152 Beach Road, #21-01/04 Gateway East, Singapore 189721, Singapore

Preface

From 1978 to 2008, the great cause of China's reform and opening up has been carried out for 30 years. In the past 30 years, profound changes have taken place in the level of economic growth, economic structure and market economic system. So, after 30 years of reform, what significant changes have taken place in China's economic growth level and economic structure? What are the internal relations between these changes and the institutional changes brought about by reform and opening up? What historical value orientation and method should be used to evaluate the effect of market economy reform? What criteria should be used to evaluate the marketization process and economic development mode of China's economy? That is to say, with the great institutional reform of China's reform and opening up, what changes have taken place in the institutional mode of China's social and economic development? What are the characteristics of this institutional change itself? Did the system change promote socioeconomic growth, if so, how? Is this economic growth based on increased efficiency? In other words, has the reform promoted the unprecedented acceleration of economic growth, and does such growth have real development significance and sustainability? Can the historical justice and progress of reform be proved in the sense of liberating and developing China's productive forces? Looking ahead, what are the main drivers of China's long-term sustainable economic growth? In a word, how to understand and evaluate China's socialist marketization process? How is the relationship between the level of economic growth, the change of economic structure and the improvement of economic efficiency in China's socialist marketization process? This is the central theme of this book. In other words, we should understand and analyze the rationality and progress of economic system reform from the perspectives of economic growth and economic development, expansion of economic scale and improvement of economic quality, acceleration of economic speed and improvement of economic efficiency. At the same time, it further reveals the historical requirements for the in-depth reform of the system, which is the basic issue of this book. Around this core proposition, this book is divided into the following three parts to discuss the development of China's market economy.

Part I: Characteristics of China's Socialist Market Economy Reform Process and the Value Judgment Criteria.

Firstly, this part discusses the value judgment of the reform effect. Along with the historical process of reform, profound changes have taken place in China's economy. On the one hand, unprecedented achievements have been made in the progress of modernization and the improvement of people's living standards. On the other hand, the contradictions in the social process are more complex and acute. It is hard to avoid controversy over reform, at least when it comes to consensus: Should we continue to reform? What historical standards should we use to evaluate reforms that have taken place? What historical values should we use to promote reform? All these have become issues that people are generally concerned about and urgently need to be resolved in social development. The research results of the book have been theoretically studied and answered.

Secondly, this part systematically explains the justice and progress of institutional change in theory. From the divergence and opposition between value theory and different market economy philosophies, this part examines the divergence of value orientation in economic theory regarding whether or not market system should be established and how to establish market system.

Thirdly, this part discusses the evaluation of China's marketization process and economic development mode. What historical stage has China's economic development reached and what are the salient features of this stage? It is always a controversial issue to measure the level of a country's social and economic development. According to the two basic indicators of economic quantity and economic quality, this part judges the level of China's economic development and concludes that China's economy is in a period of accelerating industrialization from the longitudinal perspective. Horizontally, China is now slightly higher than the average level of middle-income developing countries in the world. On this basis, the prominent characteristics of this stage after 30 years of reform and opening up, and economic development have been summarized and refined. This part summarizes the transformation characteristics of China's economic development using empirical method from several aspects, including ownership structure adjustment, changes in resource allocation mode, technological innovation and system evolution.

Fourthly, this part analyzes the relationship between the process of factor marketization and economic growth. The prominent feature of China's current marketization process is to accelerate the marketization of factors. Among the two basic growth factors, labor and capital, capital is more scarce in developing countries, so it is more significant to improve the efficiency of capital. So, the marketization of capital factor appears more important. From the perspective of China's reality, not only is the level of factor marketization far behind that of commodity marketization, but in the process of factor marketization the level of capital factor marketization is lower than that of labor factor marketization. This part reveals the reform path of China with banking and financial institutions as the main body in a comprehensive and in-depth way, puts forward a series of targeted reform suggestions and empirically studies the impact of the reform of the capital market and its financing mode on the actual economic growth.

Part II: Economic Growth Cycle and Aggregate Regulation in China's Socialist Market-Oriented Reform Process.

Firstly, this part discusses the long-term strategic objectives of China's economic growth and possible problems. Since the reform and opening up, China has maintained long-term high-speed economic growth. In 2002, China set a new long-term economic growth target of quadrupling its GDP in 20 years, and in 2007 it set a target of quadrupling its per capita GDP by 2020. This part analyzes and studies the possibility, trend, growth rate and possible problems of China's long-term economic growth from the aspects of the comparison between China's economy and East Asia's economy, resident disposable income, and the impact of China's future economic growth on China's international economic status. It reveals a series of problems that determine China's long-term development goals, such as urbanization, the contradiction between short-term surplus and long-term shortage of production capacity, energy and environmental constraints, and education and scientific and technological development.

Secondly, this part analyzes the characteristics of the economic periodic fluctuation in the system transition. With the deepening of marketization, the law of the economic cycle has begun to play a role in China. An important task of macro-control is to reduce the negative impact of such an economic cycle on economic growth through counter-cyclical operation. This part studies the performance, quantitative characteristics and formation mechanism of China's economic cycle, and points out how to make macro decisions according to the characteristics of China's economic activities at the present stage. Due to the historical process of China's industrialization and marketization and other development factors and institutional factors, the imbalance in China's current economic growth has a series of new complexities; the subject system reveals the main factors causing economic fluctuations.

Thirdly, this part analyzes and evaluates the macro-economic policy effects in the system transition. The part makes a systematic analysis of the complexity of contradictions in China's macro-economic operation since the reform and opening up, evaluates the effect of the use of macro-policy in stages, and reveals the factors that determine and influence the effect of the use of macro-policy tools. At the present stage of China's economic development and system, under the historical background of reform, a series of new characteristics have emerged in the macro-economic imbalance, and the corresponding macro-economic policies have also produced a series of new characteristics. The limitations of demand management have become increasingly apparent, and the requirements for supply management have become more and more obvious. This part puts forward and demonstrates the judgment of the transition from demand management to supply management in the new stage of development and new argumentation, putting forward the policy proposal that passes argumentation according to the current macroscopical economy situation.

Part III: Structural Changes and Growth Efficiency in China's Socialist Market-Oriented Process.

Firstly, this part analyzes the evolution path of China's economic structure since the reform and opening up from the quantitative and qualitative perspectives. From the perspective of the high level of industrial structure, the process of industrialization entered an accelerated period after 1998. By 2006, China's industrialization process had gone through a little more than one-third. This part analyzes the main influencing factors of China's industrial structure changes since the reform and opening up. Besides, it also studies the significance of industrial structure change to economic efficiency improvement from three perspectives. These studies show that in the 30 years from 1978 to 2008, although the changes in industrial structure once made a significant contribution to China's economic growth, with the improvement of marketization, the contribution of industrial structure changes to economic growth shows a decreasing trend, gradually giving way to technological progress. Especially after 1998, China's economic growth model has increasingly reflected its own sustainability.

Secondly, this part empirically analyzes the relationship between industrial structure, ownership structure, regional structure and China's economic growth. This part studies the correlation between industrial structure, ownership structure and China's economic growth through empirical analysis. Using the empirical data from China's reform and opening up, this part empirically investigates the role of market institutions as the goal of institutional change in resource allocation. Besides, this part tries to explain what kind of value orientation the market system should embody in order to adjust the reasonable economic structure through the market. Through the empirical analysis of the industrial structure, ownership structure and the interaction between the industrial structure and ownership structure of China's economy, it is found that the economic structure is unilaterally affected by the industrial structure or ownership structure, and also that the value orientation of market system plays a key role in the adjustment of economic structure through market.

Thirdly, this part analyzes the improvement of efficiency in China's economic growth since the reform and opening up and its impact on economic growth from two perspectives: factor productivity (labor productivity, total factor productivity) and input-output efficiency. Here, technological progress and industrial structure change are decomposed from factor productivity, and the contribution of industrial structure change to China's economic growth is empirically measured and compared with that of technological progress. Empirical research shows that in the 30 years from 1978 to 2008, although the changes of industrial structure once made a significant contribution to China's economic growth, with the improvement of marketization, the contribution of industrial structure changes to economic growth shows a decreasing trend, gradually giving way to technological progress. That is to say, the power of marketization embodied in the change in industrial structure will gradually give way to the power of technological progress. In addition, the study also found that the weakening of the effect of structural change does not mean that the benefits of market-oriented reform will disappear, and some development and institutional factors still hinder the further improvement of the efficiency of resource allocation. From this perspective, China still has a long way to go in improving the market mechanism. In addition, this part analyzes the change trend of China's intermediate consumption level since 1992 by using the input-output data over the years. The effects of technological progress, industrial structure change and price change on the intermediate consumption level of the whole national economy are studied through the direct consumption coefficient matrix and the intermediate demand consumption matrix time series of the three industrial sectors. The research shows that during this period, technological progress contributed to the reduction of the intermediate consumption level of the national economy and the improvement of economic growth efficiency. However, due to the change of price relationship and the increase of the proportion of sectors with higher intermediate consumption levels, the intermediate consumption rate of the entire national economy reflected by the current price increased instead. In order to change this trend, maintain the sustainable development of China and improve the input-output efficiency of various sectors, we should combine it with the adjustment and upgrading of industrial structure.

In a word, the basic logic of this book is as follows: firstly, it makes an essential analysis of the institutional changes brought about by China's economic reform. At the same time, the prominent historical changes brought about by the reform itself are discussed in particular. From the analysis of the system changes and the characteristics of the reform itself, the historical value orientation of the system changes, namely the development criteria of historical materialism, is clearly understood. Then, according to this historical materialism, we can judge the basic value criteria of the justice and progress of social productive forces development in the change of social production relations, and analyze the economic growth in China's institutional change, including the pace of economic growth and the particularity of the total imbalance in the process of growth. At the same time, it examines the particularity of macro-control on the total imbalance in the process of the reform of China's socialist market economic system, and then recognizes the growth and balance of market-oriented transition. Further, it is to investigate the effectiveness and quality improvement of this growth process in depth. Usually, people have less doubt about the pace and scale of economic growth in China's reform. That is to say, to a large extent, they acknowledge that reform has brought about growth, but there are more doubts about whether effective development has been achieved. Based on China's experience (1978–2008), this book, on the one hand, analyses the evolution of structure resulting from China's economic growth, and at the same time examines the structural benefits of structural changes. On the other hand, it demonstrates the effect of efficiency improvement on China's economic growth from two aspects: factor productivity and input-output efficiency. On the basis of the above investigation, this book makes an analysis of the institutional causes of China's economic growth and development, and puts forward the requirements of institutional changes for the change of China's economic development mode and the realization of sustainable development.

The main contribution of this book, or more prominent innovation, lies in the following aspects. (1) From the perspective of value theory, it reveals the basic motivation of arguing the justice of institutional change in economic theory, and clearly judges the value standard of reform progress from the analysis of the characteristics of China's reform historical process, so as to answer why the process of institutional change is always accompanied by the development of economy. The debate about basic theory, scope, especially value theory? Why does the system change need to support from the aspect of axiology? (2) How to explain the causes of the increasing institutional change? How does China's experience of economic growth explain the relationship between institutions and growth? What are the particularities of the total imbalance in the system transformation? In view of these particularities, what is the particularity of the aggregate demand and supply management, what is the significance of the aggregate supply management to the transitional society, and what are the system requirements? The answers to these questions not only deepen the understanding of China's reform and development experience, but also, more importantly, make distinctive discussions on macro-economic theories based on China's experience. (3) The most important is whether China's growth is the growth based on efficiency gains and therefore sustainable. This book not only makes an empirical analysis of the efficiency characteristics of China's economic growth from the aspects of the evolution of industrial structure, factor efficiency, input-output efficiency, etc. but also examines the motivation of the institutional reform behind the efficiency improvement, and then makes a more profound demonstration of the necessity and rationality of the reform. It is this emphasis on structural efficiency and total factor efficiency of economic growth. In the macro-analysis, besides considering the aggregate demand, the supply analysis is emphasized, and the macro-economic regulation and control mode, policy orientation and the corresponding micro-based market mechanism and order are further explained based on the demand of aggregate demand and aggregate supply and structural equilibrium.

This book is the final result of *Research on China's Market Economy Development*, one of the major research projects in the philosophy and social science research of Ministry of Education of the People's Republic of China. Liu Wei is the chief expert on this subject. The members are Xu Xianchun, Sun Qixiang, Huang Guitian, Lin Shuanglin, Wang Yuesheng, Liu Yi, Li Shaorong, Cai Zhizhou, Su Jian, Zhang Hui, et al. As a phased research results, around this basic theme "China's market economy development", four monographs were published in recent years; in addition, 34 academic papers were published in *Economic Research Journal, Social Sciences in China, China Industrial Economics, Journal of Financial Research, Journal of Peking University (Philosophy and Social Sciences), Journal of Management World, Economic Perspectives, Economic Science* and so on. Among them, Prof. Liu Wei, the chief expert on the subject, has published 11 papers and one monograph.

This book is mainly based on the research results independently completed by Prof. Liu Wei from 2002 to 2008 and the research results completed in cooperation with Huang Guitian, Cai Zhizhou, Li Shaorong, Su Jian, Zhang Hui, et al. It is also the systematization and deepening of the research results of these 7 years.

Beijing, China Wei Liu

Main Members of the Research Group

Yuesheng Wang
Qixiang Sun
Shaorong Li
Jian Su
Hui Zhang
Guitian Huang
Zhizhou Cai

Translation Team

Translators: Chi Wei Su, Yannong Xie
Senior Proofreader: Jinyan Hu

Contents

Part I
Characteristics of China's Socialist Market Economy Reform Process and the Value Judgment Criteria

This part consists of three chapters. Firstly, it discusses the progress and characteristics of the historical practice of China's economic reform, the historical evolution of the reform itself which brought about institutional changes, and value orientation and divergence of the reform from the analysis of the process of institutional change and reform evolution (Chap. 1). Then, it discusses the debate of economic theory on institutional change, especially on institutional reform and value orientation aiming at market economy (Chap. 2). Furthermore, on the basis of the analysis of the value orientation of the reform in practice and theory, this chapter examines the profound changes brought by the reform in China's economic development mode, and points out the internal relationship between the change of this economic development mode and China's economic growth and development. Or in other words, it analyses the reasons for the growth of China's economy from the changes of development mode, in order to clearly demonstrate the fundamental basis of the justice of reform in methodology (Chap. 3).

Chapter 1
What Historical Value Orientation Should We Take to Understand and Promote the Reform

With the historical progress of reform, China's economy has undergone extremely profound changes: on the one hand, the development of modernization and the improvement of people's living standards have achieved unprecedented achievements; on the other hand, the contradictions in the social progress are sharper and more complex. Therefore, it is inevitable that there will be controversy about the reform, at least, there will be serious difficulties in the consensus on the reform: Should we continue the reform? What kind of historical value orientation should be used to evaluate the reforms that have taken place? What historical values should we use to promote reform? All of these have become some issues of general concern. At the same time, they are also the problems that need to be solved urgently in the social development.

1.1 Social Economic Changes Brought by the Reform and the Historical Changes of the Reform Itself

1.1.1 The Social and Economic Changes Brought by the Reform Are Mainly Embodied in the Institutional Change and Economic Development in China

As far as institutional change is concerned, after 30 years of the reform and opening up, market mechanism has basically replaced planned system as the main mechanism of resource allocation in China, and price signal has replaced quantity signal as the main signal to guide resource allocation. Although there are still serious problems

---

The content of this chapter was published in the 5th issue of *Economic Perspectives* in 2006, as a stage achievement of the subject. Later, it was reprinted in the 16th issue of *Xinhua Digest* in 2006.

W. Liu, *Research on China's Market Economy Development*,
https://doi.org/10.1007/978-981-97-1398-1_1

such as disorder and unfair competition while at the same time people still have different opinions on the quantitative judgment of the specific degree of China's marketization process, there is a general consensus that the market mechanism has fundamentally replaced the status of the planning system.[1] Besides, it is generally acknowledged that the speed of China's marketization is faster than that of all countries in transition, especially in comparison with Russia's economic transformation. China's marketization index or economic liberalization index is generally considered higher than Russia's; in international trade practice, more than 70 countries have recognized China as a market economy country.[2]

In terms of economic development, China's economic reforms have contributed unprecedentedly to China's economic development, whether in terms of quantitative indicators of economic growth or qualitative indicators of structural changes in the economy, the degree of economic development or the level of social development, the progress of absolute indicators or the improvement of relative indicators, the social and economic progress of China since the reform and opening up has been unprecedented. The level of GDP, whether in total or per capita, has increased more than 10 times compared with the level before the reform and opening up, with an average annual growth rate of more than 9.8% in comparable terms. The proportion of agricultural employment has dropped from 80% at the beginning of the reform and opening up to about 43% at present. The proportion of food expenditure (Engel coefficient) in the household consumption structure of urban and rural residents has entered a well-off society (over 40%) after subsistence-level (over 50%) from the poverty state at the beginning of the reform and opening up (over 60%). These profound changes are indeed unprecedented in the history of China's economic development. In terms of the pace of development, it is rare even in the comparison of the history of world economic development.

In fact, in order to achieve a social consensus on reform, we must first answer the following questions: Do we acknowledge that reform has promoted China's social

[1] Scholars in China have made abundant achievements on the progress of China's marketization, such as Lu Zhongyuan, et al., "The Impact of Marketization on China's Economy", *Economic Research Journal*, No. 12, 1993. Jiang Xiaowei, et al., "Exploration of China's Market Economy", *Journal of Management World*, No.6, 1995. Former State Development Planning Commission Research Group, "Judgment of China's Economic Marketization", *Macroeconomic Management*, No.3, 1996. Gu Haibing, "The Latest Estimation and Judgment of China's Marketization Degree", *Journal of Management Science*, No. 2, 1997. Chang Xiuze, et al., "The Marketization Degree and Development Thought of China's National Economy", *Economic Research Journal*, No. 11, 1998. Fan Gang, et al., "The 2000 Report on the Marketization Process of China's Regions", *Journal of Chinese Academy of Governance*, No. 3, 2001. Chen Zongsheng, et al., *The Study of Chinese Economic System Towards Market Economy*, Shanghai: Shanghai People's Publishing House, 1999. Li Xiaoxi, et al., *Report on the Development of China's Market Economy in 2003*, Beijing: China Commerce and Trade Press, 2003.

[2] In the reports of the Heritage Foundation and the Frazer Institute, the speed of marketization and the degree of economic liberalization of China ranked before Russia. In the analysis carried out by the World Bank, the speed of marketization in China was also among the top countries in transition. In the *Economic Freedom of the World:* 2000 *Annual Report* proposed by the Frazer Institute, China ranked 101, while Russia ranked 116. In the *2003 Index of Economic Freedom* published by the American Heritage Foundation, China ranked 121 and Russia ranked 131.

and economic development unprecedentedly? Does China's social and economic progress have a profound internal historical logical connection with the reform and opening up? Is social and economic development the most important or fundamental proof of the historical progress of the reform and opening up? Can contradictions and problems arising from the reform and opening up fundamentally negate its historical progress? Are the contradictions and problems in reform and development mainly caused by marketization itself, or are they mainly caused by insufficient depth of marketization and imperfect market mechanism? Is the objective existence of the contradictions and problems facing China's social and economic development a reason to negate the previous reforms or a new requirement for the further deepening of future reforms? In principle, the answers to these questions should be found and explained from the historical facts of the social changes brought by the reform and opening up in accordance with the basic methods of historical materialism.

After 30 years of reform from 1978 to 2008, we may be able to summarize the outstanding characteristics of the reform in China. In that case, the following characteristics are very prominent. (1) Basic purpose and institutional objectives of China's reform are to seek the unification of the basic system for the co-development of various ownership systems on the basis of socialist public ownership and the resource allocation mode in which the market is the basic force for allocating resources, that is, the socialist market economy with Chinese characteristics. It can be said that the real difficulty of China's reform, or its fundamental feature, lies in the unification of the public ownership of means of production and market mechanism, which is not only a breakthrough in the traditional dogma of Western economics, but also a development of traditional Marxist economics that negate the mutual integration of public ownership and market; it is not only a critique of the fundamental value of the so-called "Washington Consensus" regulated by Western value standard, but also the real difficulty of socialist economic reform. (2) The basic way and process of China's reform is to follow the principle of gradual progress, rather than the "shock therapy" advocated by Western scholars. This "gradual" reform is not only the price reform or some other specific reform that has taken a gradual approach, but also a gradual progress in an all-round way: under the conditions of significant urban–rural differences characterised by a dual economy, we should adopt the comprehensive reform of gradually transferring from rural to urban areas; under the condition that enterprises and governments are facing important institutional defects at the same time, we should first take enterprise reform as the core and then gradually transfer the reform core to reforms of government and social security system; in the process of enterprise reform, we should shift the reform core from state-owned enterprise reform to non-state-owned enterprise system innovation and reform; in the two interrelated but differentiated aspects of enterprise reform and price reform, the focus is gradually shifted from price reform to enterprise reform, especially the reform of enterprise property rights, and further to promote the transformation of reform in both aspects at the same time; in the major adjustment of economic relations dealt by the reform, the reform of distribution relations has gradually deepened into the essential field of production relations, especially the property rights relations; in the process of the reform and opening up, it has been gradually deepened from coastal areas to the mainland; especially in the price reform, it has been pushed forward from the "double-track system" to the comprehensive market pricing. Generally speaking, in the way of reform, we should start from the most urgent aspects, start from the local aspects, and start from the areas where consensus is relatively easy to achieve, and gradually deepen and fully develop. On the whole, in the way of reform, we should start from the aspects of the most urgent need for reform, start from the partial parts, and start from the areas where consensus is relatively easy to achieve, and gradually deepen and fully develop the reform. (3) The basic logic and fundamental goal of China's reform is that basing on the requirements of development and promoting development. If reform as a system change belongs to the transformation of production relations, then, according to the basic principles of historical materialism, the nature and movement of production relations fundamentally depend on the nature of social productive forces and the requirements of development. From the very beginning, China's reform has clearly taken liberation and development of social productive forces as its fundamental purpose, and made it clear that "development is the absolute principle" and "development is the first priority". That is to say, all reforms should radically obey the requirements of development. The objectives and processes of reform should be done according to the requirements of development, and the results of reform should be tested by development.

1.1.2 The Historical Progress of Reform Gives New Features to Reform

Reform is historical, so, after 30 years of reform progress from 1978 to 2008, what historical changes have taken place in the reform itself? Or rather what new features have been given to the reform by the historical progress?

1.1.2.1 Whether the Core of Reform or the Key to the Successful Reform Lies in Enterprise Reform? In Particular the State-Owned Enterprise Reform should be Transformed to Government Reform, Especially to the Transition of the Function of the Central Government

At the beginning of the reform and opening up, we clearly pointed out that the core of the reform and opening up in the new era is to invigorate enterprises, especially the reform of state-owned enterprises. The clarity of this reform core is fundamentally different from the core issues dealt by the previous system adjustment in China. However, after the reform progress since 1978, can we still say that the key or core proposition of China's reform is enterprise reform, especially the reform of state-owned enterprises? It should be said that with the progress of denationalization,[3] the proportion of assets of state-owned enterprises has continued to decline, and the position and role of state-owned enterprises in the national economy have undergone fundamental changes. Therefore, the key to deepening reform is not so much the reform of enterprise, especially state-owned enterprises, but the reform of the government, especially the central government, including the transformation of government functions and policy transmission mechanism.

Taking enterprise reform as the core, especially the core link of all reforms all made up of the reform of state-owned enterprises, not only had great revolutionary significance, but also was the stipulation of historical conditions at that time. As early as 1978, before entering the new period of the reform and opening up, China in the planned economy era had made several major economic restructurings, but the basic problem it dealt with was the relationship between the central government and local governments, which did not really involve enterprises in terms of system, let alone take enterprise reform as the main content. The important reason is that in the course of the formation of our traditional planned economic system, although taking the Stalin model of the Soviet Union as a paradigm, we have not established our planned economic system in full accordance with the Stalin model based on different national conditions. What is important is that we have not emphasized the vertical centralized management of the central government as the Soviet Union did, that is, the so-called "Sectoralism" or "direct management". But we implemented the policy of "walking on two legs" While emphasizing the vertical management of the central government. Under the premise of the centralized plan of the government, local governments at all levels have a considerable amount of power, that is, the so-called "combination of direct and indirect management". Therefore, on the one hand, compared with the traditional Stalin model, it is more conducive to mobilizing the enthusiasm of local governments and more dynamic; on the other hand, there is a long-standing problem of "conflicts between direct and indirect management" in China's planned economic system. Coordination of this contradiction has accordingly become the main task of previous institutional adjustment under the planned economic system, while enterprise reform is ignored. What is different from the past is that the reform objectives put forward by the Third Plenary Session of 11th Central Committee of the Communist Party of China (CPC) held in the autumn of 1978 have clearly defined the indispensable position of enterprise reform in the whole economic reform from the very beginning. And it was proposed that, at present, a serious defect of China's economic management system is that the power is too centralized, which should be boldly delegated under leadership, so that local governments and enterprises can have more autonomy in operation and management under the guidance of the unified national plan. Efforts should be made to reduce economic and administrative institutions at all levels and to delegate most of their functions and powers

[3] According to the latest economic census, the proportion of capital of state-owned industrial and commercial enterprises in the total capital of enterprises has decreased from nearly 90% at the beginning of the reform and opening up to about 48% in 2004.

to enterprise-based specialized companies or joint ventures.[4] It is because of the enterprise reform as an important part of the entire economic reform, the system reform in the new period is incomparable with the system adjustment in both depth and breadth.

After 30 years of reform from 1978 to 2008, the reform of state-owned enterprises has gone through several important stages. The first stage is from the Third Plenary Session of the 11th CPC Central Committee in 1978 to the 14th CPC National Congress in 1992. The basic content of the reform of state-owned enterprises in this stage is to "streamline administration and delegate power, decentralize power and transfer profits". Various measures have been taken to expand the authority of enterprise management, and various ways, such as profit retention, replacement of profit delivery by taxes and contract system have been adopted to expand the interests of enterprises and standardize the distribution of interests between enterprises and the government. The second stage is from the 14th CPC National Congress in 1992 to the 16th CPC National Congress in 2002. The features and main contents of the reform of state-owned enterprises at this stage lie in the following aspects: Firstly, since the 14th CPC National Congress has clearly established the socialist market economic system as the institutional objective of the reform, the reform of state-owned enterprises should be carried out systematically and consciously around how to meet the requirements of the socialist market economy, so that the main content of the reform of state-owned enterprises will be expanded from the general management authority and the adjustment of distribution relations to the reform of property rights system and ownership relation. Therefore, it is an important task to reform the modern enterprise system of state-owned enterprises, especially large and super-large state-owned enterprises. In particular, the Third Plenary Session of the 14th CPC Central Committee held in 1993 made a clear summary of the acquisition of this modern enterprise system and the basic principles for the construction of modern enterprise system in China. It pointed out that "clearly established ownership, well-defined power and responsibility, separation of government administration and enterprise management, and scientific management" are the basic institutional characteristics of the reform of modern enterprise system in state-owned enterprises in China.[5] Secondly, since it is clear that the socialist market economic system is based on public ownership and the long-term cooperation of multi-ownership economy is taken as the ownership basis, it is not only necessary to develop various non-public economies, but also necessary to denationalize enterprises in the reform of the state-owned enterprises, especially the small and medium-sized state-owned enterprises in a considerable number of competitive fields, which is called "retain the large, release the small". The report of the 15th CPC National Congress of the Communist Party of China gives a systematic explanation of the ownership basis of China's socialist market economy. The third stage is from the 16th CPC National Congress held in

[4] See Communique of the Third Plenary Session of the Eleventh Central Committee of the Communist Party of China.

[5] See Communique of the Third Plenary Session of the Fourteenth Central Committee of the Communist Party of China.

2002 to the present. The basic content of the reform of state-owned enterprises in this stage is to promote the transformation and construction of the corporate governance structure of state-owned enterprises on the basis of promoting the reform of the modern enterprise system of state-owned enterprises, especially the property right system of enterprises, and to carry out the construction of joint-stock system to meet the requirements of market and international open economy. On the basis of adjusting the state-owned economy's control over the whole national economy, we should implement the principle of "where to advance and where to withdraw, what to do and what not to do", accelerate the ownership transformation of small and medium-sized state-owned enterprises in the process of promoting the strategic transfer of the state-owned economy, and make strategic structural adjustment of the whole state-owned economy and the distribution of state-owned enterprises.

Besides, while carrying out the transformation of the modern enterprise system and the construction of the corporate governance structure of large and extra-large state-owned enterprises, we should promote the improvement of the industrial organization of state-owned enterprises. While relatively clarifying the rights and interests of state-owned asset investors and exercising the rights of investors at different levels, it has promoted the restructuring and merger of state-owned enterprises, improved the status of industrial organization, and improved market competitiveness and the effectiveness of market competition.

With the deepening of the reform of state-owned enterprises themselves, the economic operating environment faced by state-owned enterprises has also changed significantly. Firstly, except for a few industries such as oil, railway, aviation, electricity, steel and automobiles, which still retain some mandatory plans, most state-owned enterprises have been pushed into the market. Market price signal has become the main signal to regulate the whole social and economic operation, including state-owned enterprises. Market competition mechanism has begun to become the basic mechanism to regulate the conduct of enterprises. Secondly, the rapid growth of the non-state-owned economy and the continuous improvement of openness to the outside world, especially after China's accession to the World Trade Organization (WTO), have put more and more market competition pressure on the state-owned enterprises. Thirdly, financial and tax system has gone through tax for profits, tax farming system, and tax distribution system to the reform and adjustment of the new tax system. In terms of tax system, not only does the institutional preference of state-owned enterprises no longer exist, but also its institutional burden has become an important factor affecting its competitiveness. Fourthly, with the reform of state-owned enterprises changing from decentralization to contracting, from joint-stock system reform to modern enterprise system construction and non-state-owned enterprises transformation, the government's direct administrative intervention in state-owned enterprises has been gradually weakened. Fifthly, with China's entry into WTO and the increase of capital inflow, the competition between foreign capital and state-owned enterprises in China's domestic market is intensified, and the state-owned enterprises are further pushed into international competition. Sixth, from allocation to loan and from debt to equity, from the development of direct financing market to the cultivation of indirect financing market, from the independence of the central bank to the construction of commercial banking system, from the political separation of banks to the construction of multi-type joint-stock banks, the investment and financing system and mode of state-owned enterprises have undergone profound changes. The market conditions for investment and financing have gradually improved, and the market binding force has gradually strengthened.

Of course, the reform of state-owned enterprises still has a series of difficult problems to be solved urgently so far. Firstly, how to realize the separation of state-owned enterprises from government effectively and make them accept the economic qualitative rules of the market first rather than the constraints of the ultra-economic administrative rules, that is, how to integrate the separation of government and enterprise scientifically with the separation of government and capital? Secondly, how to construct the governance structure of state-owned enterprises effectively and make the state-owned enterprises form effective restriction in power, responsibility and interests while not lacking sufficient incentives?

However, after 30 years of reform from 1978 to 2008, compared with the initial stage of reform, the position of the reform of state-owned enterprises has changed historically in the whole economic reform. For the construction and reform of the socialist market economic system in China, the transformation of government functions and the changes of the macro-control mechanism and mode made by government on national economy have increasingly become the key to restrict and determine the deepening of the marketization reform; the establishment and perfection of the social security system, including education, medical care, pension and unemployment insurance, have increasingly become a prominent contradiction in the social system changes. It can even be said that the position of the reform of state-owned enterprises in the whole economic reform has not only changed historically. The core proposition of the whole reform has not only gradually shifted from the reform of state-owned enterprises to the reform of government and society, but also relied on the transformation of government functions and the reform of government regulation mechanism to a considerable extent to effectively solve the new problems faced by the reform of state-owned enterprises. The reform of public finance system and monetary policy system in particular, depends on the perfection of social security system and market environment.

1.1.2.2 Does the Basic Content of the Reform Change from the Construction of Socialist Market Economy System to the Perfection of Market Economic Order?

The basic task of the economic reform is to replace the planned economy system with the market economy system as the basic system of allocating resources, and to replace the quantity signal with the price signal as the main signal of allocating resources. Therefore, it is a historical necessity for the reform to take price reform as the forerunner and market conduct system (enterprise system) reform as the primary task.[6] After decades of reform, it can be said that at present, although there are still differences in understanding the degree of progress of China's market economy, it has become a common consensus to recognize that market mechanism has replaced the planned mechanism in the national economy. After decades of reform, the market has replaced the dominant position of the plan in terms of the dominant power of allocating resources and the scope of the market mechanism; in modern economic life, even if the market mechanism is the main resource allocation force, there cannot be a complete market economy, and there will always be areas where market fail to function, so the market progress is always limited; in other words, the improvement of fairness and order of market competition, or the quality construction of market economy, cannot be realized fundamentally within decades, but without limitation. Therefore, after decades of marketization advancement, China's reform process with socialist market mechanism as its institutional objective has changed from giving priority to quantity construction, that is, broadening the space of market mechanism, to giving priority to quality construction, that is, enhancing the fairness and effectiveness of market competition. After all, the improvement of the quality of market mechanism is the construction and continuous improvement of market order. Firstly, the subject order of market competition answers the question of "who is competing", whose essence is the enterprise property right system; secondly, the transaction order of market competition answers the question of "how to compete", whose essence is the price-determining system; the unification of the subject order and the transaction order constitutes the internal competition mechanism of market economy. Like the internal competition mechanism, the external environmental order construction of market economy is also indispensable. The first is the rule of law order of market economy, that is, how to protect market competition mechanism and order with legal system and rule of law. After all, market economy is a law-governed economy, because market economy implements legal power in content and adopts universal contract in form. The second is the moral order of market economy, that is, how to support market economy civilization in moral spirit. After all, market economy is a credit economy, so the moral order with integrity as the core is the objective requirement of the process of market economy civilization; the unification of rule of law order and moral order constitutes the most important and basic external order of market economy. Obviously, the construction of the internal competition order and the external environmental order of social economy is a very long historical process.[7]

Focusing on the quantity construction and scale structure of market mechanism to the quality construction and order improvement of market mechanism, we need to understand the historical characteristics of the market economic order construction in China:

[6] Although there are disputes about which is more important in price reform or enterprise reform, it is a common understanding that the primary task of reform is to cultivate the internal competition mechanism in the market.

[7] See Liu Wei, "*The Cultural View of Market Economy in China*", cited from *My View of Market Economy*, Nanjing: Jiangsu People's Publishing House, 1993.

(1) The dual transition of China's economy has sharpened the contradictions faced by the market economic order construction. In the history of developed capitalist countries, commercial revolution is usually carried out first, then industrial revolution is promoted, that is, marketization system is realized first, and then industrialization is completed under the institutional conditions of market mechanism. In other contemporary countries with economic transition, industrialization is usually completed first, and then marketization transformation of the system is carried out. That is to say, industrialization has been realized under the traditional planned economy system, and then marketization reform is promoted on the basis of industrialization development. In short, industrialization and marketization should be separated and dealt with respectively in terms of time. But China is different. While China has achieved industrialization, it has promoted marketization, that is, at the same time as the economic development model has undergone rapid changes, the economic system has also undergone profound changes. This dual transition of development mode and system mode has brought us a series of special contradictions in the process of marketization. On the one hand, the rapid deepening of industrialization and the profound changes in the economic structure have resulted in social contradictions that require the rapid improvement of economic system order to improve the institutional capacity to deal with development contradictions. At the same time, chaos and disorder may arise because various institutional changes lag behind the requirements of economic development. On the other hand, the process of reform and marketization brings about the progress of industrialization and the liberation of productivity. At the same time, the conflicts of interest and the resulting social instability triggered by reform may seriously undermine the process of industrialization and development. In this special historical process of "double transition", how to effectively and orderly promote the construction of market economy order in accordance with the historical requirements of economic development constitutes an important particularity of the construction of socialist market economy order in China.
(2) The reform of enterprise system and the reform of market price system are promoted simultaneously, which makes the historical process of market order more uncertain. In the history of economic development, almost all marketization has been carried out on the basis of private capital ownership, including the Federal Republic of Germany and Japan after the Second World War. They vigorously promoted market reform without price control, and took the existing capitalist private ownership as the fundamental system foundation. The transition of price system in these countries is based on the free enterprise system which already has the basis of private capital ownership. In other words, when these countries promote the reform of market transaction order (price system), the order of transaction subject (enterprise property right system) is clear and established. But China is different. The process of marketization in China is to promote the reform of enterprise property right system and market price system at the same time. On the one hand, how to construct the modern enterprise property right system and corporate governance structure required by the socialist

market economy based on the fundamental system foundation in which public ownership is the main subject and multi-ownership economies develop together is a difficult problem that needs to be explored in depth, especially in practice. Under the condition that the enterprise property right system is not clear, it is very difficult for the conduct of market to be really constrained by market planning in the property right system. Thus, the result of price liberalization is not convergent, but divergent. There is no possibility that price liberalization tends to become balanced in the system. On the other hand, the disorder of market price order in transition can be explained to a considerable extent from the disorder of market order, including unfairness in market access and institutional discrimination, which lead to insufficient competition and monopoly pricing. The lack of the subject qualification and the ability of property rights responsibility to enter the market, leads to market price chaos and irresponsible indulgence and so on. All are deeply related to the chaos of the main order. In addition, the disorder of market transaction order not only makes it difficult for enterprises to follow market rules to join fair competition, but also brings about a certain sense of "adverse selection" phenomenon, that is, to expel enterprises that strive to follow market planning from the market, so as to make the market order more chaotic.

(3) How to unify the construction of internal competition order and the external social environment order of market economy is another special proposition that must be dealt with in the construction of market economy in China. In the economic history, the process of marketization requires that the society promote democratization, legalization and social spiritual changes, including various ideological emancipations and religious reforms. In fact, they all create necessary social conditions for the process of marketization. The basic content of the external social environment order of market economy is the rule of law order and moral order of market economy. As far as China's current rule of law order is concerned, the most prominent problems lie in two aspects. On the one hand, due to the drastic changes in economic life, coupled with the unique stability of the legal system construction and the lag of changes in economic life, the construction of the rule of law lags behind the changes in the economic mode of economic reform in many aspects in the process of transition, thus forming the "no law to abide by" situation in some aspects of the economic order. This phenomenon of "no law to abide by" also existed in developed countries. Due to the social and economic development and the progress of science and technology and other factors, the construction of the rule of law order is difficult to fully adapt to social development, especially to the requirements of economic development. Because China's society is in the process of dual transition, the construction of the rule of law order have to face the challenges of economic development and institutional change at the same time. On the other hand, the construction of the rule of law order should not only ensure the supply of the legal system and make the society observe the law, but also cultivate the spirit of the rule of law, that is, the conscious spirit of abiding by the law. Otherwise, there will be a general "failure to observe the law", a lack of spirit of the rule

of law, which deepens the disintegration of the rule of law order in the market economy. China has thousands of years of feudal tradition. The real construction of socialist market economy has only lasted about decades. The cultivation of the spirit of the rule of law is still a long way to go. The lag of the cultivation of the spirit of the rule of law has brought serious difficulties to the construction of market economy order in China, and has greatly increased the social cost of the construction of market economic order. The core of moral order in market economy is "honesty", because market economy itself is a credit economy based on credit relationship. Without "honesty", moral order will be chaotic, and it will be difficult to form a market economy order as a credit economy. It is generally believed that in the traditional natural economy society, the core of its moral order is "loyalty". In the modern market economy society, the core of its moral order is "honesty". In the process of institutional transition, moral "anarchy" is the most common phenomenon. That is to say, with the change of traditional economy, the "loyalty" criterion begins to fail. And because the development of market economy needs a long historical period and the transformation of social morality has a hysteretic nature, the moral order with "honesty" as the core, which is in line with market economy, has not been really established, so it may lead to people's lack of "loyalty" and "honesty" among themselves, resulting in serious "indulgence" in the social moral order. The rule of law order and moral order of market economy are deeply connected, and there is inherent unity between the rule of law and the rule of virtue. On the one hand, the moral order of market economy is the social spiritual basis of the construction of the rule of law order, and the cultivation of the legal spirit of society directly constitutes the important content of the rule of law order in particular; on the other hand, the rule of law order is an important constraint on the moral anarchy. In the legal system, the act of losing morality and credibility must bear the corresponding cost, which is also a powerful constraint on the act of losing morality. The construction of moral order in market economy needs not only to guide people to "refuse to cheat", but also to make people "dare not cheat".

1.1.2.3 Has the Key Point of the Historical Process of Reform Changed from Product Marketization to Marketization of Factors?

China's marketization progress is relatively rapid, but through further analysis it can be found that in 30 years, from 1978 to 2008, the key point of China's marketization progress is commodity marketization, including the marketization of investment products and consumer goods. If we take how to price as the basic criterion to judge the marketization, then we can say that the degree of marketization of commodities in China is quite sufficient at present. The price of at least 90% of commodities are determined by the market instead of the government. This is a fundamental change compared with the initial stage of the reform and opening up. The root of the problem lies in the fact that the more important content of marketization is in factor liberalization, including labor, capital, land and other factors. Moreover, the institutional changes required by factor liberalization are far more profound than the marketization of commodities. From the perspective of China's reform process, labor marketization is relatively fast in the development of various factor markets. Most of the wages (price) are determined by the market no matter it is rural or urban labor force. The proportion of the government's administrative decision on wage level is very low, although the fairness, orderliness and effectiveness of China's labor market competition still need to be improved. Relatively speaking, the degree of capital marketization in China is relatively low; the growth rate of both direct and indirect financing markets is also relatively slow. As far as the development of direct financing market is concerned, firstly, the scale is small. Less than 5% of the capital formation of industrial and commercial enterprises comes from direct financing market. The second is disorder, and it is an indisputable fact that China's stock market is too speculative; as far as the development of indirect financing market is concerned, the first is that the price (interest rate) is basically determined by government administration rather than the market, and the second is that the state-owned financial capital occupies an absolutely dominant position. Therefore, the prominent contradiction in the process of China's marketization lies in how to accelerate and deepen the capitalization, though interest rate control has begun to relax and considerable progress has been made in the reform of banking system. Compared with the capital marketization, the marketization degree of land factor in China is lower, including urban land and rural farmland no matter in the property rights system or in the trading system; the conditions of market allocation of land factor are far from available no matter in price determination or in the legal system. The lagging development of factor liberalization is a prominent contradiction in deepening reform process with the socialist market economy system as its basic objective, which fundamentally restricts the marketization of China.

It is because of the historic changes in the reform itself (which do not involve the objective economic development basis and changes in various social environments that the reform faces), that the reform must be deepened historically in the way, in the motive force, or the focus and scope of reform. Any stagnation, any denial of deepening reform, is unacceptable in the historical process of China's social development.

1.2 The Pluralism of Evaluation Criteria and the Complexity of Requirements for the Reform

With the development of social economy and the historical changes of economic reform itself, the socioeconomic development constantly puts forward new requirements for system reform, and the reform itself has formed a series of new characteristics. Therefore, people's evaluation criteria and requirements for the reform will be more diversified and complicated objectively. The value judgment criteria of the social reform performance have begun to change from a single and clear one to a more comprehensive and systematic standard. At the beginning of the reform, the contradictions of social development that need to be solved are relatively clear, and the requirements for development of productive forces are relatively explicit. For Chinese society without solving the problem of food and clothing, the most urgent requirement is to secure adequate food and clothing. Therefore, development, especially economic development, the liberation of productive forces and improvement of people's living standards which brought by development have become the most direct and convincing basic criteria for judging the reform. However, after many years of reform and development, the social economy has been lifted out of poverty, and secure adequate food and clothing, entered a moderately prosperous society in all respects. At the same time, the contradiction of social development is more complex, the social problems caused by unbalanced development are more acute, how to understand and deal with the relationship between fairness and efficiency is more uncertain, and the different demands of different interest groups for social change are more profound. As a result, the evaluation criteria of social reform are becoming more and more comprehensive, and the objectives of deepening reform are increasingly diversified. How to deepen the reform in the historical changes of comprehensive evaluation standards and diversified objectives and requirements is a new historical proposition we are facing.

At this stage, people's evaluation criteria for reform can be summarized into at least three categories. The first category is institutional criterion, which judges the historical value orientation of reform and to examine the nature of historical progress of reform with certain institutional characteristics; the second category is the developmental criterion, which measures and judges the historical justice of reform by the impact of institutional changes on social development, especially on social and economic development; the third category is interest criterion, which measures and judges the nature of reform progress by the improvement of interest and the change of interest structure. These three kinds of evaluation criteria are not separated from each other, but have profound internal relations. Usually, when people evaluate the reform, they also try to proceed from the unification of the three kinds of criteria above. However, when analyzing and judging the value orientation of the reform, different aspects are usually emphasized, which leads to different criteria of the reform.

Judging the direction and nature of the reform from the institutional criterion and standardizing the reform with the requirements of the institutional criterion have its historical objective necessity. Because China's reform is aimed at establishing a socialist market economy, the institutional evolution promoted by the reform must first maintain the direction of socialism, and the economic system established must have the basic nature of a socialist society. Adhering to the socialist orientation of reform is not only the belief of the reform and opening up led by the CPC, but also the objective trend proved by Chinese history. There are two problems: on the one hand, what is socialism? At least until now, in the theory and practice of the development of scientific socialism, it is still a proposition to be discussed. Therefore, if we start from abstract doctrine, from established theory and from the so-called basic institutional characteristics, we may suffocate the reform fundamentally by seeking the nature and characteristics of socialism and use them as the criteria to measure whether the reform is correct, just and progressive. The cause of socialism is, first and foremost, China's great practice, and reform itself is an important historical way to create the great practice of socialism. Firstly, the socialist cause is China's great practice, and reform itself is an important historical way to create the great practice of socialism. On the other hand, the close historical integration of the socialist cause and China's destiny shows that the socialist road meets the requirements of China's historical development, but at the same time, it also shows that only the system that truly and effectively solves the contradictions and problems in China's social development is socialism with Chinese characteristics, and that the socialist social system with Chinese characteristics should not be an abstract doctrine divorced from China's reality, but should be a package which includes all the institutional arrangements and tools that are conducive to the development of China's modernization cause. Therefore, the characteristics of the system itself shouldn't be used as the characteristics of judging the reform in isolation and motionlessness, because the progressiveness of all systems needs to be proved by practice. We can't simply say that only socialism can develop China, but we should establish the notion that only developing China is socialism.

Evaluating reform from the perspective of developmental criterion has its historical rationality. Because from the basic point of view of historical materialism, whether the reform, as a change of social production relations, is progressive or successful basically depends on whether it can truly and effectively promote the development of social productive forces, and promote the progress of social civilization as a whole on the basis of the liberation and development of social productive forces. It is in this sense that Deng Xiaoping said that "development is the absolute principle", because it is the fundamental principle of historical materialism. After all, the historical progress of institutional change is not proved by the characteristics of the system itself, but by the results of the development and liberation of social productive forces brought by institutional change. However, the problem has two aspects: on the one hand, the development itself has the problem of how to develop, and the growth itself also has the problem of the growth mode. That is to say, behind the development lie the problems of the development concept and the growth mode. The scientific development view and the choice of the effective growth mode are more of an institutional innovation rather than a technological innovation. Scientific development view is not people's subjective desire, but a development path with social, economic, political and cultural system guarantee; effective economic growth mode is not the inevitable result of general technological progress, but the result of competitive institutional innovation. On the other hand, even if effective social and economic development has been achieved, there still exists the problem of how to distribute development achievements in all aspects of society. Distribution is deeply related to development, but they are different propositions. As far as development is concerned, institutional change is required to bring about institutional conditions for improving efficiency for development. As far as distribution is concerned, there are not only problems of how to distribute more conducive to improving efficiency, but also problems of how to distribute more fairly and rationally. Therefore, separating itself from the efficiency criterion associated with institutional innovation, separating itself from the social equity criterion associated with the distribution of development achievements, simply and mechanically using development as the criterion for measuring reform, using development, especially the change of economic development indicators in a certain period of time in isolation and simplicity, as proof of the progress of reform has its limitations.

Judging the rationality and fairness of the reform from the interest criterion has its social necessity, because society is always a collection of interest relations. People's value judgment of institutional change in reality depends first on how it affects their own interests. But the problem is that if people judge the progressiveness of reform from their own interests and demand reform accordingly, it is likely that reform will be divorced from the fundamental interests of social development, and there will be great divergence in judging the progressiveness of reform based on their own interests. But if we take the fundamental interests of society as the criterion to judge the reform, there are problems of how to recognize the fundamental interests of society and who will represent the fundamental interests of society. If the interest criterion is taken to measure the progressiveness of reform, then it must be the fundamental social interest, which must be the interests of the majority at the same time, not the partial and individual interests of the minority. Only by effectively enhancing the interests of the majority, can the unity of fairness and efficiency be possible. But the question is, how to identify, embody and guarantee the fundamental interests of society? Especially how to ensure that they are not eroded by individual private interests. This requires a series of economic, political, cultural, administrative, legal, news and other system guarantees of our society, not just a simple problem of interest distribution mechanism. Therefore, it is difficult to give a correct answer to judge the fairness and rationality of the reform only from the distribution of interests. It is even more difficult to give a reasonable explanation to evaluate the overall process of the reform from the perspective of individual interests.

Therefore, the three kinds of judgment criteria above have their own necessity, rationality and inevitability, but if one of them is used in isolation and unilaterally, it will inevitably have its limitations, or it will be difficult to really reveal the historical value orientation of reform scientifically. Especially if different kinds of judgment criteria are set against each other, it will be impossible to make a convincing analysis of the progressiveness of reform. All kinds of criteria must be unified organically. This unification is not only the need for theoretical analysis, but also, more importantly, the need for the historical progress of China's reform and development. However, it must also be emphasized that this unification is not just listing criteria mechanically, but an organic structure in which different types of criteria should have different positions. At least among the three criteria mentioned above, development, especially the liberation and development of productive forces, should have the most fundamental and indispensable position. Although there are limitations in using development, especially the developmental criterion of productive forces for judging the rationality of reform's progressiveness, it is impossible to deny the fundamental position of productivity development in proving the rationality of institutional change and progress. Because the historical progressiveness in the sense of institutional criterion should fundamentally be proved by the development of productivity, and the historical rationality in the sense of interest criterion should basically be supported by the development of productivity.

1.3 The Issue of Equity in Income Distribution and the Rationality of the Reform

Reform promotes development, especially improves the level and efficiency of economic development, which is agreed by people and can be confirmed by China's practice for many years. However, with the progress of the reform and opening up, it is also an indisputable fact that the gap of income distribution in China is widening. While promoting development and improving efficiency, the impairment of the objective of fair distribution of social income has become the main reason for people's doubts and disputes about the value orientation of reform.

The objective of fair income distribution contains at least two meanings. On the one hand, fairness refers to a right, which refers to the equal right in front of prior opportunities with the nature of legal power; on the other hand, fairness also includes the meaning of equity or equality, which refers to the equality in the subsequent results. In the process of social development, the realization of the fairness includes not only the fairness in the sense of legal rights in advance, but also the gradual realization of the equality in the subsequent results. However, under different historical conditions, the emphasis and the degree of realization of the two objectives will be different. For the society in transition, as far as the relationship between marketization progress and income distribution is concerned, there is inequity in the sense of unequal opportunities in advance. The important reason is that marketization is not profound and perfect enough, which makes it difficult to implement the rules of law. There are many privileges to monopolize opportunities or conduct unfair competitions in various ways, thus widening the income gap. However, as for the inequality in the sense of unequal subsequent results afterwards, the important reason of it has profound relation with marketization. Because the more the market competition efficiency is emphasized, the more prominent the inequality will be afterwards under certain conditions. The equality and efficiency in income distribution are difficult to achieve at the same time, which mainly refers to the conflict between the objective of equal income distribution afterwards and the objective of competitive efficiency, instead of the conflict between prior equality of opportunities and efficiency objective. The goal of fairness and efficiency in front of prior opportunities is consistent. The key lies in the perfection of market mechanism and the adequacy of competition. Complicated is the relationship between the objective of equal income distribution and the objective of efficiency in the subsequent results. Overemphasizing the objective of equal income distribution may deprive people of their competitiveness and reduce efficiency. However, the fact that the gap is too large will not only damage fairness, but also sharpen various social contradictions, which will seriously affect efficiency. That is to say, the fact is that the widening income gap does not necessarily lead to efficiency improvement. For example, in the previous years of Russian reform, the Gini coefficient tripled to 0.5 in 1993, but the economy stagnated and declined seriously in the same period.[8] After 2001, the Gini coefficient dropped below 0.4, but the economic growth began to accelerate in the same period.[9] In Japan after the Second World War, from the 1960s to the 1980s, Japan's Gini coefficient declined gradually, but at the same time, it was also a period of sustained and rapid economic growth in Japan.

From the historical process of China's reform and development, in the early stage of reform, China started from the hierarchical basis of planned economy and transformed into market mechanism in terms of system; China transformed from a state of extreme backwardness and universal poverty with emphasis on equalitarianism to an economic takeoff accelerated by industrialization in terms of development, coupled with China's feudal tradition of more than 2,000 years. Therefore, the important task of reform is to emphasize equality in advance, break ranks and privileges, encourage equal competition, in order to improve efficiency and get rid of poverty as soon as possible. Therefore, it is necessary to observe the principle of "take efficiency first, and give consideration to equality", and "take fair opportunity first, and give consideration to equal results". So, with the deepening of China's reform and development, under the current level of development and institutional conditions, whether it comes to an era when more emphasis has been placed on fairness, especially on the equality of subsequent results, while the objective of efficiency or pre-equality has become secondary?

It must be admitted that with the sustained and rapid growth of China's economy, the gap in social income distribution is actually widening. Firstly, the income gap between urban and rural residents is widening. Especially since the 1990s, urban per capita disposable income was 2.2 times that of rural per capita net income in 1990. By 2003, it was 3.23 times that of rural per capita net income, and the gap was enlarged by about 50%.[10] Secondly, the income gap between different classes is widening. According to the data from the sample survey of about 50,000 households conducted by the National Bureau of Statistics, the per capita disposable income of the highest-income group was 4.2 times that of the lowest-income group of urban residents in 1991. However, by 2004, it expanded to 8.87 times, which doubled within seven years.[11] According to the research group of the National Bureau of Statistics,

---

[8] Grzegorz W. Kolodko: *Incomes Policy, Equity Issues, and Poverty Reduction in Transition Economics, Finance and Development*, IMF, September 1999, Volume 36, Number 3.

[9] World Bank: *Beyond Economic Growth: An Introduction to Sustainable Development*, Second Edition, 2004 Chiaki Moriguchi and Emmanuel Saez: *The Evolution of Income Concentration in Japan*, 1885–2002: *Evidence from Income Tax Statistics*, Working Paper.

[10] There are differences between the net income of rural residents and the disposable income of urban residents, so they can't be directly compared, but their growth rates can be compared with each other. The data refer to the National Bureau of Statistics: *China Statistical Yearbook*, 2004, 2005.

[11] Data Source: *China Statistical Yearbook*, 2004, 2005.

the Gini coefficient of urban and rural residents in China has reached 0.45 in 2005, which exceeded the level of the safety line. And it was not only significantly higher than that of contemporary capitalist welfare states, such as Norway and Sweden (the Gini coefficients range from 0.2 to 0.3), but also higher than that of contemporary developed capitalist countries, such as Britain, the United States and France (the Gini coefficients range from 0.3 to 0.4).[12]

Then, what on earth are the main reasons for the widening income distribution gap in China since the reform and opening up? To sum up, there are four main reasons:

Firstly, developmental reasons, that is, the imbalance of income distribution caused by the imbalance of economic development is aggravated, especially the duality of economy, which is an important manifestation of the imbalance of development in developing countries. The profound reason for the widening gap of income distribution in China at the present stage is also the strengthening of the duality of development. According to statistics, the level of per capita GDP in China is highly correlated with the urbanization rate (the ratio of urban population to the total population) of various regions (the correlation coefficient is as high as 0.9140).[13] The higher the urbanization rate, the higher the speed and level of economic development correspondingly. Therefore, the widening of the urban–rural gap has become an important development reason for the widening of the income gap. If we only look at the Gini coefficient of urban residents, it is only about 0.32, not only at the normal level, but also not significantly increased in ten years compared with 0.30 in the 1990s. If we look only at the Gini coefficient of rural residents, it is only about 0.35, compared with 0.34 in previous years, it is not much improved, and it is still in the normal level of safety; but if we mix the Gini coefficients of urban and rural areas into a unified one, the Gini coefficient of the whole society has reached 0.45, which obviously exceeds the safety margin.[14] This shows that the expansion of income distribution gap in China is mainly due to the expansion of the gap between urban and rural development and the deepening of the duality of development.

Secondly, growth reasons, is that the contribution of different factors to economic growth in the process of economic growth is different in speed and degree, which leads to different income growth speed and degree of different factor owners in income distribution. Moreover, the more deepening marketization, market competition and efficiency are emphasized, the more it is necessary to admit the differences in market competition in income distribution. Especially in the market economy system, factors participate in distribution. Therefore, the income distribution gap of different factor owners is directly related to the efficiency differences of different

---

[12] China Center for National Accounting and Economic Growth of Peking University: *China's Economic Growth Report 2006: Economic Growth in the Opening up to the Outside World*. Beijing: Economic Science Press, 2006.

[13] The date of GDP of various regions are from the Statistical Bureau: *China Statistical Yearbook* (2004). Population and urban–rural composition of each region is calculated according to the data of the Fifth National Population Census, based on the cross-sectional data of 2000 for these two indicators, the correlation coefficient is 0.9140.

[14] Liu Wei, "The Unbalance of Income Distribution is Fundamentally the Unbalance of Development", *New Economics*, 2005(11).

factors in competition. Through the Cobb–Douglas production function, we have analyzed the interrelationship of various factors of production of China's economic growth in the 20 years of the reform and opening up (1978–1998), and found that with the improvement of degree of marketization and denationalization in China, the efficiency of the two basic factors, labor and capital, has increased obviously, and the contribution to economic growth has increased continuously under the same input. However, in contrast, the impact of institutional changes on capital factors is significantly greater than that on labor factors (estimated to be more than 900 times the difference between the two). That is to say, China's reform has had an impact on the efficiency improvement of capital and labor, but the efficiency improvement of capital and the corresponding contribution of capital to economic growth is much higher than that of labor.[15] Therefore, if the income distribution is directly related to the contribution of the factors, the growth speed of the income of the masters of capital factors will be hundreds of times higher than that of the labor factors correspondingly, thus it inevitably enlarging the income distribution gap. The enlargement of this gap is not only the inevitability of different contributions in growth, but also the inevitability of marketization. It is also the inevitability of the unbalanced promotion of factor efficiency in growth, and the inevitability of deepening the process of market institutional transformation.

Thirdly, the reasons for institutional change are that in the process of institutional transformation, the degree of progress and perfection of marketization are different in different aspects and fields, so the adequacy and fairness of market competition are different, and the degree of equality of opportunity in advance is different. The exclusion of legal rights by corresponding privileges, the denial of monopoly to competition, the transaction of power and money and the emergence of various corruption will inevitably expand the gap of income distribution in the process of market transition. In a sense, the expansion of this income gap is caused by insufficient and imperfect marketization progress, including the imperfection of the rule of law system, which is compatible with the requirements of market economy civilization, rather than the marketization, and is not inevitability of marketization. This is due to unequal opportunities in advance, resulting in the widening of the virtual income distribution gap afterwards.

Fourthly, the structural reason of income is that along with the reform and opening up, people's income sources are becoming more and more diversified. Besides labor, people's assets income is increasing. Besides general physical labor, the difference formed by human capital input is becoming an important reason for income difference. In addition, risk income, operating income and so on are beginning to become the important root causes of widening income gap of different social strata. Especially with the reform of ownership system, the accumulation of private capital and the reform of property right system of state-owned enterprises, assets and investment income have increasingly become the important income base of the high-income stratum in society, and its proportion is increasing gradually, unlike in developed

[15] Liu Wei and Li Shaorong, "The Ownership Change and the Economic Growth and Upgrading of Factors Efficiency", *Economic Research Journal*, 2001(1).

countries, the proportion of assets income has entered a relatively stable period. The disparity of asset possession among different strata is widening day by day. According to the latest economic census, the proportion of state-owned capital in the capital of industrial and commercial enterprises has dropped from nearly 90–48.1%, and the proportion of personal capital has risen from less than 1–28%, reaching RMB5.1 trillion.[16] In particular, it should be pointed out that at the beginning of the reform, there was almost no difference in asset (capital) possession among the members of China's society. That is to say, the difference in capital possession was only formed after the reform and opening up. Unlike the traditions of Europe and America, even South America, where the landed estate owners have inherited from generation to generation on the basis of the development of large plantations, accompanied by the inheritance of their eldest son in law. To the present age, the gap between the assets of the big bourgeoisie and the general members of the society is not only huge, but also inherited from generation to generation. And the members of society can recognize and respect them to a considerable extent, at least the social contradictions caused by them are not as sharp as you think. In the 20 years from 1978 to 1998 in China, people's asset possession has expanded rapidly from basically no difference to the present situation, which is prone to intensify social contradictions and frictions. Moreover, China's tradition is a small-scale peasant economy based on cotton and rice civilization, coupled with the division and inheritance of various household, land annexation and continuous equal distribution, which leads to the opposition between large asset possession and a large number of social members who have lost their assets and it is an important source of social conflict.

It can be seen that there are many reasons for the formation of widening of income gap in China at this stage. The widening income gap caused by different reasons should be dealt with in different ways. First, the income gap caused by unbalanced development (urban–rural gap) is widening. The fundamental way to solve this problem is to improve the level of rural development, speed up urbanization. The income gap caused by unbalanced development can only be overcome by speeding up development and improving the balance and coordination of development. Any practice that sacrifices development or damages development will fundamentally undermine the realization of the goal of equal income distribution. Second, the income gap, which is caused by growth factors (differences in the speed of degree of contribution of different requirements to growth), is based on the difference in efficiency and based on the inevitability of market competition of the equal opportunities in advance. Without denying the priority to efficiency, it is emphasized that in the process of fundamental transformation of growth mode, which regards efficiency improvement as the main driving force of growth, it is not possible to improve the equality of distribution results after the event at the expense of impairing prior fairness and then reducing efficiency. Otherwise, it will not only conflict with the historical objective requirements of China's social and economic development, but also with

[16] Bulletin No. 1 of the Main Data of the First National Economic Census, *Economic Daily*, December 7, 2005.

the fundamental requirements of the socialist market economic system. The contradiction of the widening income distribution gap in the effective market competition is difficult to be solved by the market competition mechanism itself, but should be handled by non-market forces, especially the government. Third, the income gap caused by institutional factors (the difference in the degree of progress and perfection of marketization) is due to unequal opportunities in advance. In theory, the key is to realize that this is the result of imperfect marketization rather than the necessity of marketization. In practice, two aspects are important. On the one hand, it is important to deepen and improve market competition, including the reform of property right system and price system, including the cultivation of commodity market and factor market, including the reform of enterprises and government. On the other hand, it is necessary to strengthen and improve the rule of law order, including accelerating the process and quality of legal system construction, including the promotion of the authority of law, the spirit of rule of law and so on. Fourth, the key of widening income gap caused by the difference of assets lies in two aspects: firstly, the relationship between ownership structure with public ownership remaining dominant and market mechanism must be dealt with scientifically and effectively in theory and practice; secondly, the role of government in achieving the goal of fair and equal distribution in society must be further strengthened to improve the harmony of all aspects of society.

Chapter 2
Theoretical Debate Focus Regarding the Rightness of Institutional Transformation: Rethinking the Theory of Value and Conflict of the Two Economic Philosophies

Is the institutional change under certain historical conditions progressive? Does it promote justice and civilization? This is an important controversial proposition. The answer to this question involves basic historical value orientation, basic class position and corresponding elementary interest requirements. The value theory of economics can provide the most systematic answer and the most profound explanation to this proposition. This is the reason why all kinds of debates about the profound changes in the system often end up returning to the basic problems and categories of value theory. Although the value orientation recognizes that the market economic system is impartial, progressive, just and effective under certain historical conditions, there are deep divergences on what kind of economic philosophy should be followed in the order arrangement of the market economic system. Almost all economists and theories that recognize the historical existence of market economy can be divided into two opposing positions, economic liberalism and rational interventionism, in the view of economic philosophy, that is, the value orientation of market economic order. That is to say, the debate of theory of value focuses more on the progress and justice of market system in the evolution of human system, that is, to answer the question of whether to adopt the civilized form of market economy system. Then two different economic philosophies around the order of market economy are to answer the question of how to build a market economy system. In other words, it answers the question of which value orientation should be adopted in the process of practicing market economy system civilization.

W. Liu, *Research on China's Market Economy Development*,
https://doi.org/10.1007/978-981-97-1398-1_2

2.1 The Theory of Value and Debates on the Rightness of Institutional Transformation

The category of value does not exist as an economic category in the first place, but it has a very special significance in economics. Any economic theory or economist has their own unique theory of value, which is the strongest cornerstone of all their theories. The historical value orientation reflected by the theory of value is the most essential manifestation of the historical view of economics. The radical opposition of different camps in economics is not only the difference of specific economic analysis tools and methods, but also the difference of values behind them. Certain analysis and proof of economics is only an economic explanation of specific historical values. That's why economics has scientific significance in history. The essence of theory of value lies in the economic proof of the historical necessity, rationality, justice and harmony of the existence and development of the subordinate class and the social production mode represented by the class. That's why the theory of value of economic research has real motivation.

2.1.1 Why Has Labor Theory of Value Dominated the Mainstream for a Long Time in the History of Western Economic Thought

In the history of economic thought, western scholar's understanding of theory of value, or the replacement of the mainstream status of different theory of value, follows such a clue: first, labor theory of value was the mainstream. The labor theory of value proposed by classical economics has supported western economics for a century, and it has become the mainstream theory of value in the first Industrial Revolution. Then the utility theory of value became the mainstream, marked by the marginal revolution in 1871, before which the objective utility theory of value was the mainstream, and then the subjective utility theory of value was the mainstream. Later, Marshall's equilibrium value-price theory became the mainstream, which realized the substitution of price theory for value theory based on comprehensive subjective and objective utility theory. Since then, western scholars who entered the 20th century have further supplemented and developed the theory of equilibrium price on the basis of Marshall's theory of price instead of theory of value.

The reason why the labor theory of value represented by classical economics can become the mainstream theory of value in more than one hundred years before and after the first industrial revolution of capitalism lies in two aspects.

Firstly, during the first Industrial Revolution, capitalist mode of production as a new mode of production in history, and bourgeoisie as a representative of the new mode of production, its dominant position in history has not yet been stable. Whether human historical development can truly recognize capitalist society, whether capitalist mode of production can occupy a dominant position, or whether capitalist system should replace feudal system, are still propositions to be proved. Therefore, as the representatives of bourgeois ideology, including economists, philosophers, jurists, sociologists and historians, the times and the interests of their classes required them to prove the same proposition in different ways and different academic languages and logic, that is, to prove the inevitability and rationality of capitalist society. Then, how did economists prove this proposition through economic analysis? Thus, theory of value became the basic problem of economics in that era. In the sense of economic philosophy, if we want to prove the necessity and rationality of capitalist mode of production, we must prove whether this mode of production has philosophical value, and only if it has value can it be inevitable. In the sense of economics, if we want to prove the necessity and rationality of capitalist mode of production. It must be proved whether this mode of production is fair. From an economic point of view, how can we prove this fairness? Because the capitalist mode of production is a market society of exchange (that is, a civil society), which implements the principle of legal rights, rather than the principle of privilege. How does this principle of legal rights embody in economic life? It reflects fairness through equality in front of commodities, prices, currencies, trades and markets, that is, by implementing the principle of equal exchange. That is to say, the capitalist market society is a society of equal exchange, and therefore an equitable society. However, what is equivalent exchange, and what determines the equivalent price, and how to measure the exchange is equivalent? This involves the question of price determination, what determines the price and what is the basis of equivalent exchange. Consequently, the issue of value has become a hot topic of attention. People find that there is a force behind the equivalent exchange that decides the price, and this force is essentially value. That is to say, before and after the first industrial revolution, the fundamental purpose of bourgeois economists is to prove the historical inevitability and rationality of capitalist society from economic theory. Because the capitalist mode of production in that era did not have a stable dominant position, we need to demonstrate the historical necessity of its existence and development. In the view of economists, capitalist society is reasonable because it is fair. Why is it fair? Because it is equal. Why is it equal? Because it implements the legal rights rules of equal exchange. Why is it equal exchange? Because price is determined by value, and equal value determines the price in exchange. Therefore, the discussion of theory of value is closely related to the justification of the capitalist mode of production, and has become a hot topic of economics in that era. The urgent historical need to prove the rationality of capitalist mode of production makes theory of value of special importance in economics.

Secondly, the first Industrial Revolution era of capitalism is an era of free competition. Generally speaking, the bourgeoisie has its historical progressiveness. In order to gain the dominant position of the capitalist mode of production represented by the bourgeoisie, the main hostile force they faced was the feudal landlord class, not the proletariat. On the contrary, the bourgeoisie should unite with the proletariat to confront the feudal landlord class. In fact, this kind of alliance negates the feudal social mode of production by employing capital and labor. Therefore, in the value theory of bourgeois economists, they must give partial recognition to the rationality of the existence of the proletariat and the rationality of proletarian activities. The most concentrated manifestation of this recognition is the recognition that labor creates value. Because the source of value is labor, all labor, including the employment of the proletariat, is valuable, so it is rightous. Of course, the recognition of the justice of proletarian labor by bourgeois scholars at that time was still reserved, even contradictory. This contradiction is also reflected in its theory of value. For example, Adam Smith put forward the theory of labor value, but when further discussed the composition of value, he deviated from the labor theory of value. Smith holds that value consists of wages, profits and land rents. In fact, this is the theory of income value (Smith's faith). The reason why this contradiction exists in the theory of value of classical economics is that if the labor theory of value is thoroughly implemented, the profits obtained by capital and the land rent obtained by landowners are created by labor. Therefore, the rationality and justice of the existence of private ownership of capital and land will be questioned. In any case, bourgeois scholars will not put the justice and rationality of proletarian labor above the justice and rationality of capital possession. So while they put forward the labor theory of value, they also put forward three theories of income determining value. However, after all, the main enemy of the bourgeoisie in that era was the feudal landlord class. Therefore, while acknowledging the existence of land rent, bourgeois economists negated its justice (for example, regarding land rent as the exploitation of workers and capital by landlords, regarded as a price increase besides wages and average profits, which is a part of excess profits obtained by monopolizing land ownership, and all of these reveal their contempt for landlords). Therefore, they must give more affirmation to the proletarian labor and more recognition to the justice of labor, which is embodied in their labor theory of value. Therefore, the bourgeois economists in this era put forward the labor theory of value, whose fundamental purpose is to prove the justice and rationality of the capital employment labor system. In particular, it should be pointed out that the fundamental purpose of labor theory of value put forward by classical economists includes the consideration of the rationality and justice of labor. The main purpose is not to prove this point, but to prove the rationality and fairness of equivalence exchange in capitalist society. In order to explain what is equivalent exchange and the basis on which equivalent exchange depends, the classical economists put forward the labor theory of value. Similarly, it must be pointed out that labor theory of value can become the mainstream theory of value in this period because it does contain a considerable degree of affirmation of the justice of labor. Because before that, in ancient Greece and Rome, although labor theory of value and utility theory of value had sprouted, and in a long historical period, even throughout the Middle Ages, labor theory of value and utility theory of value had always coexisted. But in ancient Greece and Rome, economic life was subordinate to political and aesthetic interests. Besides, it was crude to study economic problems, and it only aimed at solving more important ethical and legal problems, without any economic purposes. As far as the whole era is concerned, when labor was mainly the activity of slaves, slaves cannot be regarded as just and noble. Although some thinkers at that time felt that there was some connection between labor and value, labor itself was not regarded as a noble and valuable activity. As for the understanding of medieval theologians, although they paid attention to the issue of value, they could not establish a special system of economic theory. They were merely trying to explain the codes of conduct purportedly arranged by God that required people to abide by. Theologians regard the accumulation of wealth as a sin and advocate an economic system based on the sharing of property. They praised natural economy agriculture, tolerated manufacturing with reservations, and severely condemned commerce. Therefore, it is impossible to truly recognize the capital and justice of the employment labor associated with capital and manufacturing production. Under the advocacy of classical economics, labor theory of value has gradually become the mainstream. This is not only a response to the historical emergence and development of capitalist mode of production, but also to the social mass production brought about by the industrial revolution.[1]

In a word, western classical economics put forward the theory of labor value, and the reason why the theory of labor value became the mainstream theory of value for a century before and after the first industrial revolution of capitalism lies in the need to prove the fairness and justice of capitalist mode of production. Because the development of capitalism in that era needed to argue for its stable dominance, capitalism was not really stable at that time.

2.1.2 Why Did Utility Theory of Value Replace the Mainstream Position of Labor Theory of Value, and Further Replaced the Theory of Value with the Theory of Price?

Let's first examine why the mainstream theory of value of western economics has changed from labor theory of value to objective utility theory of value. Production cost theory of value and production factor theory of value can be summed up as objective utility theory of value. It should be said that this objective utility theory of value originated from the classical economist Adam Smith. In a sense, Smith's theory of value includes the basic idea of social production cost theory of value. Later bourgeois scholars gradually developed the production cost theory of value based on this idea. Smith put forward the labor theory of value, and at the same time put forward three kinds of income-determined theory of value. How are these two contradictory theory of value unified in Smith's academic system? In Smith's view, whether it is labor, or profit, wage, rent, these three kinds of income are costs, which determine and constitute the value of commodities. The difference is that people are at different stages of history. For example, in the primitive stage, the main cost of commodity value is labor, so labor creates value. But in the later stage of capital development, the cost of commodity value includes wages, profits and land rent, so these three kinds of income constitute the source of commodity value. He believes

[1] Yan Zhijie, *A New Exploration of Labor Theory of Value,* Beijing: Peking University Press, 2001: 137–149.

that at a certain stage of capital development, labor theory of value will give way to income-determined theory of value. Smith's cost theory of value certainly has a series of profound theoretical contradictions, especially the contradiction between income determinism and labor theory of value. He confused the relationship between value creation and value distribution. At the same time, it is difficult to explain the objective existence of the value of means of production by dividing the whole value into three kinds of income according to the income-determined theory of value (which is also an important reason why it is difficult for Smith to put forward the reproduction theory). More importantly, Smith's income-determined theory of value includes the demonstration of the legitimacy and rationality of the existence of capital and land rent, which is determined by his class attribute. According to his labor theory of value, land rent and profit are the exploitation of the value created by labor, so there is no fairness. According to its income-determined theory of value, it not only embodies the compromise of the landlord class, acknowledges the rationality and legitimacy of the existence of land rent, but also demonstrates the justice of capital gaining profits. Since profits and rents, like wages, constitute the composition of value and are the source of value, they all have the same fairness from the perspective of theory of value. Obviously, the basic purpose of Smith's cost (income) theory of value is to prove the rationality and justice of capital existence.[2]

The direct reason why the mainstream position of labor theory of value gave way to production cost theory of value was the bankruptcy of the Ricardian School. After Smith, David Ricardo deduced the labor theory of value put forward by classical economics to the extreme that bourgeois scholars could reach. Ricardo believed that the source of value lay in labor. Utility and factors of production do not determine the value of goods. Especially natural conditions such as capital and land can only affect the production of use value, but it does not affect value creation and does not constitute a source of value. The only source of value is human labor. Ricardo insisted on the monistic labor theory of value, demonstrating that land rent is only the exploitation of the value created by labor. And then he pointed out the opposition between industrial capital society and feudal society, which provided a strong theoretical basis for anti-feudalism. However, his unitary labor theory of value also contains the opposition between capital and labor. Because if the only source of value was labor, then the profit earned by capital was undoubtedly the exploitation of the value created by labor. Obviously, this was not Ricardo's original intention as a representative of bourgeois ideology. Ricardo should not only oppose feudalism, but also demonstrate the historical rationality and inevitability of capitalism. In this way, Ricardo's theory has to face a fundamental contradiction: insisting on labor theory of value is conducive to anti-feudalism, but at the same time means denying the rationality of capital itself. Recognizing the rationality of capital gaining profits means abandoning or shaking the labor theory of value fundamentally. Moreover, in theory, Ricardo attributed the source of value to the only living labor. But it is difficult for Ricardo to give a convincing explanation to the actual phenomenon of deviation

[2] Adam Smith, *An Inquiry into the Nature and Causes of the Wealth of Nations (Chinese Version)*, Volume 1, Trs. Guo Dali, Wang Yanan, Beijing: The Commercial Press, 1974.

between price and value in capitalist economic reality, especially to some phenomena which consume almost as much labor as other while due to various factors, the price are quite different. So that Ricardo's followers, on the one hand, out of class instinct to justify the rationality of capital, and on the other hand, because of the theoretical need to explain the deviation between price and value, had to regard dead labor, especially as the accumulation of value created by labor-capital, as the source of value creation. They even regarded the role of natural forces as a source of value creation, which led to the bankruptcy of the Ricardian School. The disintegration of the Ricardian School directly led to the change of mainstream theory of value from labor theory of value to production cost theory of value.[3]

Production cost theory of value was systematically put forward by the French economist Jean-Baptiste Say in the early 19th century, and until the 1940s eventually replaced the mainstream position of labor theory of value. Later, John Mill made a complete statement on the value theory of production cost. Say's theory of value is a mixture of production factor theory, supply and demand theory, production cost theory and utility theory, but its foundation is the factor theory and utility theory. Say believes that value is utility, that is, creating value is creating utility. And how is the value created as utility? Say thinks that value (utility) is the common creation of labor, capital and nature (land). As far as value creation is concerned, like labor, both capital and land are productive.[4] Later, John Mill made a complete statement on the value theory of production cost.[5] So far, the labor theory of value no longer exists in the western orthodox economics, but the production cost theory of value replaces its mainstream position.

It can be seen that in the history of western economic thought, the substitution of production cost theory of value for labor theory of value, or the change of mainstream theory of value from labor theory of value to objective utility theory of value, is due to the need of bourgeois economists to demonstrate the rationality, necessity and justice of capital existence.

Next, we will examine why the mainstream position of objective utility axiology has been replaced by subjective utility axiology in the history of western economic thought. There are many scholars who have put forward the theory of subjective utility value, and their ways of argumentation are different, but their core idea is to attribute value to utility. However, it is emphasized that this utility is not the utility of objective things, but the utility of the degree of satisfaction of human desires. This desire and satisfaction can be attributed to people's subjective evaluation and feeling of the utility of things. Therefore, they attribute the essence of commodity value to the subjective evaluation of human beings. Value is no longer an objective existence,

---

[3] David Ricardo, On the Principles of Political Economy and Taxation (Chinese Version), Trs. Guo Dali, Wang Yanan, Beijing: The Commercial Press, 1962.

[4] Jean-Baptiste Say, A Treatise on Political Economy (Chinese Version), Trs. Chen Fusheng, Chen Zhenhua, Beijing: The Commercial Press, 1963.

[5] John Mill, Principles of Political Economy: With Some of their Applications to Social Philosophy (Chinese Version), Trs. Zhao Rongqian, Sang Bingyan, Zhu Yang, Beijing: The Commercial Press, 1991.

but a subjective feeling of people. In this way, this view not only contradicts labor axiology, but also objectively utility theory of value.

The initial proposition of subjective utility theory of value is also based on the disintegration of Ricardo's labor theory of value. However, after the disintegration of Ricardo's labor theory of value, the objective utility theory of value was developed and perfected first. Subjective utility theory of value is still in its infancy. After the marginal revolution in 1871, subjective utility theory of value rose to the mainstream, replacing the position of objective utility theory of value. The main analysis method of subjective utility theory of value is marginal analysis, that is to say, value is determined by people's subjective evaluation of the degree of satisfaction of their desires. But as people's desires are constantly satisfied, the degree of satisfaction that the same thing brings to people is different in subjective perception, and there is a law of diminishing degree of satisfaction utility. Therefore, the subjective evaluation that determines the value is not the general subjective feeling, but the marginal utility, that is, the degree of satisfaction brought by the last increase.

Why did subjective utility theory of value replace the mainstream position of objective utility theory of value? The most fundamental reason is that objective utility theory of value is difficult to explain and support the development of capitalism since the late 19th century. In the late 19th century, the dominant position of the capitalist mode of production has been relatively stable, and the various institutional contradictions inherent in the capitalist mode itself have begun to sharpen. Especially after several major economic crises, people find that the capitalist mode of production is not harmonious. The repeated emergence of economic crises of large-scale overproduction makes people doubt not only the idea advocated by objective utility theory of value that production naturally creates demand so supply and demand will be naturally balanced, but also whether the capitalist system is a harmonious and appropriate one. This requires bourgeois economists to prove theoretically whether the capitalist system is a suitable and harmonious system, and how to achieve a balanced and harmonious capitalist system. Therefore, they have to pay special attention to the problem of demand and the balance between demand and supply. Accordingly, in the study of value theory, they naturally put human desire and satisfaction of desire into a very important position, even attributed to the essence of value. The purpose is to show that the capitalist mode of production is valuable and just, because it can satisfy people's desires to the greatest extent and make the whole social and economic life reach a harmonious and balanced state by satisfying people's desires. It can be seen that the basic motive of the marginal revolution and the substitution of subjective utility theory of value for objective utility theory of value is also the need to prove the rationality of capitalist system.

However, the marginal utility theory of value has not been in the mainstream for a long time, and its mainstream position was soon replaced by Marshall's neoclassical comprehensive theory of value. As mentioned earlier, Marshall's theory of value is a synthesis of objective utility theory of value and subjective utility theory of value. The most fundamental reason why this kind of integration is possible is that whether it is the labor theory of value of bourgeois scholars, the objective theory of utility value or the subjective utility theory of value, it is essentially a justification for the justice of the capitalist system. The change of mainstream status is also due to the historical needs of the development of capitalist society. The neoclassical comprehensive theory of value can explain the rationality of capitalist system more fully and effectively. The class nature and mission of this doctrine make it possible for it to be integrated. Of course, the reason why they can be synthesized includes some common points in theory and some common points in analytical methods.

The essence of Marshall's comprehensive theory of value is that theory of price replaces theory of value. It can be said that since Marshall, the mainstream of western economics no longer pays attention to the true original theory of value, but to the equilibrium price theory. Marshall himself proposed the partial equilibrium price, on which the contemporary western economists further discussed the general equilibrium price. Their focus is: what is the equilibrium price and how to find the equilibrium price.

Why is there such a change from theory of value to price theory? The direct theoretical reason is of course from Marshall's comprehensive analysis, but the more profound historical reason is the following: the capitalist mode of production at the end of the 19th century and the beginning of the 20th century has firmly gained a dominant position. Comparatively speaking, it is of no greater significance to demonstrate the rationality and justice of this system, and then to argue theoretically for its establishment and dominance. Because its rule has become a thing of the past. More importantly, it is necessary to demonstrate how to use the capitalist mode of production and how to use the capitalist market mechanism in order to make the allocation of economic resources more effective. Therefore, the important issue is no longer the proposition of value, no longer the discussion of whether capitalism is valuable or not, no longer the discussion of which activities in capitalist society create value, the rationality and justice of capital existence need no more theoretical proof, so there is no need to explain whether capital creates value, nor to prove the justice and harmony of capital by demonstrating the relationship between capital and value source. What is important is how to ensure the harmonious operation of the capitalist system and realize the effective allocation of resources, so as to prove the effectiveness and superiority of its system. And this effective and harmonious state of operation is precisely summarized as a balanced state. So how to find the equilibrium position and how to approach the equilibrium state has become the fundamental task of western economics. Thus, the discussion of equilibrium price replaces the discussion of theory of value. This substitution is actually a transformation from answering why we should choose the capitalist system to answering how to use it.

It can be seen that the basic logical clue in the evolution of the mainstream status of western economic thought, from the labor theory of value of classical economics to the utility theory of value, from the objective utility theory of value to the subjective utility theory of value, from the utility theory of value to the comprehensive value-price theory, is to comply with the need of demonstrating the rationality, fairness, justice, validity and harmony of the capitalist system. This is why the fundamental mission of western economics is to study theory of value. Accordingly, we can say that the fundamental purpose of all economics and all economists' research on value theory is to justify the historical inevitability and justice of the class they represent and the mode of production they require. This is the root cause of the profoundity of value theory and the sharp opposition, and also the principal reason led to the important position of value theory in economics. The mission of the theory of value of western economics as same as that of Marx is also originate from that. We should take this mission as the basic starting point to create and construct theory of value that meets the historical requirements of socialist market economy.

2.1.3 What Does Marx's Labor Theory of Value Really Mean?

The essence of Marx's labor theory of value is to attribute value to the social relationship between human beings and to regard this social relationship as the result of historical movement.

Marx's labor theory of value was inherited and developed on the basis of criticizing the labor theory of value of classical economics. The establishment of Marx's labor theory of value was also the time when the labor theory of value of classical economics disintegrated, and then the mainstream theory of value of western economics changed from labor theory of value to production cost theory of value.

While critically inheriting and developing the labor theory of value of classical economics, Marx deeply criticized the production cost theory of value (objective utility theory of value). It is in this kind of inheritance and criticism that Marx formed his theory of value. The basic starting point of this inheritance and criticism is that Marx insisted that value is the social and historical relationship between people, not the utility relationship between people and things.

From the point of view of Marx's labor theory of value, how does he prove that the essence of value is the social relationship between human beings? First, Marx strictly distinguishes between value and use value, and holds that commodity is the unity of opposites between value and use value. However, economics only pays attention to the use value within the scope of the material bearer of the use value. In addition, economics does not study the value of use, that is, the utility of things. This completely excludes the relationship between man and matter in theory of value. Classical economists have put forward this point, but it is far less thorough than Marx. Secondly, Marx strictly distinguished value from exchange value (price), which is an important development of Marx's labor theory of value in classical economics. Labor theory of value in classical economics, including Smith and Ricardo, confuses exchange value and value. Therefore, they only focus on the proportion of exchange (exchange value), but cannot find what is the decisive entity behind exchange value. Third, Marx scientifically demonstrated the source of value, which is confused by classical economics. Marx created the dual character of labor theory, which has special significance for Marx's labor theory of value. Classical economics regards labor only as concrete labor, and does not abstract social general labor from various kinds of specific labor. Therefore, when we insist on the labor theory of value and regard labor as the source of value, it is difficult to distinguish the different relations between labor and use value and value, thus it is difficult to attribute the source of value solely to labor. More importantly, specific labor reflects the material relationship between man and nature, and is the specific process in which man uses labor tools to act on the object of labor. The abstract labor in general reflects the social nature and historical form of people's labor. Abstract labor as a general reduction of socialization of specific labor, that is, to remove the specific form of labor and return to common abstract labor. This process itself is not only the abstraction of theory, but also the socialization of reality. It is essentially a process in which people recognize each other's work and individual work is recognized by the society to restore their specific work to the general work of the society. If the utility of the material produced by specific labor is to be of value, it must be recognized by the society and abstracted into general social labor by the society. Value is not only a kind of social relationship, but also a kind of movement process of social relationship, which is the essence of Marx's dual character of labor theory. Fourth, on the basis of abstract labor, Marx further put forward the determination of value the category of social necessary labor time. The determination of value is not determined by individual working hours, nor by the labor time consumed under the worst production conditions, as Ricardo said, but by the social necessary working hours, i.e. the social average and necessary working hours. This shows that in Marx's theory of value, whether there is value or not and how much value is determined not by individual labor, but by society. The extent to which individual labor is recognized by society and the extent to which individual labor time meets the requirements of social necessary labor time are all social processes. Therefore, value itself is the social relationship between people, not the individual relationship between people and specific things.[6] Fifth, Marx analyzed the value form of commodities and the origin and essence of money, which was neglected by classical economics. Essentially, the origin and development of value form and currency are the process of social history and the reflection of the historical changes of people's economic relations and economic systems. The analysis of Marx's value form and the origin and essence of money reveals the changes of people's mutual economic relations movement from the evolution and development of this economic system. Value and form of value, exchange and currency are only specific historical ways adopted by people's economic relations under certain social and historical conditions.

However, although value is created by labor, it is the social and economic relationship between people, value is manifested in the relationship between things, and in the domination of things over people. The production of commodity producers depends on whether their private labor can be transformed into socially necessary labor, and whether they can realize the transformation of private products into money, which

[6] When discussing value determination, Marx assumed that the aggregate supply and demand were equal. Therefore, social necessary labor time does not include the constraints of demand, but is an equalization discussed from the point of production conditions. After entering the total analysis, Marx gave a new meaning to "socially necessary labor", pointing out that social necessity includes the meaning of recognition of social aggregate demand. Because of this, there was a great debate on the transformation of Marx's value to production price at that time and later.

is spontaneous socialization rather than the subjective predictability and control of commodity producers themselves. As a result, commodity currencies are mysterious and unpredictable in front of people. Therefore, people have a superstition about the movement of commodity currency relations, that is, commodity currency fetishism. That is to say, in the process of commodity production and exchange, the inevitability and internal logic of economic relations among people are realized through the spontaneous, accidental and unknowable movement of relations between external things and objects. Originally, it is the social and economic relationship between people, and it is human labor that creates value. Commodity money is only the way of movement adopted by human economic relations under certain social and historical conditions. However, in the face of commodity currency fetishism, human activities are in turn dominated by the relationship between things and things. This is alienation and distortion. Marx's theory of commodity currency fetishism is a profound criticism of this alienation and distortion. Through this criticism, Marx further profoundly revealed the essence of commodity value and the essence of the movement of value form, which is only the movement of human social and economic relations.

Marx attributed value to the historical movement of people's social and economic relations. What should we tell people through this kind of attribution? The most important thing is to tell people in terms of values in two aspects: on the one hand, value is created by labor, and labor is the only source of value. Therefore, all gains without labor, whether through private capital or through private land possession, are the exploitation and exhaustion of labor. In spite of this, the proof and scientific analysis are carried out in Marx's theory of surplus value. But here, the labor theory of value has profoundly revealed the opposition between labor and capital, and revealed the injustice and irrationality of capital exploitation, because all materialized labor does not create value. It is for this reason that labor theory of value not only becomes the economic theoretical basis of theory of surplus value, but also becomes the basis of ethical values of theory of surplus value. On the other hand, Marx tells people in value that the social nature of human labor is realized by means of spontaneous, uncontrollable and alienated forms. Human labor is originally produced by human labor, but it is manifested in the way that human beings cannot dominate but are dominated by it. It is unreasonable that human labor should indirectly prove its value through exchange, which in itself is a kind of alienation of human economic activities. This historical distortion is due to the existence of private ownership. Under the condition of social division of labor, private ownership cuts off the direct social connection of people's production. The sociality of people's production is a circuitous and indirect external process. To overcome this alienation, the most fundamental thing is to eliminate private ownership. All commodity values, currencies and exchange relations directly related to private ownership are historical distortions. Therefore, in terms of development trend and value orientation of human ideal society, private ownership will eventually be abolished. Therefore, Marx's labor theory of value clearly denies the fundamental negation of commodity relations and market exchange. These two aspects are the fundamental purpose of Marx's analysis of labor theory of value, and we must firmly grasp them when we study theory of value.

2.1.4 What Historical Challenge Did Marx's Labor Theory of Value Meet?

2.1.4.1 Can Public Ownership and Market Economy Be Unified, or Can the Main Economy Itself Become a Market Economy in a Society Dominated by Public Ownership?

The most difficult and important thing in the construction of China's socialist market economy is not to bring the non-public ownership economy existing in the socialist society into the market mechanism, but to bring the dominant public ownership economy into the market economy. Otherwise, the market mechanism can hardly really restrain the dominant economic structure, and the whole social economy will not be called the market economy. However, if we strictly follow the logic of Marx's labor theory of value, it is impossible for a public ownership society to be called a market economy society. In fact, there is a deep internal relationship between ownership and resource allocation in a certain society. Property system is the institutional premise and fundamental motivation for the choice of resource allocation, while resource allocation is the movement form and interest realization mode of a certain social property system.

The logical clue of Marx's labor theory of value is as follows: starting from the most common phenomenon of commodity, analyses what commodity is. Commodity is the unity of opposites between use value and value. Without this contradiction, products will not become commodities. Then, why should a product become a commodity, it is necessary to make its use value and value of the unity of opposites? Because the nature of the labor process of producing commodities has changed historically. Labor process becomes the unity of opposites between concrete labor and abstract labor. Concrete labor forms use value and abstract labor forms value. It is this special contradiction in the process of labor that makes the result of labor a contradictory unity of use value and value. Then, why is the labor process the process of unity of opposites between concrete and abstract labor? Because the main contradictions in the social production process have changed. The unity of opposites between the privatization of production and the sociality of production has become the basic contradiction in social economy. The individuality of production makes the labor process of production always specific and individual, and the sociality of production requires that the labor of production have the nature of general social necessary labor, and that individual labor must be recognized by the society from the beginning. Then, why does the contradiction of social production and the nature of production stipulated by it change like this? Why is there a contradiction between private and social production? Because the basic institutional conditions in the development of human society and economy have changed with the development of productive forces, the social division of labor system and the private ownership of means of production have emerged. Private ownership makes people's gross production private and for private interests, but social division of labor requires people to exchange products with each other, which requires that private production must have the sociality of providing products for others. As a result, social production has become a contradictory movement of the unity of opposites between the private and the social. It is through the logical analysis of this contradiction that Marx's labor theory of value reveals how commodity value, as a social relationship between people, happens and moves systematically and historically. The most profound reason for the emergence of value category lies in the emergence of private ownership. Because here the logic of thought is consistent with that of history. If we replace the private ownership with the public ownership, which is the most fundamental historical logical basis of Marx's labor theory of value analysis, can a series of special contradictions that constitute commodity relations be established? In this sense, it can be said that the logic of Marx's labor theory of value is to integrate commodity, market economy category and private ownership, and fundamentally negates the possibility of the unity of public ownership and commodity relationship and market economy.

For the theoretical and practical exploration of socialist economic reform, we have to face two traditional doctrines at the same time, one is from western economics. All western economics, whether it is the history of ideological development since classical economics or the active schools of contemporary economics, no matter how many differences exist among them, is consistent in linking commodities, currencies, market economy and private ownership, especially capitalist private ownership. In their view, market economic relations can only exist and develop under the private ownership of capital, and no society that abolishes private ownership can have a market. Another is the traditional dogma from Marx. In Marx's view, economic relations such as commodity and money markets are only a certain form of movement adopted by the private capital system and a product of private ownership. The abolition of private ownership means the abolition of commodity, currency and market relations. Therefore, public ownership is fundamentally opposed to commodity, currency, value, market and other systems. The logic of Marx's labor theory of value analysis completely negates the historical possibility of the organic unification of public ownership and market.

The practitioners of socialist public ownership society initially followed this tradition and opposed the market to socialist public ownership. Under the public ownership, they negated the relationship between commodities and currencies and the market mechanism. But it has paid a very high price. Practice has made people realize that it is a historical choice to reform the traditional system and explore the market mechanism on the basis of public ownership. It can be said that the practice of reform in various countries, initially and for quite a long time, revolved around the historical proposition of how to unify public ownership and market mechanism. But up to now, this proposition has not really been solved. Although China has clearly put forward and adhered to the socialist market economy as the reform goal, that is, under the premise of the system of public ownership as the main body, to make the market a basic force for allocating resources, and to unify public ownership and market economy. But on the one hand, this choice needs to be deeply analyzed and discussed in economic theory, on the other hand, more importantly, it needs to be explored and proved in practice. Establishing market economy in public ownership society is a historical problem that Marx's labor theory of value negates, and that is what we need to practice at present. For a long time, the theory and practice of economic reform in the Stalin-style planned economies of the Soviet Union, Yugoslavia, Eastern Europe and later Russia revolved around the proposition of how to unify public ownership, especially state ownership and market mechanism. However, the various theories and schemes put forward by them fail to achieve the unity between the public nature of property system and the requirement of market-oriented resource allocation in practice. Finally, in order to obtain market efficiency and make market mechanism the basic way to allocate resources, public ownership has been abandoned one after another, which makes the nature of reform change fundamentally.

However, the fundamental historical problem to be dealt with in the theory and practice of socialist economic construction in China lies precisely in the unification of the property system with public ownership as the main body and the allocation of resources based on market mechanism. This is a problem that has never really been solved in human history, and it is also a proposition that Marx's economic theory, especially Marx's theory of value, fundamentally negates. If we adhere dogmatically to the viewpoint of Marx's labor theory of value and mechanically adhere to the logic of Marx's labor theory of value, it means that we theoretically deny the historical possibility of public ownership and market economy system as well. Obviously, such a theory cannot support the great practice of China's socialist market economy.

2.1.4.2 Should a Society Dominated by Public Ownership Take Market Mechanism as the Basis for Allocating Resources, or Should It Affirm the Historical Progress and Justice of Market Economy in Socialist Society?

Value theory is not only an economic analysis, but also a historical value orientation. The fundamental problem it aims to illustrate is to prove the historical fairness or unfairness of certain social production modes from the perspective of economics. Marx's theory of value, broadly speaking, includes two parts: labor theory of value and theory of surplus value. Through his labor theory of value, Marx not only reveals the opposition between capital and labor, but also negates the fairness of all societies with private ownership and market. Because Marx's labor theory of value holds that all commodities, currencies, values and market relations are alienation of human labor. The sociality of human labor needs to manifest and dominate people's economic activities through the category of market exchange. This is a distortion and inversion of human labor, which is unreasonable and inconsistent with the historical ideal of human social development. Therefore, in the ideal society of public ownership in the future, the sociality between people does not need the intervention of exchange, commodity, currency, value, market and so on. Through his theory of surplus value, Marx criticized capitalism and negated the rationality and fairness of capitalist society. He believed that under the condition of capitalist employment of labor, labor became commodity, and then surplus value and capitalist exploited surplus value. Therefore, capitalist society is fundamentally unjust.

Therefore, Marx's labor theory of value not only fundamentally negates the possibility of market relations in a public ownership society, but also completely negates the rationality and justice of market relations in a public ownership society in terms of values. However, the task of China's socialist economic reform and development practice is to unify the socialist public ownership and market economic mechanism and deal with this unprecedented historical proposition. We should not only answer the question of whether it is impossible to unify in practice, but also answer the question of whether it should be unified in theory.

The overall goal of the reform and opening up is to establish a market economic mechanism based on the long-term common development of multi-ownership economy with public ownership as the main body. In theory, from the traditional opposition between socialist public ownership and market economy, to the gradual acceptance that socialist economy is the dominant and subsidiary theory of planned economy, supplemented by market regulation, to the combination of planned economy and market regulation in socialist planned commodity economy, the 14th National Congress of the CPC clearly put forward that the goal of reform is to establish a socialist market economic system. Our understanding of the historical inevitability of the existence of market economy in the public ownership society is becoming clearer and clearer with the practice of reform. Practically speaking, in the past 30 years from 1978 to 2008, the market-oriented speed of China's economic system has been relatively fast in all countries in transition. According to a calculation of the World Bank, in the mid-1990s, the average market index of all countries with institutional transition was 4.4, while that of China was 5.5, which was 1.1 percentage points higher than the average. China has made tremendous progress both in the marketization of commodities and in the marketization of labor force. In the aspect of capital marketization with slow progress, although capital market has become a very complex proposition due to various reasons at home and abroad, many substantial progress has been made in the practice of the reform and opening up in China. Including the direct financing (stock market) market from scratch; the independence of the central bank, the construction of state-owned professional banking system, the development of joint-stock banks; the gradual opening up of the financial services market; the gradual market fluctuation of interest rates, and so on. It can be said that by the beginning of the 21st century, the market mechanism has replaced the planned mechanism. Although it still has a rather arduous historical task in improving the market order, it has become a basic force in the allocation of resources in China. Corresponding to this marketization process, China's ownership structure has undergone profound changes. The proportion of state-owned enterprise assets has dropped from about 87% at the beginning of the reform to less than 40% in 2002; and private economic assets have risen from less than 1% at the beginning to about 7% in 2002. In the gross national product, the state-owned economy has dropped from about 70% to less than 30%, while the private economy has risen from a negligible level to more than 20%, and the rest are mixed economy (about 30%)

and foreign investment.[7] Along with the market-oriented allocation of resources and the diversification of social ownership structure, great changes have taken place in income distribution. Firstly, the income distribution gap between regions, enterprises, urban and rural areas and strata in the market competition is widening; secondly, the capital ownership and the ability of operating capital itself become the legitimate source of income, so that the income distribution mode has undergone profound changes; thirdly, how to deal with the contradiction between fairness and efficiency in personal income distribution becomes more and more complex under the condition of increasingly complex interest relations. It's getting more and more complicated, and so on.

In the socialist society and economy with public ownership as the main body, the way of resource allocation is market-oriented, the structure of ownership is diversified and the way of distribution is diversified. Is this series of institutional changes just or the progress of civilization? This is a question that all humanities and social sciences, including economics, must answer. Because of this, the issue of theory of value in economics has become a hot topic again. Because the theory of value answers the question of historical rationality and fairness of certain mode of production and its vicissitudes. However, if we mechanically follow Marx's theory of value, the logical conclusion is to deny the historical fairness and rationality of introducing market mechanism reform. Therefore, we must proceed from practice, adhere to the scientific analysis method of Marxism, develop and explore new theory of value, in order to support the practice of socialist market economy in theory. This is not only a historic challenge to Marx's labor theory of value in terms of values, but also a brand-new proposition that needs us to deal with and create.

2.2 Divergence Between Two Conflicting Market Economic Philosophies and Market-Oriented Value Orientation

2.2.1 Two Different Philosophical Views of Market Economy

In the ideological and practical history of human market economy, there are always two different philosophical views, or two different value orientations, around how to construct market economy system. That is, market spontaneous competition mechanism theory based on economic liberalism and state intervention mechanism theory based on rationalism. One emphasizes the independence of the market subject, the spontaneity of the market, the freedom of competition and the voluntariness of trading; the other emphasizes the overall intervention in the market economy, stresses the regulation and control of decentralized market behavior by the state as the overall coordinator of the national economy, and especially emphasizes the correction and

[7] Liu Wei, "Why Economics Should Study Value", *Economic Theory and Economic Business Management*, 2003(5).

restraint of the spontaneity and freedom of market competition. Economic liberalism holds that the order formed spontaneously by market economy has the function of automatically coordinating decentralized market activities and various results. Under the automatic coordination of this spontaneous order, market decentralization can tend to overall harmony or equilibrium. The more the market system guarantees the rights of market actors and the freedom of competition, the more vigorous and efficient market economy competition will be. At the same time, on the whole, it is more likely that the economy will automatically tend to equilibrium, and the more likely that the economy will maintain the unity of efficiency and order. Any destruction and denial of the spontaneous coordination function of market mechanism and the free and voluntary nature of market competition will lead to the loss of resource allocation, destroying both efficiency and harmony. Any intervention that denies market spontaneity and competition freedom in super-economy and supermarket market will result in more serious losses than the defects of market itself. The theory of state rational intervention holds that it is difficult to achieve equilibrium state in a free and spontaneous competitive economy depending on the market itself. The state must provide clear criteria for decentralized market competitors, and regulate the decentralized behavior of market competitors through a series of national forces and government means.

From the second half of the 15th century until now, there have been five stages in the debate about the philosophy of market economy in western economic thought. The first stage was from the rise of mercantilist state intervention theory in the 15th century to the establishment of market economy liberalism philosophy in classical economics in the 18th century. This stage was a process in which the classical economic liberalism philosophy overcame the feudal autocratic theory and the mercantilist state intervention policy. The second stage was the initial doubt and criticism of the economic liberalism concept of classical economics from the second half of the 19th century. That is to say, in the second half of the 20th century, the German Historical School and the American Institutional School introspected and criticized the market spontaneous competition theory of economic liberalism in classical economics with their preference for national power and their emphasis on the role of the state, government, law, policy and public opinion in system design and arrangement. The third stage was the Great Depression in the late 1920s, which made the theory of market failure popular. The result was the establishment of the theory of state intervention represented by Keynesian economics, supported by the practice of Roosevelt's New Deal. The fourth stage was the theory of state failure which became popular in the mid and late 1970s. Especially in the case of increasingly serious economic phenomena such as stagflation, on the one hand, people had a comprehensive reflection on Keynesianism, on the other hand, they had a new perspective on the capitalist market mechanism by neo-liberalism, so that economic liberalism can be revitalized under the new historical conditions. The fifth stage was marked by the global economic crisis triggered by the current US financial crisis. People reconsider the limitations of free and spontaneous competition in the market and the contradictions arising therefrom. In order to overcome the most serious economic crisis since the 20th century, countries not only themselves but also in the international arena have intensified government intervention in policy unprecedentedly. This also indicates an unprecedented deep reflection on neo-economic liberalism in economic theory and an unprecedented emphasis on the theory of state intervention.

2.2.2 Historical Motivation of the Debate Between Two Different Philosophical Views of Market Economy

Classical economics emphasizes that the historical motivation of economic liberalism is clear. As the bourgeoisie's basic revolutionary purpose is anti-feudalism, in the process of overthrowing the feudal mode of production, it must use equality against hierarchy and legal power against privilege. Therefore, economic liberalism constitutes the fundamental philosophical view of classical economics and the profound understanding of all economic theories and capitalist production methods by classical economists. As far as economic theory is concerned, the economic liberalism of classical economics is not only anti-feudal, but also aims to deny the previous theory and policy of state intervention of French mercantilism, so as to establish a more solid position for the freely competitive capitalist mode of production. Therefore, classical economics holds that, first of all, the market economic system is spontaneous, is based on individual human nature requirements, and is therefore natural and eternal. Economic life is governed by objective natural laws, rather than being changed by the arbitrariness of the authoritarian. The most profound foundation of the freedom and spontaneous competition of the market economy lies in the natural rights of human beings, including the inalienable right of individuals to own property, the right of individuals to work, and the right of individuals to pursue their own interests. Obviously, this view is not only aimed at feudal autocracy, but also at the cumbersome state intervention policies of mercantilism. Secondly, the more spontaneous and free market competition is, the more likely it is to achieve fairness, especially to ensure the fairness in trading conditions. On the one hand, wealth does not originate mainly from circulation as mercantilism believes, but from production. Therefore, classical economics opposes commercial fraud and the pursuit of prosperity and full competition by selling or not buying only. On the other hand, the fundamental reason for transaction fairness lies in price fairness, and the institutional condition of price fairness lies in freedom and full competition. So the more free and spontaneous it is, the more just it is. Finally, the more free and spontaneous market competition, the more efficient it is. Because free competition can make scattered and spontaneous individuals more creative, and the more free competition, the right of freedom and independence itself will restrict individual's decentralized behavior. The clearer the right is, the clearer the responsibility is, and the more harmonious the creative individual behavior is in the overall result. As Adam Smith said, the natural order of market competition, as a free system, has the function of realizing the balance of human economic activities spontaneously. This function is just like an invisible hand, which urges everyone to pursue the realization of personal goals while achieving goals that are not his original intentions.[8] Obviously, the economic liberalism of classical economics emphasizes the spontaneous freedom of competition, the adequacy and fairness of competition, the effectiveness of competition and the harmony on this basis. The motive of economic history lies in the denial of feudal mode of production and mercantilist policy propositions.

In the second half of the 19th century, the German Historical School and the American Institutional School began to conduct preliminary reflections and criticisms on the market outlook of classical economic liberalism. This kind of reflection and criticism is carried out under two backgrounds. On the one hand, it is the basis of the history of economic development. Classical economics originated in Britain, where the capitalist system and social productivity were the most developed. At that time, the development of the British economy did not require state intervention and protection, nor fierce competition from other countries, and did not need to rely on the power of the state and government to support its national economic development. However, Germany and the United States were different in the middle and second half of the 19th century compared with Britain and France at that time. They were backward countries in the capitalist world. If they allowed free competition, their national capital competitiveness would be far inferior to that of Britain and even lag behind that of France. Therefore, they could not rely on the spontaneous and free competition of the market to achieve their development goals. They needed the state to protect and support the national capital economy, so they expressed doubts about economic liberalism in their economic thoughts, and paid special attention to the need for state intervention. It is for this reason that the so-called "national economics" originated in Germany, which originally proposed to maintain economic order by the state.[9] On the other hand, it is based on different understandings of human nature. The liberal market view of classical economics is based on the assumption of rational human behavior, that is, as an economic person, people will consciously accept the constraints of objective economic conditions, and under such constraints, strive to maximize the degree of realization of personal goals. Driven by this rationality, scattered individual behaviors will eventually automatically tend to overall harmony and convergence of results, thus creating a balance of freedom, efficiency and competition. However, historians and institutionalists have different understandings of human nature. They pay more attention to the irrational aspects of human beings. They believe that since human beings are irrational, the market competition mechanism cannot be realized spontaneously by human rationality, but must concentrate the power of social rationality and establish the corresponding order by law and system by relying on the power of the state. As an external coercive force, the state also acts as a general rule which overrides the decentralized competition in the market to regulate and restrict the individual's decentralized behavior. It is in the economic history background and

[8] Adam Smith, *An Inquiry into the Nature and Causes of the Wealth of Nations (Chinese Version), Volume 2*, Trs. Guo Dali, Wang Yanan, Beijing: The Commercial Press, 1974.

[9] In the history of thought, it is generally believed that the founder of the early German Historical School, F. List, originally proposed "National Economics", referring to his *The National System of Political Economy (Chinese Version)*, Trs. Chen Wanxu, Beijing: The Commercial Press, 1961.

philosophical thought background of the above two aspects that they criticized the economic liberalism of classical economics. It points out that, first, human behavior is not a rational spontaneous act bound by objective natural law, but dominated by spiritual will, so there is no natural order in line with objective law. The formation of order can only depend on the will, that is, the rationality of the centralized society, and this concentration of rationality is the "will of the state", and the realization of the will of the state depends on the law and power system. Second, only through the state power and system, can individual interests and national interests be developed in a balanced way. The principle of private economy is different from that of national economy, and it is difficult to coordinate automatically. Only by relying on the power of the country can personal interests obey national interests, personal goals can converge to the overall goal, and the national economy can develop in a coordinated manner. Third, most of the individual's abilities come from the social system and environment in which they live. Without a certain social system and environment, no matter how diligent, thrifty, creative and intelligent a person is, he cannot achieve great success, and such a system and environment must also rely on national power to establish.[10] Of course, the Historical School emphasizes that it relies on the will and power of the state to construct market order, which is not a fundamental negation of private interests and freedom, but a principle of coordinating national interests and individual interests on this basis. In fact, they especially emphasize that the foundation of the spirit of freedom lies in private ownership. In their view, technology and commerce are constantly transferring between countries and regions, and it is always tyrannical to expel them. They are always attracted to freedom, and this spirit of freedom needs institutional guarantee, and the key of institutional guarantee lies in the recognition and protection of private ownership. Private ownership is the most powerful lever for the spiritual development of human society. Without private ownership, society will become lifeless, and lose the diversity and development of personality. To effectively protect private ownership, we can only rely on national strength. Therefore, when the dispersed personal interests conflict with the national interests, the individual economic interests should be subordinate to the overall interests of the country.[11]

However, the theory of rational intervention of the will of the state in the market truly became the dominant ideology and policy proposition after the 1930s. There are two backgrounds here. One is the background of economic history. The Great Depression appeared in the capitalist world around the 1930s required people to adopt various policies and ways to get rid of the depression. Relying on free competition and spontaneous actions in the market is almost ineffective. Government intervention must be introduced to overcome market failures and limitations, so the "Roosevelt New Deal" system was proposed and implemented in the United States. On the other hand, it is the background of the history of economic thought. Based on the reality of the Great Depression, people had to doubt the traditional "invisible hand" in

---

[10] F. List, *The National System of Political Economy (Chinese version)*, Trs. Chen Wanxu, Beijing: The Commercial Press, 1961.

[11] Chen et al. (1981), p. 233.

economic theory and the market view of economic liberalism, and then put forward the revolution of unimpeded economic liberalism. Therefore, the corresponding the Keynesian Revolution took place historically. The Keynesian Revolution is embodied in three aspects. First, the revolution of the research object and method of economics, i.e. the emergence of macroeconomics, extends the study of economics from classical micro-behavioral analysis to total analysis. Second, the revolution of assumptions and principles of economic behavior, i.e. the law of diminishing return on investment. The demonstration of three psychological principles, namely the law of diminishing consumption utility and the existence of flexible preferences, makes the conclusion that effective demand is insufficient negate the traditional view that supply and demand tend to balance automatically. Third, the revolution of economic policy tendency, that is, the normal situation of insufficient effective demand under the market mechanism. It is proposed that the government should take the initiative to use fiscal and monetary policies, especially the fiscal policy system to intervene in the economy and stimulate demand, so as to change the role of government policy in economics from the traditional "watchman" to the role of active intervention.

After the 1970s, from the perspective of economic history, Keynesian economic theory and policy encountered difficult problems. Since the 1950s, when Keynesianism began to prevail, doubts about its effectiveness have arisen. New problems such as "stagflation" in the economy after the 1970s further prompted people to strengthen this suspicion. People have seen that while market failures exist, there are also "state failures". Firstly, the motivation of government action does not necessarily represent the interests of the whole society. The interests of the parties involved in government actions are also established in the relationship of social interests, and it is not necessarily noble. It is not necessarily fair to rely on the government to establish market mechanisms and competition order. Secondly, relying on the state to establish market mechanism and competition order does not have sufficient information basis. The highly dispersed market information makes it technically difficult for the country to possess all the information in time. In addition, access to information has to pay a price, not free goods available at any time. Therefore, the spontaneous horizontal transmission of information through the market may be more effective than the conscious vertical transmission of information through the country. Thirdly, relying on the state to establish market order, there is objectively a "paradox of voting", or it is difficult to reach agreement, or to achieve justice. Fourthly, the efficiency of directly running enterprises and projects by the state is low, because it is difficult for state-owned enterprises to follow the basic market competition principle that marginal cost equals marginal income. Based on the historical facts of Keynesian failure, and on the basis of the gradually popular "theory of state failure", the market view of economic liberalism began to revitalize. Various economic schools and doctrines based on economic liberalism have become popular, such as modern monetarism, rational anticipation, public choice, property right economic theory and so on.

Since 2007, an unprecedented and profound financial crisis and corresponding global economic crisis have taken place throughout the Western world. On the one hand, in policy practice, governments including the United States, the European

Union and other countries have introduced unprecedented strong government intervention measures to overcome or alleviate the economic imbalance and serious recession caused by market mechanism failure. Especially in the decades since the 1970s, the government has relaxed the government's supervision of the market, resulting in excessive competition, excessive imbalance, excessive bubbles and excessive speculation. At the same time, the continuous deregulation and the macroeconomic policies that constantly reduce the efficiency conditions and competitiveness requirements of entering the market, especially the monetary policies of loosening money and reducing interest rates to stimulate demand, and expanding the scale of market economy transactions and stimulating market demand to increase the economic growth, constantly reduce the economic quality and the profitability and competitiveness of enterprises. As costs continue to rise and the corresponding real interest rates rise, a large number of enterprises and projects that could survive or even be profitable under the requirement of low interest rates in the past will become difficult to survive. As a result, a large number of bubble economy phenomenon are formed. Under the influence of financial derivatives and the corresponding market transaction economy, this kind of bubble will have a great multiplier effect on the economy and greatly aggravate the distortion and imbalance of the economy. In fact, this crisis is the total outbreak of the contradictions between macroeconomic policies based on economic liberalism in the western world since the 1970s, which makes people have to rethink the rationality and effectiveness of economic liberalism market theory and policies. On the other hand, how to analyze the root causes of the global crisis from the perspective of economic theory, especially macroeconomics and institutional analysis, and find a theoretical way out from this analysis. This means that the market outlook of neo-economic liberalism and various economic theories with the philosophical tendency of economic liberalism are facing unprecedented challenges. Meeting this challenge may mean another great change in economic theory, or another sharp debate between the two different market economic views of economic liberalism and state interventionism.

It needs to be pointed out that in the history of western economic thought and economic development, the opposition and divergence between the two different market economy philosophies are identical in the following two aspects. First, no matter what kind of economic philosophy, it is based on the recognition of private capital ownership and market competition mechanism as the basic system. It does not deny private ownership and competition, nor does it deny market and freedom, but there are differences on how to better and more effectively realize capital private ownership and market competition effectiveness. One pays more attention to individual rights and market spontaneity, while the other emphasizes overall coordination and government spontaneity. Second, in the debate of two different market economic views, no matter in any period, which market economic view has a slight advantage or mainstream, it is out of the need to solve the main contradictions in the operation of capitalist market economy and the development of social economy more effectively. In other words, the alternating changes of the dominant position of different market economic concepts in the ideological history are only a response to the changes in institutional arrangements that highlight contradictions in the development of capitalist social economy. This is also the fundamental economic motive for the two different market economy philosophies to argue for a long time and take turns in holding the mainstream position.

2.2.3 The Choice of Market Economy View in the Process of Economic Reform in China

The construction of a socialist market economy in China is not only a process of introducing and learning advanced technology and experience of economic development from western developed countries, but also a process of criticizing and drawing lessons from their market economic system during the process of reform. However, with regards to China's characteristics are concerned, the following aspects deserve special emphasis. Firstly, China's socialist market economy system is based on a basic system with public ownership as the main body and common development of multiple ownership economies, rather than simply on the basis of capitalist private ownership. The most fundamental institutional characteristics of the socialist market economy with Chinese characteristics are embodied in this. The fundamental difficulties of China's socialist market economy are also concentrated here. Therefore, China's market values in the process of marketization are fundamentally different from any camp in Western economics, including economic liberalism and state interventionism, because they are based on the recognition of private capital ownership. Secondly, the proposition of a socialist market economy itself contains profound requirements for the organic unity of national macro-control and free market competition. "Socialism" itself emphasizes "society" as a whole, while "market economy" clearly points out that the basic force of resource allocation lies in market competition. Therefore, the socialist market economic system of China is not the centralization of the fundamental interests of the society as a whole, the fundamental mechanical opposition and separation between the market and the decentralized market subjects, but an organic and internal unity as a whole. The proposition of "socialist market economy" is a brand-new generalization of the economic system with long macroeconomic equilibrium. Whether from the perspective of western economic thought or the development of Marxist economic theory, "socialist market economy" is a new interpretation of the relationship between government and market. Although this interpretation has just begun and needs to be explored more arduously for a longer period of time, the reform practice of China's socialist market economy is indeed a great historical creation. Thirdly, the proposition of a socialist market economy includes not only the requirement of system, but also the requirement of realizing economic equilibrium in the relationship between government and market. It also contains the requirement of fair and reasonable distribution of welfare brought about by balanced growth and development, so that the majority of members of society can enjoy the benefits of development reasonably, fairly and effectively.

2.2.4 *Attention Should Be Paid to the Impact of the Current Global Economic Crisis on China's Economic System Reform*

From the real estate market crisis in the United States to the financial crisis in the United States and even the global economic crisis, the impact on China's economic growth is more and more extensive and profound. Especially under the condition of insufficient growth of domestic demand for many years in China's economy, especially the relatively weak growth of consumer demand, the impact of the global economic recession on China is more significant, which has increasingly attracted the attention of the government, enterprises and residents. The macroeconomic policies adopted by China to combat the crisis and curb the sharp decline in the growth rate are becoming faster and stronger, including fiscal policy and monetary policy, demand management policy and supply management policy, macroeconomic intervention and microeconomic intervention. The intensity and systemicity of the government's economic intervention policies have also been greatly enhanced and strengthened. In the face of the global crisis and the profound international economic background, almost all western countries have unprecedentedly strengthened government intervention in the market. So, what impact will this background of economic history have on China's economic system reform? Especially in the critical period of the reform and opening up, we should pay enough attention to this issue, that is, we should not only pay attention to the impact of the crisis on China's economic growth, but also pay attention to its impact on China's economic reform.

The main problems lie in two aspects. On the one hand, the global economic crisis does show the institutional limitations of the western capitalist market mechanism in allocating resources and achieving balanced growth, indicating the limitations of its government's macro-control, indicating the profundity of its market failure, and the necessity of the state and government to intervene in market failure, but with this shake and deny the market-oriented goal orientation of China's economic reform? On the other hand, although China's market-oriented reform has only lasted for decades, especially when the socialist market economy is clearly put forward as the reform objective, it is only after the 14th National Congress of the CPC in 1992, but is it excessive?

For the first problem, the author's answer should be "no". From the perspective of economic development history, including Chinese and foreign economic history, it has been fully demonstrated that market economy civilization is the most effective way to allocate resources. Although the capitalist market mechanism, as a historical mode of production, has a series of profound and sharp contradictions, the social progress and civilization progress brought about by this historical civilization is unparalleled by all previous human social systems. Although there are many deep conflicts and contradictions to be further dealt with in the reform process of China in the past 30 years from 1978 to 2008, which is oriented by market economic mechanism, the development of Chinese society in the past 30 years, especially the development of basic social economy and productivity on which social development depends, is unprecedented in Chinese history.

For the second problem, it may be more complicated, but in general the answer should be "no". During the 30 years of reform and opening up in China from 1978 to 2008, there is indeed a tendency of over-marketization in some fields and aspects. However, this excessive tendency is not so much the excessive progress of marketization, it is the introduction of marketization in regions that should not be marketized, and the introduction of market mode in areas where contradictions and interests should not be dealt with by market means. In more aspects of existing problems and contradictions, the important reason is not so much market-oriented as insufficient, in-depth and imperfect market-oriented process. Generally speaking, the reform of China's socialist market economic system is far from complete. From the point of view of the core link of the reform, although the enterprise reform, especially the reform of state-owned enterprises, has begun to shift gradually to the reform of government and social public system, the fundamental proposition of the enterprise reform still needs to be dealt with in depth, including the property right reform of state-owned enterprises and the improvement of corporate governance structure, including the institutional construction of non-state-owned enterprises and the creation of fair competition conditions. At the same time, the transformation of government functions, the reform of macro-control methods and the corresponding reform of social public system are also in urgent need of further development. From the perspective of the main task of the reform, although the commodity marketization has been basically realized and gradually turned to the factor marketization reform, institutional discrimination against non-state-owned enterprises, and monopoly issues in industrial organization need to be processed. At the same time, the contradictions faced by factor marketization are more difficult. The institutional discrimination in labor marketization, the lack of deepening capital market and the lack of land marketization need to be promoted. From the point of view of the main difficulties in the reform, although the market mechanism has replaced the traditional planned economy in its role, the main resistance in the process of marketization has ceased to be the force of the traditional planned economy, and the main difficulties in marketization have gradually shifted from the expansion of the scale of the role of market mechanism to the improvement of the quality of market mechanism, the structure of market mechanism is still extremely incomplete. And under the influence of domestic and foreign contradictions, there is a considerable possibility of institutional "return". More importantly, the fairness and quality of market mechanism need to be improved, including the cultivation of market mechanism's main order, trading order, legal order, moral order and so on, which still need a very long historical process.

Therefore, we must attach great importance to the possible impact of the global economic crisis on China's reform of the system. We must see, in terms of long-term development, in order to truly realize the sustainable development of China's economy, efforts must be made to change the mode of economic development. The fundamental of the transformation of development mode is to make the long-term development truly change from relying mainly on the expansion of factor input to relying mainly on the improvement of factor efficiency, and to make the members of society fairly share the benefits brought by the improvement of efficiency, so as to ensure the continuous improvement of efficiency. Therefore, we must rely on innovation, including technological innovation and institutional innovation, especially institutional innovation. After all, system is more important than technology. The fundamental of institutional innovation lies in deepening reform. The basic goal of deepening reform is to construct and improve the socialist market economic system. It is an important proposition to deal with the relationship between government and market scientifically and historically. It is hoped that the impact of the global economic crisis will not only not shake and confuse the direction and principles of socialist market economic reform, but also make it deeper, more scientific, more sober and more effective.

Chapter 3
Historic Changes of Economic Development and Reform and the Fundamental Changes in Development Pattern

China's economic development and economic reforms have progressed to a new historical stage, which has presented us with a series of special development propositions and reform propositions. To deal with this particular proposition, what matters is that transforming the mode of economic growth. The transformation of the mode of economic growth lies first and foremost in technological innovation, while the fundamental of technological innovation lies in institutional innovation. The key to the transformation of economic growth mode driven by technological innovation and institutional innovation is to make efficiency increase the primary driving force for growth. With efficiency as the primary driving force for sustained growth, the important contradiction that needs to be addressed is the expansion of the income distribution gap, because under certain conditions, there will often be deep contradictions between efficiency and fairness. For the expansion of the income distribution gap, different corresponding measures should be taken according to different reasons, with the aim of better coordinating the relationship between fairness and efficiency. The purpose of this chapter is to point out that institutional change is the fundamental driving force for the change of social economic development mode. Besides, the basic test standard of the change effect of social economic development mode lies in its promotion of the development and liberation of social productive forces.

The basic time frame for writing this chapter is 2005. The basic content of this chapter was published as a stage achievement of the project in the third issue of *Economic Research Journal* in 2006, and was later reprinted by *Xinhua Digest* in the seventh issue of 2006.

W. Liu, *Research on China's Market Economy Development*,
https://doi.org/10.1007/978-981-97-1398-1_3

3.1 The Historical Stage of China's Economic Development and What the Particular Features of This Stage

Measuring the level of social and economic development in a country has always been a controversial issue. However, no matter what kind of differences exist, two types of economic indicators are indispensable in measuring the level of economic development. The first is the economic quantity index for GDP as the core, including the total GDP and per capita level, the growth rate of GDP, and the degree of expansion measured at constant price. The other is economic quality indicators with economic structural indicators as the core, including industrial structure, regional structure, employment structure, and input–output relationship. The economic quantity index with GDP as the core directly reflects the growth of economic quantity and the expansion of economic scale, and thus has significant growth significance. However, growth is different from development. The important difference is that development must reflect a structural change in the state in the economy, while structural change is long-term, it is because of technological innovation and institutional innovation just the corresponding change. Simple growth can rely on the increase in the number of factor input in the case of constant technology, the same system, and the same efficiency, and achieve the growth of output under the condition of constant economic structure. But this growth is different from development, and development must be an evolution of structural state.[1]

If we measure the level of China's economic development based on the two basic indicators of economic quantity and economic quality, vertically, in 2005, China's economy was in an accelerated period of industrialization. Horizontally, China is slightly higher than the average of middle-income developing countries in the world. According to the released economic census data, the total current GDP price of China at the end of 2004 was RMB1,5987.8 billion, which was converted into US$1,931.7 billion at the official exchange rate, accounting for 4.4% of global GDP in the year,[2] ranking sixth in the world. The per capita GDP level is around US$1,500 (population growth was close to the average natural growth rate of 6.4‰ from 2001 to 2004), and the average natural growth rate in 2004 was 6.4%. This per capita level is slightly higher than the average of the lower middle-income developing countries in the contemporary world. From the perspective of economic quality indicators, especially from the perspective of the changing state of labor force employment structure, the proportion of the agricultural labor force in the total labor force at present is about 47%. This level is also slightly higher than the average of the lower middle-income developing countries in the contemporary world (54%). In terms of economic quantity and economic quality indicators, China's current economic development is in a state of transition from the lower middle-income developing country to the

[1] Liu Wei, *Research on Industrial structure in the Process of Industrialization*, Beijing: China Renmin University Press, 1995.

[2] The report by Li Deshui from the National Bureau of Statistics at a press conference held on December 20, 2005 at the State Council Information Office of the People's Republic of China. See the *People's Daily* on December 21, 2005.

middle-income developing country's average level. The basic problem dealt at this stage of economic development is to realize the modernization with industrialization as the main content and realize the accelerated development of industrialization.[3]

So, what are the outstanding characteristics of economic development at this stage?

(1) The social economy during the accelerated period of industrialization usually means that the economy has entered a fairly long period of sustained high growth, as seen in the economic history of industrialized developed countries, as well as in the reality of contemporary newly industrialized countries. As far as China's practice is concerned, from 1978 to 2005, the average economic growth rate has remained above 9.8%, and it has continued its rapid growth for decade. If there are no particularly special international and domestic uncontrollable socio-political, economic, cultural, military, and natural accidents, from the possibility of economic growth, at least until 2030, it is very realistic for China's average annual economic growth rate to remain above 7.2% (it is estimated that the average is 8–9% from 2001 to 2010, 7–8% from 2011 to 2020, and 6–7% from 2021 to 2030). This means that China's economy will continue to grow at a high rate for more than 20 years until 2030, and the Chinese economy is in the middle of a period of sustained high-speed growth for more than 50 years. According to this growth trend, by 2010, based on constant price calculations, taking into account the natural population growth level (estimated at 8.8% during the 11th Five-year Plan period), China's per capita GDP level will double that of 2000 and will exceed the average level of developing countries with moderate incomes. By 2020, it will increase the per capita level by about 4 times compared to 2000 and achieve the development goal of building a well-off society in an all-round way. It will reach the average level of the middle-income developing countries in the contemporary world. By 2030, GDP per capita will be 10 times higher than in 2000 which is equivalent to the level of developing countries with high income in the contemporary world. It will become a modern industrialized country and has completed the modernization with industrialization as its basic content. After continued development, China as the economy of the post-industrial era will enter the ranks of medium-developed countries by the middle of the 21st century. China's economy is experiencing rapid growth. Due to the rapid growth of high speed, a series of high-speed growth contradictions will inevitably arise, and the contradictions arising from high-speed growth can only be solved with sustained high-speed development.

(2) The period of accelerated industrialization is a period of dramatic changes in the structure of the national economy. From the perspective of economic history, the accelerating period of industrialization in various countries is the period of the most rapid changes in technological structure, employment structure, industrial structure, regional structure, income structure, and market organization structure. On the one hand, the growth rate of industrial manufacturing will

[3] China Center for Economic Research, *China Economic Growth Report 2005*, Beijing: China Economic Publishing House, 2005.

accelerate sharply, which will drive profound changes in the structural quality of the entire national economy. In the traditional industry, especially in the primary industry, under the condition that the relative labor productivity of the industry is increasing, and the market demand is relatively narrow, the proportion in the national economy is rapidly and continuously decreasing, forming a very serious problem of "agriculture, rural areas and rural residents". Especially for China, in a short period of time, industrialization has accelerated the pressure of hundreds of millions of agricultural labor transfer. In the past 30 years of reform and opening up from 1978 to 2008, China has transferred more than 200 million labor from agriculture. At the same time, at least 150 million agricultural labor remain to be transferred to meet the needs of agricultural production. On the other hand, industrialization accelerates to a certain extent, industrialization itself will be deepened from general processing industry to labor object industry and means of labor industry. Therefore, the tendency of heavy industry and heavy chemical industry is increasingly prominent, and the capital and technical problems raised by this become more serious. Resources, environmental issues, capital exclusion of labor, etc. will be further acute. At this stage, China's debate on whether to re-industrialization and how to promote heavy industrialization in theory and practice is a reflection of the sharpening of this series of contradictions. In addition, in the period of acceleration of industrialization and deepening of marketization, what is the position of the tertiary industry, how to deal with the relationship between the development of the tertiary industry and the secondary industry, how to deal with the relationship between the development of the tertiary industry and marketization, how to improve the internal industry structure, how to deal with the structural relationship between the traditional service sector and the modern service industry in the tertiary industry, to what extent the development of the tertiary industry has the direct significance of promoting economic growth, and to what extent it has the direct significance of promoting marketization, etc., These problems are the structural propositions that must be faced during the acceleration of industrialization.[4] The structural change was supposed to occur gradually over a long period of time, but in the period of industrialization acceleration, such long-term changes can be formed in a relatively short period of time, which makes the social contradictions more acute. Because of the structural changes that have occurred in the long run and the resulting changes in social class structure, income structure, and interest structure, society can gradually adapt and adjust accordingly in a long period of time, but if profound structural changes were to take place quickly in the short term, the society is often difficult to adapt. From the perspective of economic history, the period of industrialization acceleration is the period with the highest structural change. The reason why the accelerating period of industrialization in various countries is the most acute period of contradiction in the development process is extremely profoundly related to this structural reason.

[4] Liu Wei, Yang Yunlong, "Industrialization and Marketization: The Dual Mission of China's Tertiary Industry Development", *Economic Research Journal*, 1992 (12).

(3) The period of industrialization acceleration is also a period of rapid rise in social development costs. On the economic front, from the perspective of micro-resource allocation, the acceleration of industrialization is often a period of rapid increase in the consumption of resources, and the entire economic development will be increasingly constrained by resources. In China's case, since 1990, over the past decade or so, the external dependence of China's economy on major mineral resources has increased from 5% to over 50%. Especially in the case of technological progress and management science lag behind the situation, the efficiency of input–output is slow, and the consumption ratio of resources is bound to rise further, thus increasing the cost of development. Take China's energy elasticity coefficient as an example (energy consumption growth rate/ GDP growth rate), from 1991 to 2000, it was 0.2, and from 2001 to 2004, it reached 1.29, of which 2004 was as high as 1.6.[5]

From the perspective of macroeconomic operation and regulation, during the period of accelerated industrialization, on the one hand, the imbalance of macroeconomic aggregates will show a series of new complexities. Imbalances are often not simply a contradiction in the amount of aggregate demand greater than or less than aggregate supply, but also accompanied by a series of structural contradictions that are contrary to the usual economic logic. Judging from China's current macroeconomic imbalances, it cannot be said that aggregate demand is greater than aggregate supply, so it cannot be said that anti-inflation is the primary macroeconomic policy goal. However, it is also difficult to say that aggregate supply is greater than aggregate demand, so it cannot be said that expansion of employment is the primary macro policy goal. At present, there are at least three major paradoxes in China's macroeconomic imbalances, that is, the market's aggregate demand growth is weak, while the demand for fixed-asset investment is increasing too fast. As the price level rises, people's expectations for inflation are high, and the rate of economic growth is relative to the previous period. The rate of economic growth relative to the previous recovery significant, at the same time, the unemployment rate continued to climb.[6] This makes macroeconomic policies difficult to expand and difficult to tighten, thus increasing the difficulty of overcoming macroeconomic imbalances. On the other hand, during the period of industrialization acceleration, it is also a period of increasing difficulties in the realization of macroeconomic goals, whether it is the anti-inflation target or the goal of alleviating the unemployment rate, it will encounter a series of new resistance. In terms of anti-inflation, the inflation rate of low-income developing countries is very low. This is mainly due to low development speed, low marketization and low degree of economic monetization. However, once entering the lower and middle income stage of development, the inflation rate has risen remarkably due to the acceleration of industrialization and marketization. From the history of economic development after the Second World War, the inflation rate

[5] Zhang Zhuoyuan, "Transforming the Mode of Economic Growth and Maintaining a Sound and Rapid Development of the Economy", *Social Sciences of Beijing,* 2005(11).

[6] Liu Wei, "Three Paradoxes to Analyze China's Macroeconomic Imbalances", *Academic Research,* 2005(9).

of the developing countries at this stage has reached an average of more than double digits, and the average years in high years have reached more than 30%. Entering the stage of development of middle and upper income, the average inflation rate is higher, which is more than double the average in the lower and middle income stage. In the high years, the average inflation rate of the upper middle income developing countries reached more than 60%. Only after the high-income development stage, that is, the newly industrialized countries and the completion of the dual economic transformation, the inflation rate fell back to one-digit. Within the whole process, the whole process presents an inverted "U" shape.[7] As far as anti-unemployment is concerned, during the period of accelerating industrialization, on the one hand, due to the acceleration of technological progress, the contradiction between unemployment and vacancies has become more acute. On the other hand, due to the deep marketization, a large number of hidden unemployment has become explicit unemployment. Take China as an example. In the mid-1980s, for every 1 percentage point increase in China's economy, more than 2.4 million new jobs were created. Up to now, for every 1% increase in GDP, the number of new jobs is less than 1 million.[8]

Undoubtedly, this microscopic and macroscopic contradiction and the intensification of difficulties will greatly increase the cost of economic development. Moreover, other social costs have not been fully included here. For example, the contradiction between fairness and efficiency in the period of industrialization acceleration, the serious conflict between development and environment, and the coexistence of unemployment and vacancies will aggravate the difficulties in realizing development during this period.

3.2 The Key to Promote Development Through Reform is to Change the Pattern of Economic Development Through the Reform and Opening up

Dealing with a series of developmental problems and institutional contradictions faced by China in the new period of reform and development, the transformation of development mode is of fundamental significance. Because the key to solving the problems of development and reform lies in the transformation of China's economic growth and development from the expansion of the main factor-based investment to the improvement of efficiency. As far as development is concerned, whether it is to maintain sustained high-speed economic growth or to alleviate structural contradictions in high-speed growth, whether to improve development efficiency or reduce

---

[7] The World Bank used the statistics of countries from the 1960s to the 1980s as a sample to explain this trend in the history of the factory's economic development. See World Bank, *World Development Report 1989*, Beijing: China Financial and Economic Publishing House, 1990, p. 164.

[8] Zhu Zhixin, "Economic Growth is Significantly Weakening Employment", *China Youth Daily*, April 29, 2004.

development costs, it depends on the improvement of efficiency and the transformation of growth mode. The ultimate goal of the reform is to promote economic development by deepening the process of the socialist market economic system. The internal unity between reform and development lies in the effective treatment of the proposition of development through institutional reform. Through reforms, we will promote the fundamental transformation of the growth mode from the system and make the necessary institutional conditions necessary for efficiency improvement.

The transformation of the development mode first involves technological innovation, especially the improvement of independent innovation capability. Without technological advancement and technological innovation, it is impossible to increase the efficiency of growth and realize the transformation of the mode of economic growth. However, technological innovation is not so much a technical issue as it is an institutional issue. From a certain social sense, it can be said that the improvement of technological innovation capability is based on the premise and guarantee of the improvement of social system innovation capability.

From the perspective of resource allocation, the essence of institutional innovation is the improvement of the socialist market economic system. The key to efficiency gains lies in the development of competitive factor markets. On the one hand, from the perspective of the internal competition mechanism of the market economy, it includes: the order of the market entities, especially the hard constraints on the enterprise in the property rights system, the clarity in the subject and boundary of the property rights. The order of market trading, the justice and fairness of the price order is of great significance to the technological innovation of enterprises. On the other hand, from the external environment of the market economy, the order of legal governance, especially the legal protection of intellectual property rights. Moral order, especially the integrity support for innovation. These have extremely profound social significance for the improvement of corporate innovation capabilities. From the perspective of China's economic development history, improving the ability of technological innovation, transforming the mode of economic growth, and realizing the development model of stimulating economic growth with efficiency improvement has been a long-standing theory or policy. However, the key reason why it hasn't worked for so long lies in the lack of sufficient market competitiveness in the system. Since the reform and opening up, in the process of high-speed economic growth in China, the factor efficiency, especially the efficiency of capital, has been significantly improved because of the reform of the system and the deepening of the marketization. The more the elements are incorporated into the competition, the higher the competitive efficiency. Empirical studies show that institutional changes play a crucial role in improving the efficiency of factors in China's economic growth.[9]

Promote technological innovation with institutional innovation, and then realize the fundamental transformation of the economic growth mode to solve the new problems facing China's economic development. The key to this historic transformation is increased efficiency, including microscopic factor efficiency, structural efficiency

[9] Liu Wei, Li Shaorong, "Changes in Ownership and Economic Growth and Improvement of Factor Efficiency", *Economic Research Journal*, 2001(1).

in the highly evolved economic structure, and stability efficiency in the motion of macroscopic total quantity. Then, with the continuous improvement of efficiency as the primary driving force to drive sustained economic growth and development, what is the most important social constraint? For developing countries, efficiency is the primary driving force for development, and it is often difficult to meet the requirements of the social income distribution fairness goal at the same time. Therefore, with efficiency as the primary driving economic the sustained and high-speed economic growth, the important social constraint is how the social contradictions formed by the widening of the income distribution gap formed in this process can be effectively controlled within the tolerance of society. That is to say, the transformation of the growth mode has extremely profound requirements for social harmony. A balanced relationship must be established between efficiency and fairness.

3.3 Changes of Ownership Structure and Development Pattern

Ownership constitutes the institutional basis for economic development, and changes in ownership constitute the most profound source of changes in economic operating mechanisms. The motivation for the change of China's economic development mode can also find an institutional explanation in the change of ownership.

Since the reform and opening up, the outstanding characteristics of China's ownership structure change are two aspects. First, the proportion of state-owned economy has continued to decline. According to the 2004 national economic census data, the proportion of state-owned capital in paid-in capital of all enterprises as legal persons has dropped from nearly 90% at the beginning of the reform to 48.1%. However, there are two characteristics that must be pointed out in the process of declining the proportion of state-owned assets. Firstly, although the proportion of state-owned assets has continued to decline since the reform and opening up, the growth rate of state-owned assets is significantly higher than the traditional system of state-owned assets. That is to say, the reform and opening up has promoted the growth of state-owned assets, but only because the increase in the growth rate of state-owned assets is lower than the growth rate of non-state-owned assets in the same period. Secondly, although the proportion of state-owned assets is declining, its distribution structure still reflects effective control over the national economy. In the industrial distribution of state-owned assets, social infrastructure has been sharply reduced, such as railways, air transportation, telecommunications, road traffic adjustment, municipal infrastructure, etc., it can be said that more than 95% are state-owned economic control. In the field of energy power and raw material production, such as electricity, oil, steel, coal, etc., it can be said that nearly 95% is controlled by the state-owned economy. In important and key areas of the national economy, such as automobile manufacturing and finance, more than 90% are state-owned economic control. Second, the proportion of non-state-owned economy, especially the private economy, has risen significantly. In the paid-in capital of corporate legal persons, the share of private capital rose from less than 1% at the beginning of the reform and opening up to over 28% at the current stage. In terms of its distribution, the non-state-owned economy is mainly concentrated in the general competitive field. The most prominent feature is its rapid growth, especially since the mid-to-late 1990s, China's private enterprises have achieved remarkable development. In the past decade, the number of private enterprises has increased by 33 times, the registered capital of private enterprises has increased by 52 times, the output value created by private enterprises has increased by nearly 48 times, and the retail sales of consumer goods in the private sector has increased by 56 times.[10]

This kind of ownership structure's change, has the following four aspects influence to China's economic growth at least.

(1) The role of the non-state-owned economy has risen markedly in economic growth. Firstly, in terms of total GDP, the state-owned economic sector accounts for about 25%, the private economy accounts for about 25%, the mixed economy accounts for 30%, and the foreign-funded enterprises provide less than 20%. Secondly, in recent years, the contribution of the non-state-owned economy has been the most important. The state-owned economy has contributed nearly 30% to its economic growth, while the non-state-owned economy has contributed more than 70% to its economic growth rate.

(2) The role of the non-state-owned economy is increasing in overcoming the imbalance in economic growth. From the perspective of controlling inflation, the development of the non-state-owned economy has eased the pressure of inflation from at least five aspects: Firstly, agriculture, the dominant sector of the non-state-owned economy, has developed steadily for many years and has played an extremely important role in stabilizing prices. Among the added value of China's current primary industry, more than 97% is contributed by the non-state-owned economy, and the contribution of the state-owned economy is less than 3%. Secondly, the non-state-owned economy has relatively less credit funds. Both in terms of scale and proportion, they are much lower than the state-owned economy, and the capital turnover rate is relatively fast. Therefore, it plays an active role in promoting the balance and mutual balance of the aggregate supply and demand of funds and the aggregate supply and demand of commodities, alleviating the pressure of the contradiction between aggregate supply and demand on price increases. Thirdly, the non-state-owned economy has continuously increased taxes, and its proportion has also increased. At the same time, the non-state-owned economy has low direct dependence on finance. Especially under the condition that the transformation of public finance has not been realized, the development of non-state-owned economy is not the cause of increasing fiscal deficit, but alleviates the contradiction of fiscal revenue and expenditure and thus alleviates the inflationary pressure caused by the increase in fiscal deficit. Fourthly, the budgetary constraints of the non-state-owned economy are more stringent than those of the state-owned economy. In the process of

---

[10] *China Private Economy Yearbook,* 2002–2004. Beijing: China Zhigong Press, 2004.

transition, the market's restraint on its behavior is relatively higher, and its overall market efficiency is relatively high, which is conducive to promoting balanced economic growth. Fifthly, the rise in wages and welfare levels in the non-state-owned economy is generally more stringent and more closely linked to operating condition of the enterprise. Therefore, the cost-push inflationary pressure caused by the excessive rise in wages is also alleviated to some extent.

(3) Another aspect of the rise of the non-state-owned economy in overcoming economic imbalances is the reducing of unemployment. On the one hand, with the rapid development of non-state-owned economy, the contribution rate to economic growth is getting higher and higher, and it has become the primary force to drive economy, which creates more employment opportunities. According to statistics, in the past decade or so since the 1990s, just the number of employees recruited by private companies has increased by 12 times. On the other hand, due to various developmental and institutional factors, the average cost of absorbing a single employee in non-state-owned economy is significantly lower than that in state-owned economy. According to estimates, in the non-state-owned economy, it spends about half as much on fixed assets and wages and benefits as in the state-owned economy. This further enhances the ability of the non-state economy to absorb employment.

(4) The change in ownership structure has produced profound to China's economy productivity promotion.

If we assume that the output elasticity of capital and labor factors does not change, that is, the productivity is required to be constant, the provinces of our country are used as sample units, and the ownership structure and industrial structure data of each province are taken as the characteristics of their economic structure. Through the Cobb–Douglas production function model, we study the impact of changes in China's economic structure on productivity. We can obtain a model of the impact of economic structure on China's economic scale and factor productivity. By performing regression analysis on this model, we can obtain an estimation model of the production function containing the characteristics of economic structure (industrial structure and ownership structure)[11]:

$$\hat{Y} = K^{0.68+0.038x_1} L^{0.30+4.07\times10^{-5}x_1} e^{0.91-0.52x_2}$$

The economic implications of this estimation model indicate that at this stage in China, changes in industrial structure and ownership structure have a profound impact on production, but this effect is different. The change in industrial structure affects the scale of economic production, that is, the production possibility curve of the national economy. If the industrial structure is highly improved in the process of industrialization, and the proportion of the primary industry shrink the production possibility curve of the entire economy will move outwards, that is, the production

[11] Specific model settings, data sources and model estimates can be found in: Liu Wei, Li Shaorong, *Economic Growth and Economic Structure in Transition*, Beijing: China Development Press, 2004, pp. 97–103.

scale of the national economy will expand. Changes in ownership structure affect factor efficiency. From the perspective of China's reform practice, when the proportion of non-state-owned economy expands, the output elasticity of factors, especially the elasticity of output of capital, will increase, and the efficiency of production factors will also increase.

According to the empirical research on the relationship between ownership structure change and economic growth in China at present, on the one hand, it is assumed that the industrial structure is unchanged, but the ownership structure changes, especially the proportion of non-state-owned economy exceeds a certain level (the added value created by non-state-owned economy accounts for the proportion of GDP in 2001 reached 62.32%. The proportion of employees in urban non-state-owned units accounts for town employees reached 68.09% in 2001[12]). The production of the national economy will be manifested as economies of scale. And the reason for the formation of this scale economy is mainly due to changes in ownership structure, such as the improvement of factor efficiency, especially the improvement of capital efficiency. On the other hand, the degree of influence of ownership structure changes on the efficiency of capital factors and labor factors is very different. The results of econometric analysis using actual data from China show that the impact of changes in ownership structure on capital factors is significantly higher than the impact on labor factors (both more than 900 times). That is to say, the institutional changes in this aspect of ownership structure are mainly to improve the efficiency of capital elements, or to say that the level of capital efficiency improvement is slightly higher than the efficiency of labor factors. Therefore, a further question is raised. It is assumed that income is distributed according to the principle of market competition, that is, according to the contribution of factors, if the state of direct primary distribution of the market is not fully reallocated, with the reform of ownership and the corresponding market-oriented in-depth, the efficiency of capital factor improvement is far greater than the improvement of labor factor efficiency. The level of remuneration received by the corresponding capital element holders and the growth rate of remuneration will be significantly higher than the labor factor, that is, the remuneration and growth of capital is significantly higher than the income of labor, and the income gap between capital and labor will rapidly expanding. It is necessary to pay high attention to this. Perhaps this is also the income distribution of the goals of equality and efficiency of the contradictory movement in China at this stage of a manifestation.

In short, the change of ownership structure is an important part of the historical process of China's socialist market economy. The remarkable feature of this institutional change is that the proportion of state-owned system has continued to decline, and the proportion of non-state-owned economy has continued to rise. The impact of this remarkable feature on the economy is reflected in many aspects. In terms of the growth of economic problems, the non-state-owned economy has grown to become the main force driving economic growth and employment. In terms of the balance of economic growth, it is to urge the national economy to accept more

[12] Source: *China Statistical Yearbook*, 2002.

market constraints. In particular, the non-state-owned economy, which is expanding its proportion, is more strongly constrained by the market, thus weakening the ups and downs caused by administrative interventions under the centralized planned economy. In terms of improving the efficiency of micro-factors, it promotes the improvement of capital and labor factors, especially the improvement of capital efficiency. Therefore, changes in the ownership structure, especially the rise in the non-state-owned proportion and the corresponding deepening of the marketization level, have led more and more elements from the past administrative control field to the market competition field. This institutional change has a special ability to explain non-state-owned economic growth. This ability to interpret is not only generally reflected in the quantity of growth, but more particularly in the balance and efficiency of growth, and particularly, this institutional change has significantly increased capital efficiency. For developing countries where capital is particularly scarce, it is an effective way to improve the efficiency of capital through this kind of institutional change, and not to obtain the economic development and improve the absolute standard of people's life by means of the large investment of capital. However, it must also be clearly seen that this will widen the income gap between capital and labor. As a lasting way to develop the economy, while pursuing institutional change to bring about the goal of efficiency improvement of the factor, we must pay attention to the equal goal of income distribution from all aspects. At the time of initial distribution and redistribution, attention should be paid to the coordination between fairness and efficiency. In the process of achieving the goal of efficiency improvement, it is the nature of the social market economy that the whole society, especially the majority of workers, can truly enjoy the benefits brought about by development.[13]

3.4 Advances in Technology and Economic Growth of China

Institutional innovation has liberated productive forces, released the potential of China's economic development, and fundamentally changed the face of China. Table 3.1 lists China's GDP, employed population, and the original value of fixed assets from 1978 to 2004 and the comparison between them.

These time series reflect three trends:

(1) Labor productivity. If labor productivity is defined as the average GDP of each employed person, we can see that after the reform and opening up, China's labor productivity has increased quite rapidly. In 2004, it was 5.33 times that of 1978. The improvement of labor productivity can also be reflected in the labor elasticity time series of GDP. During this period, the labor elasticity values for each year are decreasing, and significantly less than 1, indicating that labor productivity is constantly improving.

[13] Liu Wei, Li Shaorong, *Changes in Ownership and Economic Growth and Improvement of Factor Efficiency*, *Economic Research Journal*, No. 1, 2001.

Table 3.1 China's GDP, original value of fixed assets and employment from 1978 to 2004

Year	GDP		Employed population		Original value of fixed assets		Labor productivity (RMB)	Labor flexibility	Capital elasticity
	Billion RMB (price in 1978)	Growth rate (%)	10,000 people	Growth rate (%)	Billion RMB (price in 1978)	Growth rate (%)			
1978	362	–	40,152	–	888	–	903		
1979	390	7.62	41,024	2.17	1,001	12.72	951	0.29	1.67
1980	420	7.79	42,361	3.26	1,123	12.18	992	0.42	1.56
1981	442	5.19	43,725	3.22	1,236	10.07	1,011	0.62	1.94
1982	483	9.11	45,295	3.59	1,368	10.71	1,065	0.39	1.18
1983	535	10.90	46,436	2.52	1,517	10.91	1,152	0.23	1.00
1984	616	15.19	48,197	3.79	1,698	11.90	1,279	0.25	0.78
1985	700	13.50	49,873	3.48	1,904	12.14	1,403	0.26	0.90
1986	761	8.81	51,282	2.83	2,132	11.98	1,484	0.32	1.36
1987	850	11.60	52,783	2.93	2,389	12.05	1,609	0.25	1.04
1988	946	11.30	54,334	2.94	2,657	11.21	1,740	0.26	0.99
1989	984	4.09	55,329	1.83	2,870	8.03	1,779	0.45	1.96
1991	1,116	9.20	64,749	1.15	3,360	8.43	1,578	0.12	0.92
1992	1,274	14.20	66,152	1.01	3,677	9.44	1,703	0.07	0.67
1993	1,452	14.00	66,808	0.99	4,068	10.64	1,926	0.07	0.76
1994	1,643	13.10	67,455	0.97	4,528	11.31	2,174	0.07	0.86
1995	1,822	10.90	68,065	0.90	5,051	11.55	2,435	0.08	1.06
1996	2,004	10.00	68,950	1.30	5,630	11.45	2,676	0.13	1.14
1997	2,190	9.30	69,820	1.26	6,243	10.89	2,906	0.14	1.17
1998	2,361	7.80	70,637	1.17	6,917	10.81	3,137	0.15	1.38
1999	2,541	7.60	71,394	1.07	7,640	10.45	3,343	0.14	1.38
2000	2,754	8.40	72,085	0.97	8,431	10.35	3,558	0.12	1.23
2001	2,983	8.30	73,025	1.30	9,320	10.55	3,820	0.16	1.27
2002	3,254	9.10	73,740	0.98	10,331	10.84	4,084	0.11	1.19
2003	3,579	10.00	74,432	0.94	11,541	11.71	4,413	0.09	1.17
2004	3,941	10.10	75,200	1.03	12,933	12.07	4,809	0.10	1.19

Source China Statistical Yearbook, 1979–2005

(2) Investment efficiency. It is clear that the improvement in investment efficiency is lower than the labor efficiency. As can be seen from the last column of Table 3.1, the capital elasticity coefficient of GDP for most years is greater than 1, indicating that the efficiency of investment has decreased during these years. Overall, investment efficiency is also decreasing.

(3) Technological progress. Technological progress can be examined from different perspectives. The narrow technological advancement refers only to the impact of technological innovation on the production process, and Solow's definition of broad sense technological advancement (Solow 1957) includes not only technological innovation, but also social organization, institutional innovation and many other factors. We use the method of total production function to analyze China's economic growth after the reform and opening up.

Under the assumption of neutral technological progress, the real GDP (Y),[14] the employed population (L), and the original value of fixed assets (K)[15] (see Table 3.1) for 1978–2004 are fitted to the Cobb–Douglas production function:

$$Y_t = A_0 e^{\gamma_t} K_t^{\alpha} L_t^{\beta} \tag{3.1}$$

It is assumed that the relationship between the output elasticity coefficient α of the capital K and the output elasticity coefficient β of the labor L satisfies the relationship $\alpha + \beta = 1$, which has the following relationship:

$$Y = 0.3314 K^{0.9083} L^{0.0917} \tag{3.2}$$

The goodness of fit for Eq. (3.2) is 0.99, passed the significance test. The economic explanation for this equation is that under the assumption of neutral technological progress (assuming that the amount of labour and capital needed to increase per unit of output remains the same), then, from 1978 to 2004, the contribution of capital to China's economic growth is significantly greater than the contribution of labor. Specifically, for each additional unit of output, the labor input required to increase is only 9%, and the increased capital investment is 91%. The contribution of capital is 10 times that of labor. This also explains why China's high-speed economic growth is always accompanied by a higher growth rate of fixed-asset investment. On the other hand, it also proves that the reform of the property rights system is of great significance to economic growth.

The comparison between Eqs. (3.1) and (3.2) are obtained:

$$A_0 e^{\gamma_t} = 0.3314 \tag{3.3}$$

If $A_0 = 1$ is assumed, the coefficient of technological progress during this period is $\gamma = -1.1044$. It reflects that technological progress has not contributed to economic growth during this period. In other words, a coefficient of technological advancement of less than 0 indicates that during this period of time, for each additional unit of output, the required input in production factors is incremental. From the specific numerical analysis, in 2004 China's real GDP increased by 9.87 times compared

---

[14] Calculated according to the price of 1978.

[15] Based on data of capital construction investment, renovation and renovation funds, total social fixed assets investment since 1953, and total fixed capital formation since 1978, adjusted estimates are made. Calculated according to the fixed price in 1978.

with 1978, the employment of the three major industries increased by 87%, while the original value of fixed assets increased by 13.57 times. This shows that in China's economic growth, labor efficiency has improved rapidly and significantly, but the output of fixed assets per unit has declined. This also explains, to some extent, the improvement of the level of productivity caused by China's institutional innovation. Overall, the main reliance is on the rapid expansion of scale rather than technological progress. In other words, economic growth is more dependent on the increase in capital input rather than the efficiency of the use of production factors.

This conclusion is close to our realistic feeling. After the reform and opening up, in order to change the face of backwardness, China first proposed the economic growth target of quadrupling GDP. Therefore, the growth rate of GDP has become the main task of economic activities in China and various regions. And through what kind of approach to achieve this task, for a long period of time, is not the focus of our attention. From the perspective of development practices in various regions, the most important way to achieve higher GDP growth rates is to attract investment. What attracts investors to invest is the comparative advantage of these regions in terms of production factors, especially labor, land, energy and other advantages. The technology transfer realized in this process of funds transfer is often a technology that is no longer advanced in more developed countries or regions. This makes economic growth much more dependent on scale expansion than on technological progress. The advantage of this is that it allows us to achieve faster scale expansion in a shorter period of time. The disadvantage is that such a growth pattern may lead to a series of sustainable development problems such as environment and resources.

High-speed economic growth requires China to solve a series of developmental problems and institutional contradictions in the process of modernization. To maintain sustained, stable and rapid growth of the Chinese economy, the transformation of growth patterns is fundamental. In this sense, the key to solving the development problems and reform problems lies in the transformation of China's economic growth and development from the expansion of the main factor-based investment to the improvement of efficiency. As far as development is concerned, whether it is to maintain sustained high-speed economic growth or to alleviate structural contradictions in high-speed growth. Whether to improve development efficiency or reduce development costs, it depends on the improvement of efficiency and the transformation of growth mode. The transformation of the growth mode first involves technological innovation, especially the improvement of independent innovation capability. Without technological advancement and technological innovation, it is impossible to increase the efficiency of growth, and it is impossible to achieve a change in the mode of economic growth. In the market economy system, enterprises are the main market players. Therefore, enterprises should not only be the micro-subjects of resource allocation, but also the main body of technological innovation. In this sense, the so-called independent innovation refers to independent innovation at the enterprise level, not independent innovation by the state (or government). Of course, from the individual enterprise, not all the technologies required by a single enterprise are independently developed by themselves, and some technologies or even all technologies can be obtained through market mechanisms. But on the whole, technological innovation must be organized by the corporate sector. The experience of developed market economies shows that the enterprise sector in the technological innovation system is indeed the main body of independent innovation. *The 2003 China Statistical Yearbook of Science and Technology* shows that the corporate sector is the mainstay of research funding. The research funding comes from the enterprise sector accounting for 66.2% of the total research funding in the United States, 28.7% from the government, and 5.1% from the others. Japan is 73, 18.5, and 8.5% respectively. Germany is 66, 31.5, and 2.5% respectively. The corporate sector is also the main body of research funding. In terms of research funding, the US corporate sector accounted for 72.9%, research institutions accounted for 7.6%, and universities accounted for 14.9%. Japan is 73.7, 9.5, and 14.5% respectively. Germany is 70, 13.5, and 16.5% respectively. The technical level and technological innovation capability of an enterprise not only directly determine the market competitiveness of the enterprise itself, but also play a fundamental role in the upgrading of various industries and their national economy. Through the independent innovation of the enterprise, not only the innovation project is directly oriented to the enterprise and its market demand, but also the achieved results can be directly industrialized.

If we say that in the technological innovation system, the ability to cultivate independent innovation mainly refers to cultivating the independent innovation capability of enterprises, what kind of independent innovation capability is cultivated?

Strictly speaking, from the perspective of industrial organization, only large enterprises or enterprises that have reached the scale economy required by competitive markets can have stronger and sustained technological innovation capabilities because: Firstly, only large companies have the financing capabilities required for technological innovation, while ordinary small and medium-sized enterprises (SMEs) do not. SMEs not only have to face the financing difficulties of high-risk technology innovation projects, but also the financing required to maintain general reproduction is relatively difficult. The problem of financing difficulties for SMEs not only occurs at the present stage in China, but also is a universal problem in the world, and sustained technological innovation must have strong financing capabilities. Secondly, only large companies or companies with a considerable share of the market can decentralize the cost of high-risk technological innovations, that is, share a small proportion of research and development (R&D) expenses in the sales of unit products. At present, the proportion of R&D investment in GDP in the 20 innovative countries in the world is on average more than 2% (that of China in 2004 was 1.35%). The reason why there is such a high proportion, the important microscopic reason is that dispersing the risks systematically. In particular, although the R&D expenses of large enterprises are absolutely large, they are equally low in the proportion of unit products. The scale of the enterprise, especially the large enterprises, distributes the risk of R&D in the whole society. In a society with strong innovation ability, the costs of enterprises investing in research and development are usually equivalent to about 10% of their market sales. Most enterprises do not meet the usual international standards. Among other reasons, SMEs makes it difficult to disperse the risk of high-investment research and development. Thirdly, only large enterprises, or enterprises with strong comprehensive strength, can make technological innovations free from the limitations of the product life cycle. Large enterprises may have a strong ability to counter the product life cycle. The reason why the average SME lacks sustainable technological innovation ability is that the life cycle of SMEs often coincides with the life cycle of a certain product and can even be reversed. The reason why such SMEs exist and develop is because the founders have the technology research and development and production of this product. The life cycle of an enterprise is accompanied by a life cycle movement of research and development, commissioning, and exit of this product. It is difficult for SMEs themselves to break the constraints of this product life cycle. Large enterprises can rely on financing capabilities and the advantages of decentralized R&D risks to enable innovation to break through the limitations of the product life cycle and promote continuous development of the enterprise through continuous technological innovation.

So, what role do SMEs play in the process of technological independent innovation? (1) SMEs have the function of more quickly commercializing certain relatively independent technological innovations, especially those technological innovations in which social connections and technological linkages are not very complicated. SMEs can quickly commercialize them, and large enterprises often have lag behind. Whether in decision-making or in scale, there are always some uneconomic aspects of large enterprises, and SMEs have the advantage in this respect. This is also an important reason why the production cycle of many SMEs is closely related to the product cycle formed by a certain technological innovation. In the modern economic society where the speed of technological advancement is increasing, technology innovation brings new product innovation, and then new products make the new SMEs grow faster and faster. In the world, the life expectancy of SMEs is usually about 3 to 5 years, while in China, it is only about 2 to 3 years. (2) SMEs have the function of more quickly promoting the socialization of certain technological innovations, especially in the market system is relatively complete, knowledge (technology) property rights protection is more adequate. At the same time, the economic costs, technical barriers and transaction costs of obtaining technical patents are within the conditions that can be tolerated. Through the authorization of manufacturing, SMEs can become an important force in the expansion and promotion of technological innovation products. The key here is the completeness of the patent market, the full legal protection of intellectual property rights and the feasibility of obtaining economic and technical authorization. (3) SMEs have the ability to professionalize in technological innovation in industrial organization more systematically. That is to say, although large enterprises are the main driving force for technological innovation, the industrial chain and a professional set implemented around core technological innovations may not be economical if they are directly completed by large enterprises themselves. And through the division of labor system in the whole society and even the whole world, mainly by SMEs to join the industrial division of labor chain, it may be more effective, but also more professional. Of course, this requires a systematic industrial organization. At the same time, it must be noted that the added value of the industrial chain finally obtained by the industrial division of labor that is not the source of core technological innovation is also very limited. However, the specialization effect must be recognized.

Therefore, the main body of independent innovation should be the enterprise. As the main body of innovation, the driving force of the sustainable innovation ability of its core technology lies mainly in the large enterprises. SMEs have a role to play in technological innovation, but they are not primarily innovations in core technological capabilities. Therefore, how to cultivate large enterprises and how to improve the innovation ability of large enterprises is an important link in the transformation of China's economic growth model.

However, technological innovation is not so much a technical issue as it is an institutional issue. The improvement of technological innovation capability is based on the premise and guarantee of enhancing the ability of institutional innovation. In this sense, institutional innovation in China's economic system reform still shoulders an arduous task.

From the perspective of resource allocation, the essence of institutional innovation is the improvement of the socialist market economic system. The key to efficiency gains lies in the development of competitive factor markets. On the one hand, from the perspective of the internal competition mechanism of the market economy, the market subject order (hard constraints on enterprises in the property rights system, clarity on the subject and boundary of property rights) and the market transaction order (justice and fairness in the price order) are of vital importance to the technological innovation of enterprises. On the other hand, from the external environment of the market economy, the rule of law (especially the legal protection of intellectual property rights) and the moral order (especially the integrity support for innovation) have extremely profound social significance for the improvement of corporate innovation capability. From the perspective of China's economic development history, improving the ability of technological innovation, transforming the mode of economic growth, and realizing the development model of stimulating economic growth with efficiency improvement has long been a theoretical point of view or a policy claim. However, the key reason why has not been it effective for so long lies in the lack of sufficient market competitiveness in the system. Since the reform and opening up, the efficiency of the factors of some enterprises (especially private enterprises), especially the efficiency of capital, has increased remarkably. The important reason is the institutional change, and also the deepening of marketization. The more the elements are more competitively marketed, the higher the competitive efficiency.

3.5 Economic Growth, Economic Development and Sustainable Development

The key to achieving sustained high-speed economic growth is efficiency, including growth efficiency in various periods, factor efficiency on the micro level, structural efficiency in the highly evolved economic structure, and stability efficiency in macroscopic gross motion. China's institutional innovation began with the reform of the distribution system in the 1980s. The goal of the reform is to break the balance under the traditional planning system and enable China to quickly get rid of poverty. During that period, economic development meant economic growth. However, economic growth and economic development are different after all. Generally speaking, economic growth is an aggregate question, and economic development is more of a structural problem, such as ownership structure, employment, industrial structure, balance of payments, income distribution, and regional differences. With China's rapid economic growth, the issue of development becomes more complicated, so a harmonious society will become a new theme of China in the 21st century. From a development perspective, China's current task is to re-establish a balanced development on a new basis after long-term growth.

Rebalancing does not mean giving up economic growth. China's past starting point was low, and the current per capita GDP level is not high, so economic growth is still a long-term important task for China. The solution to the development problem cannot be separated from economic growth. But more complicated than in the past, the current economic growth is facing more development constraints. Furthermore, China's development must be considered in the context of sustainable development, including economic, social and environmental development.

The economic constraints on economic growth come from the following two aspects:

The first is the issue of sustainable development. Since the beginning of the 21st century, as China has accelerated into the industrialization period, this extensive scale expansion has become more apparent. Taking energy consumption as an example, Table 3.2 lists the relationship between China's energy production and consumption from 1990 to 2004, and the growth of national economy. It can be seen that from 1990 to 2000, the energy production and consumption elasticity coefficients were all below 1. The growth rate of energy production and consumption was lower than the growth rate of GDP. Especially during the period from 1997 to 2000, as China's growth relied more on the development of high-tech industries and emerging tertiary industries, energy production and energy consumption declined. However, in 2001, with the increase in the growth rate of the industrial sector, the elasticity of energy production also rapidly increased to 1.57. After that, it remained at 1.5 or above until 2004. At the same time, the elasticity of energy consumption is also maintained at a high level. At this stage, for every 1 percentage point increase in the Chinese economy, it requires more than 1.5 times more energy consumption to sustain, showing the dependence of China's economic growth on a large amount of energy consumption.

Another issue is income distribution. For developing countries, efficiency is the primary driving force for development, and it is often difficult to meet the requirements of the social income distribution fairness goal at the same time. Therefore, with efficiency as the primary driving economic sustained high-speed growth, the important social constraint is how the social contradictions formed by the expansion of the income distribution gap formed in this process can be effectively controlled within the social tolerance. In other words, the transformation of growth mode has extremely profound requirements for social harmony, and a balanced relationship

Table 3.2 China's energy production and consumption elasticity coefficient from 1990 to 2004

Year	GDP growth rate (%)	Energy production growth rate (%)	Energy production elasticity coefficient	Energy consumption growth rate (%)	Elasticity coefficient of energy consumption
1990	3.8	2.2	0.58	1.8	0.47
1991	9.2	0.9	0.10	5.1	0.55
1992	14.2	2.3	0.16	5.2	0.37
1993	14.0	3.6	0.26	6.3	0.45
1994	13.1	6.9	0.53	5.8	0.44
1995	10.9	8.7	0.80	6.9	0.63
1996	10.0	2.8	0.28	5.9	0.59
1997	9.3	−0.2	–	−0.8	–
1998	7.8	−6.2	–	−4.1	–
1999	7.6	−12.2	–	−1.6	–
2000	8.4	−2.0	–	0.1	0.02
2001	8.3	13.0	1.57	3.5	0.43
2002	9.1	14.4	1.58	9.9	1.09
2003	10.0	15.6	1.56	15.3	1.53
2004	10.1	15.4	1.52	15.2	1.50

Source China Statistical Yearbook (*2005*)

must be established between efficiency and fairness. Judging from the current reality in China, this equilibrium has not yet reached an ideal state. The income gap between people in urban and rural areas, between different cities, between different villages, and within and between cities has widened. Adjusting the pattern of income distribution through various policies is an important issue that should be resolved in China's current economic development.

From a broad perspective, the means to achieve this balance of development at a higher level mainly include strengthening socialist democracy and the construction of the legal system, improving government administrative efficiency, improving the market economic system, and strengthening macroeconomic policies (fiscal policy, monetary policy) and so on.

Part II
Economic Growth Cycle and Aggregate Regulation in China's Socialist Market-Oriented Reform Process

This part consists of four chapters (Chaps. 4, 5, 6 and 7). The basic guiding ideology of this book is to prove the rightness and progressiveness of the reform by examining the internal connection between economic development and growth and the institutional reform of China's socialist market economy, and further explain the requirements for institutional reform based on the liberation and development of social productivity. Therefore, based on the first part exploring the features and theoretical debates of China's socialist market process, the second part begins to discuss the relationship between institutional reform and China's economic growth. Firstly, this part discusses the long-term strategic objectives for achieving China's economic growth and possible problems, thus further clarifying the historical requirements for reform and the value orientation for deepening reform (Chap. 4). Then, it analyzes the characteristics and cyclical features of China's economic growth since the reform and opening up, especially in recent years, and analyzes the complexity disequilibrium in China's macro-economy in this cyclical feature (Chap. 5). Finally, in response to the particular institutional background of the institutional reform of China's socialist market economy and the particular phased background of China's economic development, it emphasizes that in China's macro aggregate regulation, while emphasizing aggregate demand management, in response to the limitations of demand management, it should also pay attention to aggregate supply management and the particular effects of supply management (Chap. 6), and create institutional conditions for effectively implementing supply regulation (Chap. 7).

Chapter 4
Long-Term Strategic Objectives for Achieving China's Economic Growth and Possible Problems

Since the reform and opening up, China has maintained long-term high-speed economic growth. In 2002, China proposed a new long-term economic growth target that quadrupled GDP in 20 years. By 2007, the goal of quadrupling per capita GDP by 2020 was proposed. This chapter analyzes the possibility, trend, growth rate and possible problems of China's long-term economic growth from the perspectives of China's economy and East Asian economic comparison, residents' disposable income, and the impact of China's future economic growth on its international economic status.

In 2002, China's GDP exceeded RMB10 trillion. Then, in 2003, China's per capita disposable income exceeded US$1,000. These two figures provide an iconic starting point for our strategic goals. If China achieved its strategic goal of quadrupling GDP in the first 20 years of the 21st century (equivalent to an annual growth of 7.2%), the GDP calculated fixed price at 2002 will reach RMB40 trillion or so by 2020. At that time, per capita GDP will be around US$3,500, and per capita disposable income will exceed US$2,000.[1] Converted to the 2020 standard, China's total GDP will be around RMB3.6 billion, and the per capita disposable income will be more than US$2,000.[2]

It is different from the strategic goal of quadrupling the GDP first put forward by China in 1982, China's economic aggregate in 2003 has quadrupled on the basis of the time. We are achieving new goals at a much higher starting point, quadrupling not only the total but also the per capita level. We have many advantages to achieve

[1] The increase in per capita disposable income is related to the ratio between GDP, population, and disposable income of residents and GDP.

[2] Assume that the price level and exchange rate are unchanged.

The basic time frame for writing this chapter is 2003. The main content of this chapter is based on the publication of "Long-term Development Strategy for China's Economic Growth" by Liu Wei, Xu Xianchun, and Cai Zhizhou, which was released as a project achievement in the 7th issue of *Journal of Management World* in 2004.

W. Liu, *Research on China's Market Economy Development*,
https://doi.org/10.1007/978-981-97-1398-1_4

this new goal. However, there may be many factors that restrict us and affect our ability to achieve this goal. Sustainable long-term high-speed economic growth is a necessary condition for China's social and economic development. Many contradictions in China's social and economic life must be resolved through the space provided by economic growth and development. It can be said that "For a boat to sail upstream, it has to forge ahead or be driven backward." Research on the problems that may be encountered in the long-term growth of the future is crucial to our strategic goal of quadrupling in the new century. In order to achieve this strategic goal and overcome the difficulties involved, it is particularly necessary to transform the economic development mode, deepen the reform and opening up, and improve the socialist market economic system. The purpose of this chapter is to emphasize the necessity of internal unity of reform and development from the perspective of long-term development and the problems faced.

4.1 The Theory of Economic Growth Limit that Challenges the East Asian Model

Observing the pattern of global economic growth, China's rapid economic growth at the end of the 20th century was not isolated. It was an important part of the rise of Asia, especially East Asia, in the second half of the 20th century. From a more historical perspective, until the Opium War in the first half of the 19th century, China was the most powerful country in the world in terms of economic aggregate. However, the new trend of the global economy from east to west has changed the pattern of the world economy. In the 200 years of the history of modern economic development in the world, China, as a country with a long history, has suffered a lot. In this process, Western European powers such as Britain, France and Germany first rose through the industrial revolution, replacing China, a centuries-old central empire, and became the most economically developed countries in the world at that time. Then, this trend continues. The United States has became the world's superpower and has maintained this status to this day. Later, this effect continued to spread, the Asian economy began to prosper again. From the perspective of the overall trend of world economic development, it is inevitable that China will rise again in the world sooner or later between the second half of the 20th century and the first half of the 21st century due to various factors. The foresight of Chinese leaders at the turn of the 1970s and 1980s enabled China to seize the opportunity to promote China's development. Judging from this background, the development of China's economy and the development of East Asian economy are related.

High-speed economic growth is a long period of economic growth, and thus changes an economy's position in the international economy. If an economically underdeveloped country or region wants to transform and catch up with the world's advanced level, it must go through a period of rapid economic growth. From the perspective of development, there are four stages to catch up with and surpass the advanced level. The first is to catch up with and surpass speed, the second is to catch up with and surpass the total amount, the third is to catch up with and surpass the per capita level, and the fourth is to catch up with and surpass the use efficiency of production factors. This shows that high-speed economic growth has two characteristics. Firstly, the growth rate is high. Generally speaking, the growth rate in the initial period will remain at around 10% or even higher. Secondly, the duration is long. In 1958, China's GDP growth was 21.3%, but in 1961 it was—27.3%, which would not be called high-speed economic growth.

After the Second World War, with the support of the United States, Japan first embarked on the road of revival and rapid economic growth and established its dominant position in the Asian economy. It has become another major economic center after Europe, the United States, the Soviet Union and the Eastern European Group. After Japan, the economies of Republic of Korea and Singapore also began to accelerate, thus driving the development of the entire Southeast Asian economy. After the 1980s, China's economy began to take off, and the pace of development has caught the attention of the world. In this context, research on the East Asian economy has become a hot topic in the field of economics. Table 4.1 lists the economic growth of China, Japan, Republic of Korea and Singapore in the year 2000. As can be seen from Table 4.1, the high-speed growth periods of Japan, Republic of Korea, and Singapore lasted for about 20 years, and the average annual growth rates during these periods were relatively close, at around 9%. If we shorten the time interval, we will find that the growth rate of the starting period is even higher. However, these countries have experienced a slowdown after experiencing a period of rapid economic growth. This is a universal law, and developed market economy countries in the West have experienced similar development processes. However, the degree of economic slowdown varies from country to country. After the period of rapid economic growth, the economic growth rate of Japan and Republic of Korea slowed down noticeably. However, the economy of Singapore continue to grow at a rate of 7%. Among these countries, Singapore belong to the urban economy, while Japan and Republic of Korea belong to the regional economy. It can be seen that the larger the size (population and economic aggregate) of a country, the more difficult it is to maintain a high growth rate after the period of rapid growth. This law will be finally reflected in China's economic growth. And keeping the rapid economic growth as long as possible is exactly what every emerging industrialized country wants to achieve.

In September 1993, the World Bank published *The East Asian Miracle: Economic Growth and Public Policy*, which explored the various causes of the East Asian miracle. Therefore, the East Asian model has become the focus of attention.

The general view is that countries and regions where East Asian miracles happened have the following characteristics:

Firstly, the government-led economic system is often accompanied by a strong and even authoritarian government.

Secondly, an export-oriented economic development strategy based on export.

Thirdly, indirect financing with bank as the main mode. For example, in the economic development of Republic of Korea, the bank loans formed by some large

Table 4.1 Economic growth rate of China, Japan, Singapore and Republic of Korea

Country	Early high-speed growth	GDP growth rate (%)	High growth period	GDP growth rate (%)	Late high-speed growth	GDP growth rate (%)
China	1952–1978	6.15	1978–2000	9.52		
Japan			1955–1973	9.22	1973–2000	2.81
Singapore	1960–1965	5.74	1965–1984	9.86	1984–2000	7.18
Republic of Korea	1953–1962	3.84	1962–1991	8.48	1991–2000	5.76

Note The Chinese data in the table is calculated based on GDP accounting data in *China Statistical Yearbook (2001)* (excluding Hong Kong SAR., Macao SAR. And Taiwan Province); the Japanese data is calculated based on constant price GDP accounting data in the Economic and Social Research Institute of the Cabinet Office of Japan (www.esri.cao.go.jp); the Singaporean and Republic of Korean data are calculated based on GDP accounting data of corresponding countries and regions in IMF: International Financial Statistics, November, 2001 (CD)

enterprises through government intervention have formed a rapid expansion in a short period of time. And in a certain period of time, it has contributed to the economic growth of the country.

Fourthly, enterprises and social culture characterized by Confucian traditional culture.

Fifthly, give play to the advantages of latecomers, catch up with the world's advanced level, and achieve high-speed economic growth.

The occurrence of the East Asian miracle is already an indisputable fact. However, there are some opposite views on the future of this miracle. Some views even believe that the above reasons for the East Asian miracle are likely to be important factors affecting the further development of the East Asian economy. The American economist Paul Krugman's The *Myth of Asia's Miracle*[3] published in 1994 pointed out that the newly industrialized countries and regions in Asia are "paper tigers." Their economic growth, like the Soviet Union in the 1950s, relied too much on large-scale labor and investment rather than increasing efficiency. Convergence at the technical level between these countries and regions and developed countries and regions did not occur. Therefore, the mystery of East Asia does not exist, and the future of emerging Asian countries and regions will not be as optimistic as imagined. In the article, he also talked about China's economic growth. He believes that if China maintains 7% economic growth, the United States maintains a growth rate of 2.5%. By 2010, China's total economic output will reach 82% of the United States. This will undoubtedly change the focus of the world economy, but it will not be as big as people expected.

The outbreak of the Asian financial crisis seems to be verifying Krugman's prophecy, which has led to rethinking the East Asian model by scholars both at home and abroad. In particular, the bank debt crisis caused by the Asian financial crisis has attracted more attention. Since the main financing method of the East

[3] Paul Krugman: *The Myth of Asia's Miracle*, http:web.mit.edu/Krugman/www/myth.html.

Asian model is indirect financing led by the government, in order to obtain funds for operating activities, enterprises must exert pressure on banks through government officials. In this case, the first phenomenon is the corruption of government officials. The bank does not decide the loan based on the risk and possible return of the project but grants the loan according to the administrative order. At a certain stage, a large number of bad debts and bad debts will form a scale, which will pose a serious threat to the entire economy and affect the further growth of the economy. This has not only been verified in the Asian financial crisis but has also been happening in the past history of East Asian countries. Some economists have come to the conclusion that the East Asian miracle has ceased to exist and that further high-speed economic growth will encounter difficulties.

In this context, China has proposed a new strategic goal of quadrupling. If this goal can be achieved, it means that China will have maintained a high-speed economic growth for 25 years at an average annual growth rate of 9% or more, and maintained a high-speed economic growth for another 20 years, raising this record to 45 years. This is unprecedented in the history of world economic development, and it will also be a direct negation of Krugman and others' theory of the economic growth limit of East Asian models. Can this goal be achieved?

We can see that China possesses several basic features of the East Asian Model:

China's current economic management system is transformed from a planned economy. Under the conditions of a planned economy, the government's leading role in economy is paramount. Now, the leading role of governments at all levels in economy is still obvious.

The development of an export-oriented economy is a major achievement after China's reform and opening up. Without China's opening to the outside world, the rapid growth of China's economy is unimaginable.

Until now, indirect financing is still the dominant financing method in China's capital markets. East Asian countries in the government-led financing in the field of phenomenon, more or less also exists in our economy.

It is considered that Confucian culture has had a major impact on East Asian economic growth, and China is the birthplace of this culture.

Catching up with advanced ambitions and latecomer advantages is an important reason for the economic take-off of East Asian countries and regions. In China, this feature is particularly evident. In the early 1990s, Guangdong Province formulated an economic development plan to catch up with the "Four Asian Tigers". China's four modernizations of agriculture, industry, national defense, and science and technology were put forward in the context of catching up in 1960s.

It can be seen that the usual summary of the reasons for high growth in East Asian countries and regions is often the same reason for their economic growth deceleration. Then, from such an analysis logic, the period of rapid growth of the Chinese economy may also end, and then it will enter the sub-high growth or slow growth. However, economic growth in a country and region is often a more complicated process. We believe that the above analysis is far from sufficient to make a final conclusion on the East Asian economy. Take a step back, if these important analyses have some truth in explaining East Asian economic growth, they may also need to consider a more in-depth analysis of China's economic growth potential when applying them to China's long-term economic growth research. China's economy does have many similarities compared to the newly industrialized economies of Asia, but it also has its own characteristics.

China's economic system is still a government-led system. However, in China, the direct intervention of the government has gradually weakened with the transition of the system. The problems caused by indirect financing of banks are also being solved.

At the same time, unlike Japan, Republic of Korea and Singapore, there is a huge gap between China's urban and rural areas and between the eastern and western regions. China's urbanization level is low. The characteristics of this cascade distribution of Chinese economy make the adjustment of industrial structure possible in different regions. Regional economic differences are unique resources in China's economic growth. The technological gap between China and Western developed countries is large, which allows China to take advantage of the late-developing advantages of the developing economy.

With about 1.4 billion people in China, improving people's lives is a daunting task. However, on the other hand, this means that China has a potentially broad market, and can expand demand by developing domestic demand.

From the perspective of natural resources, China is also unmatched by other East Asian countries.

Therefore, it is unconvincing to directly apply the factor analysis of East Asia's rapid economic growth and their subsequent development bottlenecks to explain China's past and future economic growth. Since the reform and opening up, China's economy has grown rapidly. From 1978 to 2003, the annual average economic growth rate reached 9.36%. This growth rate is roughly the same as the average annual growth rate of Japan, Republic of Korea and Singapore during their period of rapid growth. Although these countries have experienced a slowdown after the period of rapid economic growth, and this trend is also likely to be found in China, however, we believe that due to the special circumstances of China, this process in China can be postponed and it is entirely possible to maintain a high-speed economic growth for a longer period of time. In 2003, after several years of adjustment, China's economy was back above 9%, a key indicator of rapid economic growth. From the perspective of development trends, China's economy may still maintain a relatively high growth rate. After entering the 21st century, the economic growth rate may be lowered. However, if China's policies are properly implemented and the international environment and resource conditions do not change much, we can still maintain a high speed of economic growth. The first decade of the 21st century may achieve economic growth of 7.5–8.5%, while it is possible to achieve a growth rate of 6.5–7.5% in the second decade. Based on this estimation, we believe that it is possible for China to achieve the goal of quadrupling in the first 20 years of the 21st century, and it is even possible to achieve this goal ahead of schedule.

4.2 China's Economic Growth Objective from the Perspective of Disposable Income

Fundamentally speaking, economic growth is the growth of people's income. This is why classical political economists compared the strength of the country through "income" hundreds of years ago. Of course, a government of a country can make its military and production capacity stronger than the country of equal income by sacrificing the welfare of its people. However, fundamentally speaking, a country with a low per capita income level must have limited effectiveness in its efforts in this area. Therefore, using "income" or people's living standards as a measure of the overall strength of a country is still a basic method in dynamic or static comparison in economics.

The outcomes of the 25 years of reform and opening up from 1978 to 2003 are generally shared by ordinary people. If we achieve the goal of quadrupling again, or by 2022, China's total GDP at 2002 prices will reach about RMB40 trillion. What kind of level will the people's income and living standard reach then? According to the estimates of the Department of Social, Science and Cultural Statistics of the National Bureau of Statistics, when China's population reaches 1.44 billion, the annual per capita GDP will reach RMB27,800.

Per capita GDP will not all go to the households. Disposable income which is formed through a complex process of distribution and redistribution of primary inputs in GDP, is the income of the household would have. Resident disposable income will not be used entirely for immediate consumption. Some will be savings (such as bank deposits, or savings for buying insurance or investing in the securities market) and become the financial assets of residents (financial institutions will use these funds in some ways for others or businesses), the remaining will be used for consumption. Because of the financial instruments, some people will delay their own consumption, while others may be able to cash in on future consumption through personal credit. But in general, the total consumption of residents will be lower than the disposable income of residents. However, for a family, disposable income is the most important. As for consumption as a percentage of disposable income, it is the independent choice of each family. In addition to the efforts of this family, the availability of disposable income depends on many factors such as society and economy. Then, under the economic scale of 2022, what level will the per capita disposable income of Chinese residents reach?

Table 4.2 lists the 2002 per capita GDP and per capita disposable income. From this table, we can calculate that in 2002, the ratio of annual per capita disposable income to per capita GDP was 56.69%. It is assumed that the ratio of per capita disposable income to per capita GDP will remain at the level of 2002 in 2022. Then, in that year, China's per capita disposable income should be RMB27,800 $\times$ 56. 69% = RMB15,758. The per capita disposable income for the month is RMB15,758/12 = RMB1,313. If there is a family of three (from the results of the current household survey in China, the average family size in China is approaching this value, from a statistical point of view, we call it the typical family below), the monthly disposable income of this typical family will reach RMB3,939. However, the ratio of per capita disposable income to per capita GDP is likely to change. If the maximum value of this ratio is 1, the per capita disposable income will be equal to the per capita GDP, that is, the typical household disposable income calculated on a monthly basis. The man is RMB27,800/12 × 3 = RMB6,950. Of course, such extreme values will not be achieved. Therefore, the disposable income of a typical household based on the month at that time may be between RMB3,939 and RMB6,950. In other words, if we can maintain the momentum of the rapid economic growth, assume that the overall price level of living consumption remains the same, and consider the possible changes between the ratio of per capita disposable income to GDP per capita, by 2022, the income of a typical family in China will generally be between RMB4,000 and RMB5,000.

Many families in Beijing, Shanghai, Guangzhou and Shenzhen have now reached a monthly income level of RMB4,000 to RMB5,000. Many of them will intuitively feel that this number is low. By 2022, if it is still at this level, isn't the improvement of people's lives too slow? This question should be understood from the following aspects:

Firstly, up to now, as far as the national average is concerned, China's current level of per capita disposable income is still very low. It can be seen from the calculation results in Table 4.2 shows that in 2002, the per capita disposable income level in the country was only RMB4,519 yuan, the monthly income was only RMB376, and the monthly income of a typical family was RMB1,130. If it reaches RMB4,000 to RMB5,000, the income will be 4 to 5 times that of the current one. It should be said that the growth rate is very large. On the other hand, there will be a big change of China's urban and rural population structure and the characteristics of urbanization of developed countries will become more apparent. If industrialization is achieved, the proportion of urban population should reach more than 80%. In this way, the standard of living will be improved for all the people of the country, not just the residents of some big cities.

Table 4.2 Per capita GDP and per capita disposable income in 2002

Item	Population		GDP (billion RMB)	GDP per capita (RMB)	Per capita disposable income in urban and rural areas (RMB)	Total disposable income (RMB 10,000)	National per capita disposable income (RMB)
	10,000 people	%					
Urban	50,212	39.1	–	–	7,703	38,678	–
Rural	78,241	60.9	–	–	2,476	19,372	–
Total	128,453	100.0	10,239.8	7,972	–	58,050	4,519

Note (1) The data in the table is taken from the Statistical Communiqué of the People's Republic of China on the 2002 National Economic and Social Development

(2) The per capita disposable income in rural areas refers to the net income available for spending and is similar in definition to the disposable income.

Secondly, the typical family's income of RMB4,000 to RMB5,000 should correspond to the national average consumption level. Taking living conditions as an example, according to data released by the National Bureau of Statistics, at the end of 2002, the average house price in the country was about RMB2,300 per square meter. The average house prices in Beijing, Shanghai, Guangzhou and Shenzhen are much higher than this level, generally more than 2 times. The prices of some small and medium-sized towns are much lower than the national average. If house prices are used as a benchmark, only families with a monthly income of RMB4,000 to RMB5,000 in cities with an average house price of around RMB2,000 yuan will reach the goal of living standards of the first 20 years of the 21st century.

Finally, the meaning of a typical family and a high-income family is different. Statistically speaking, if the typical household income reaches RMB5,000, it means that half of the households' income is higher than this level. The income of these families is stable, with a good sense of security, and a relatively balanced income and expenditure. This is very important for improving the consumption level of the whole society and improving people's lives.

4.3 China's Economic Growth in the Future and the Prospect of Its Economic Status in the World

At present, there are many methods for international comparison, but the exchange rate is still the most commonly used method for international comparison. Because the exchange rate itself reflects the international status of a country's economy. According to the World Bank, China's GDP calculated by exchange rate method[4] in 2000 was US$1.08 trillion, surpassing Italy and ranking sixth in the world. Table 4.3 shows the GDP and related proportions of the top 10 countries in the world calculated by the exchange rate method. As can be seen from Table 4.3, China's GDP accounts for only 3.4% of world's GDP, calculated by the exchange rate method. This numerical value is 10.9% of US's GDP, 23.1% of Japan, 57.8% of Germany, 76.4% of the UK, and 84.0% of France. Then, when will China's GDP calculated by the exchange rate method catch up with and surpass these five developed countries? By the middle of the twenty-first century, what level of China's per capita GDP is?

So far, many economists have studied China's future economic growth and its international economic status. Justin Yifu Lin believes that,[5] the US can maintain a 3% growth rate for a long time is already quite good, and the Chinese economy

[4] The World Bank's GDP data for the US dollar is based on an average exchange rate for the last three years of the country, not the exchange rate for the current year. This average exchange rate takes into account exchange rate changes in the United States, the United Kingdom, France, Germany, and Japan. See Xu Xianchun, "The World Bank's Calculation Method for GNP Per Capita of Nations", *Economics News*, December 17, 1999.

[5] Justin Yifu Lin: "Exploring the Chinese Economy in the New Millennium", cited from Zhang Zhuoyuan, *Exploring China's Economic Issues in the 21st Century*, Zhengzhou: Henan People's Publishing House, 1999, p. 22.

Table 4.3 GDP and related proportions of the top 10 countries in the world calculated by the exchange rate method in 2000

Rank	Country	GDP (US$100 million)	National GDP/World GDP (%)	China's GDP/National GDP (%)
	World	313,369		
1	US	98,828	31.5	10.9
2	Japan	46,771	14.9	23.1
3	Germany	18,701	6.0	57.8
4	UK	14,134	4.5	76.4
5	France	12,863	4.1	84.0
6	China	10,800	3.4	100.0
7	Italy	10,685	3.4	101.1
8	Canada	6,895	2.2	156.6
9	Brazil	5,876	1.9	183.8
10	Mexico	5,745	1.8	188.0

Note The data in the third column of the table is taken from *International Economic Information*, issue 20, 2001. The data in the fourth and fifth columns are calculated based on the data in the third column

can maintain a rapid growth of 8–10% for about 30 years. Therefore, before the middle of the 21st century, the Chinese economy is entirely likely to surpass the US, and become the world's largest and most powerful economy. Li Jingwen et al. (1999) used the combination of system dynamics, investment output and economic measurement to predict the economic growth over the 51 years from 2000 to 2050. The following basic conclusions are drawn[6]: China's 51-year economic growth can be roughly divided into three stages. The first phase was from 2000 to 2010, and economic growth maintained an average speed of 8%. The second phase is from 2010 to 2030, and economic growth has remained at an average of 6%. The third stage is from 2030 to 2050, and the economic growth is maintained at an average of 4–5%. The scale and strength of China's economy are among the highest in the world. Under the assumption that the US economic growth rate has remained at 3% and China's economic growth rate has remained at 8%, Guo Daoli has come to the conclusion that China's GDP will catch up with and surpass the US in 47 years.[7]

In the above research results, due to different research purposes, Li Jingwen only predicted the total economic output of China in renminbi. He did not predict the total amount of China's economy in US dollars, nor did he predict the economic aggregates of the US and other developed countries. Therefore, there was no specific comparison of economic aggregates. Justin Yifu Lin and Guo Daoli's estimates are

[6] Li Jingwen, "The Measurement and Analysis of China's Economic Development in the 21st Century (2000–2050)", cited from Zhang Zhuoyuan: *Exploring China's Economic Issues in the 21st Century*, Zheng zhou: Henan People's Publishing House, 1999, pp. 41–44.

[7] Guo Daoli: "How Long Does It Take to Catch up with the United States", cited from Cao Zijian: *Recovery: China Economic Yearbook*, Lanzhou: Lanzhou University Press, 2001, pp. 75–77.

too optimistic, it is unlikely that China's economy will grow at 8% or more for 30 years or more.

Based on our analysis of the historical economic growth data and economic growth factors of the five developed countries of the US, Japan, the UK, France and Germany, and the judgment of the future situation, we assume that the future economic growth rate of the US will remain at 3%. The future economic growth rate of other countries is 2.5%. China started from 7.5% in the first decade of the 21st century, down by 1 percentage point per year, and staying at 3% in 2050. Then, under the assumption that prices and exchange rates are constant, we have the following estimates for the future economic growth of countries (see Table 4.4).

Table 4.4 Future GDP forecasts for the US, Japan, Germany, UK, France, and China (US$100 million)

Year	US	Japan	Germany	UK	France	China
2001	101,793	47,940	19,169	14,487	13,185	11,610
2002			19,648	14,849	13,515	12,481
2003			20,139	15,220	13,853	13,417
2004			20,642	15,601	14,199	14,423
2005			21,158	15,991	14,554	15,505
2006			21,687	16,391		16,668
2007			22,229			17,918
2008			22,785			19,262
2009			23,355			20,707
2010	132,817	59,871	23,939			22,260
2011			24,537			23,707
2012			25,150			25,248
2020	178,494	76,640				41,783
2025		86,711				54,609
2026		88,879				57,612
2029		95,713				67,651
2030	239,881	98,105				71,372
2040	322,381	125,583				110,839
2047	396,488					141,018
2048	408,382					145,954
2050	433,253	160,757				156,349
2055		181,882				181,251
2056		186,429				186,689
2060	582,255					210,120
2100	1,899,339					685,420

Note Based on the constant price in 2000 and the three-year average exchange rate forecast of various currencies against the US dollar in 1998, 1999 and 2000.

Comparing the predictions of national economic growth in Table 4.4, we can see that China's GDP would surpass France (US$1,455.4 billion) in 2005 based on the 2000 price and the three-year average exchange rate of the national currency against the US dollar in 1998, 1999 and 2000), reaching US$1,550.5 billion. In 2006 it would reach US$1,666.8 billion, surpassing the UK (US$1,639.1 billion). It would reach US$2,524.8 billion in 2012, surpassing Germany (US$2,515 billion). It would reach US$18,668.9 billion in 2056, surpassing Japan (US$1,639.1 billion). But compared with the US, China's GDP in 2050 would be US$15,634.9 billion, and the US GDP would be US$43,325.3 billion. At that time, the proportion of GDP between China and the US increased from 10.9% in 2000 to 36.1%, and the relative difference[8] fell from 89.1 to 63.9%, but the absolute difference[9] rose from US$8,802.8 billion in 2000 to US$27,690.4 billion. If the economic growth rate of China and the US is assumed to be 3% from 2051 to 2100, the relative difference between China and the US will remain unchanged, but the absolute difference will further increase.

However, we know that the price of each country tends to change over time. The exchange rate of the local currency against the US dollar is not fixed. Therefore, it is also necessary to consider the impact of economic growth on China's future international economic status in the context of exchange rate changes. According to the changes in the real exchange rate of emerging countries of East Asia and regions in the second half of the 20th century, we believe that the real exchange rate of the renminbi against the US dollar will rise in the next 50 years, and the rate of increase will not be lower than 50%. Therefore, we make the following two assumptions. The first assumption is that the real exchange rate of the renminbi against the US dollar in 2001–2010 was maintained at the three-year average exchange rate levels in 1998, 1999 and 2000. It will increase by 100% from 2011 to 2050, and the growth rate will be the same every year. This is equivalent to an increase of 18.92% in real terms of the renminbi against the US dollar every 10 years. The second assumption is that the real exchange rate of the renminbi against the US dollar from 2001 to 2010 is the same as the first assumption. It will increase by 200% from 2011 to 2050, and the annual growth rate will be the same. The second assumed real exchange rate increase is close to the level of Japan in the last 40 years of the 20th century, which is equivalent to an increase of 31.61% in real terms of the renminbi against the US dollar every 10 years.

The above two assumptions are equivalent to still fixing the exchange rate of renminbi against the US dollar during 2001–2010 at the three-year average exchange rate levels in 1998, 1999 and 2000. Under these assumptions, the conclusion that the Chinese economy will surpass France in 2005, the UK in 2006, and Germany in 2012 will not change. We only need to compare the Chinese economy with the US economy and the Japanese economy.

For the sake of simplicity, when comparing China, Japan, and the US, we assume that the exchange rate of the yen against the US dollar does not change. Table 4.5

---

[8] The relative difference between China and the US in GDP = (US GDP − China GDP)/US GDP.

[9] The absolute difference between China and the US in GDP = (US GDP − China GDP).

Table 4.5 China's future GDP forecast under real exchange rate changes (US$100 million)

Year	GDP	GDP
2010	22,260	22,260
2020	49,689	54,990
2025	70,819	82,449
2026	76,019	89,405
2029	94,029	114,001
2030	100,935	123,620
2040	186,408	252,658
2047	267,749	389,594
2048	281,965	414,459
2050	312,698	469,047
2060	420,240	630,360
2100	1,370,839	2,056,258

Note The data in the second column of the table is calculated based on a 100% increase in the actual exchange rate of renminbi to US dollar from 2011 to 2050, combined with the data in Table 4.4. The data in the third column of the table is calculated based on a 200% increase in the actual exchange rate of renminbi to US dollar from 2011 to 2050, combined with the data in Table 4.4

lists the results of this comparison. It can be seen that under the first assumption, the Chinese economy will reach US$10,093.5 billion in 2030, surpassing the Japanese economy (US$9,810.5 billion). In the 21st century, the Chinese economy will not catch up with the US economy. Under the second assumption, the Chinese economy will reach US$8,940.5 billion in 2026, surpassing the Japanese economy (US$8,887.9 billion) and will reach US$41,445.9 billion in 2048, surpassing the US economy (US$40,838.2 billion).

The second assumption is an overly optimistic assumption. In the last 50 years of the 20th century, only a few countries such as Japan and Switzerland increased their real exchange rate against the US dollar by 200%. Relatively speaking, the first assumption is more likely to be realized.

According to the forecast of the Department of Population, Social Science and Technology Statistics of the National Bureau of Statistics, the population of China would reach 1,359.26 million in 2010, 1,434.98 million in 2020, 1,469.56 million in 2030, 1,468.64 million in 2040 and 1,432.29 million in 2050. According to Table 4.5 and the above data, China's future per capita GDP can be predicted under the three assumptions that the exchange rate is unchanged and the real exchange rate of renminbi against the US dollar rises by 100 and 200% respectively in 2011–2050 (see Table 4.6).

As can be seen from Table 4.6, under the assumption of constant exchange rate, China's per capita GDP reached US$10,916 in 2050, catching up with Portugal's 2000 level. Under the assumption that the real exchange rate rose by 100%, it reached US$21,832, catching up with or approaching the level of Italy, Australia and Canada

Table 4.6 China's future GDP forecast (US dollar)

Year	Constant exchange rate	Rising 100% of the real exchange rate	Rising 200% of the real exchange rate
2010	1,638	1,638	1,638
2020	2,912	3,463	3,832
2030	4,857	6,868	8,412
2040	7,547	12,693	17,204
2050	10,916	21,832	32,748

around 2000. Under the assumption that the exchange rate rose by 200%, it reached US$32,748, which is close to the level of the US in 2000.[10] According to the previous section, the assumption of a 100% increase in the exchange rate is more likely. Therefore, China's per capita GDP in 2050 is likely to reach US$20,000, reaching or close to the level of Italy, Australia and Canada around 2000, but it is difficult to reach or reach the level of the US around 2000.

4.4 Possible Challenges for Achieving the Goals

The ambition of the goal is directly proportional to the difficulty of achieving it. Whether it is the level of GDP or the improvement of people's living standards, it is fundamentally guaranteed by the productivity of this society. And a better connection between production and consumption and rapid development on this basis is an important way to achieve this goal. In a nutshell, China's strategic goal of achieving its own economic growth may encounter some of the following major challenges:

Firstly, the problem of urbanization.

It can be seen from Table 4.2 that, in 2002 China's urban population accounted for 39. 1% of the national population, and the rural population accounted for 60.9%. From the perspective of population, it is still a traditional society with a rural population as the main body. However, in terms of industrial structure, the added value of the primary industry in 2002 accounted for only 14.53% of GDP.

Of course, the added value of the primary industry is not all produced by the rural population. Modern agriculture in Urban areas is also engaged in the production of this industry. The rural population is mainly engaged in agricultural production, but there is also a portion of the population engaged in other industries either locally or outside. But overall, China is still a country with a large rural population. The growth of the primary industry has been limited by further development due to years of development and constraints on natural conditions. In the long run, the transfer of agricultural population to urban areas and the transfer of agricultural

[10] According to the data released by the World Bank, the per capita GDP of the US was US$35,046 in 2000, Canada was US$22,244, Australia was US$20,738, Italy was US$18,423, and Portugal was US$10,387. See *International Economic Information*, 2002. No. 3.

labor to non-agricultural industries will be an inevitable phenomenon in the process of industrialization. It was a painful and bloody process for the UK to complete the adjustment of the labor structure in the industrial revolution through the enclosure movement. Today, it is impossible for us to complete the transfer of rural labor to cities in this way, but the road to realizing the adjustment of the labor structure and realizing urbanization still has to go. After the completion of the Industrial Revolution, the proportion of China's agricultural labor force should be below 10%, and the proportion of rural population to the total population will be below 20%. From this goal, 40% of China's rural population will likely be transformed into urban population in the next 20 years. If this is the case, China's urban population will reach more than 1 billion, more than the population of eight Japan or the United States. Then, we will encounter a series of problems, such as employment issues and related social security issues, big urbanization issues, environmental issues.

Secondly, the long-term planning of national economic development.

At the 12th National Congress of the Communist Party of China, China proposed a strategic goal of quadrupling for the first time. Compared with the present, we were quite inexperienced in terms of understanding of the market economy and macroeconomic regulation and control. Since China's transition and high-speed economic growth have occurred at the same time, and the implementation of a "wading across the stream by feeling the way" transition, many variables in the reform process are difficult to plan in practice. Today, on the new basis, we have renewed our new strategic goals of quadrupling. The advantage lies in the fact that we have experienced economic restructuring and opening to the outside world, and have established new economic systems and modern enterprise systems. The difficulty lies in the rapid economic growth of 20 or 30 years, and some of the potential of the Chinese economy has been released (for example, the rapid growth of agriculture in the 1980s is difficult to reproduce), and the unique price advantages of some factors of production factors are being lost. In this case, planning for long-term future development is particularly important. Taking big cities as an example, the problem of big cities in newly industrialized countries is a very acute problem. In the United States, the various centers of the country are diverse. For example, Washington DC is the political center, New York is the financial center, Detroit is the car manufacturing center, Hollywood is the film production center, Silicon Valley is the computer and software center, and so on. The cities of Tokyo and Seoul are often multi-taskers, integrating various centers, making the burden of the city very heavy. In China's future urbanization process, excessive expansion of large cities should also be avoided. At present, Beijing and Shanghai already have such a trend, which is exactly what we should pay attention to in our long-term planning.

Thirdly, the short-term surplus of production capacity and the long-term lack of contradiction.

After the reform and opening up, China's seller market gradually transformed into a buyer's market. An important feature of this market is the excess capacity. In the case of overcapacity, the products produced by some enterprises may not be sold, which leads to difficulties in business operations and bankruptcy. The products of these enterprises are not without social needs but lack social needs with the ability to pay. In other words, in the context of the buyer's market, on the one hand, in the long run, the existing production capacity in the society is definitely insufficient, and there is a contradiction with people's growing material and cultural life needs. On the other hand, limited by the need to be able to pay, a considerable number of enterprises will often be in a state of overcapacity, facing strong pressure from competition and operation.

Here, production, income and consumption form an interconnected cycle. For production to develop, there must be demand, especially final demand. The increase in final demand depends on the propensity to consume and the increase in disposable income. The increase in disposable income requires increased production. The problem is that production, income and consumption are carried out by thousands of enterprises. The development of social division of labor and collaboration has made enterprises more and more specialized. Factors such as savings and investment behavior, government behavior, and financial markets are playing a role. This complicates such a simple loop. To make such a cycle work, an axis is needed. This axis is now we have found, this is the market. Money and money are the lubricants for this operation. How to add lubricants and how much to add is the government's fiscal policy, monetary policy and industrial policy.

Short-term overcapacity has become a cyclical phenomenon as early as Marx's era. The later socialist planned economy was proposed against this phenomenon. However, under the conditions of the planned economy of the Soviet Union, due to the loss of subjective initiative and innovative spirit of enterprises and individuals as basic units of society, although there is no excess, the shortage still exist and are more serious. The facts have proved that the system is lacking in vitality. So, can we consider establishing a system to make this contradiction better?

Fourthly, the realization of reasonable macroeconomic regulation and control.

After the Asian financial crisis, China adopted a proactive fiscal policy to expand demand and effectively stimulate China's economic growth. However, we also know that, since Keynes proposed his macroeconomic theory, fiscal policy is an important tool for countries to stimulate the economy and solve the surplus. But there have been many cases of failure. The success of China's fiscal policy has its specific background. Fiscal policy is only one aspect of many macroeconomic policies and should also consider the coordinated application of other policies. For example, when balancing the contradictions, we mentioned above, how monetary and regional policies work. A phenomenon that often occurs now is that the use of an economic policy that encourages expansion will first play a role in economically developed regions and promote the development of these regions. By the time the economy in these areas has overheated, policies have begun to shrink, and the economy in underdeveloped regions has not yet started or just started. They do not benefit much from encouraging expansion, but they are affected by policy tightening.

Fifthly, energy and the environment.

Energy issues may be the main bottleneck in China's future economic growth. If demand and consumption are increased at the expense of energy, according to current energy consumption levels, future energy consumption will be a huge burden for China. By 2022, the number of households in China would be around 500 million.

If 1/5 of the households had family cars, then the number of family cars would reach more than 100 million. If 1/10 of the annual update is made, China's annual automobile demand is more than 10 million, which is a big demand. However, on the other hand, the energy consumption here is also amazing. China's private car ownership in 2003 was more than 10 million, and crude oil consumption was more than 200 million tons. If there are 100 million private cars, the consumption of crude oil will be more than 1 billion tons, accounting for more than 1/3 of the current international crude oil production (3 billion tons), which is equivalent to the current level of the United States. China's crude oil consumption in 2003 has surpassed that of Japan, becoming the world's second (Japan consumes 5.43 million barrels per day, China 5.46 million barrels, 1 ton = 7.3 barrels). China's current crude oil reserves are 1.8 billion tons. At that time, can we guarantee China's energy supply? We know that Japan's economic stagnation began with the oil crisis of 1973. Will this situation repeat itself in China? Can domestic resources and the international market meet our energy needs at that time? Of course, the technological revolution may bring us low-energy products. In 20 years, new energy sources may also be developed to meet human needs. But in any case, energy development and the appropriate environmental protection should be the issues we should focus on when achieving our goals.

Sixthly, the comparative advantage in the process of economic growth.

Comparative advantages are the foundation of international economic exchanges. In today's world economic integration, if developing countries have a certain foundation, such as education level, infrastructure, etc., coupled with institutional innovation, it is possible to achieve rapid development through its comparative advantages in terms of production factors such as labor, land and raw materials. Developed countries can gain more benefits than domestically through exchanges with developing countries through their advantages in capital, finance, science and technology. In this process of development, the newly industrialized countries may have a faster economic growth rate than the developed countries due to the low starting point. Countries such as Japan and Republic of Korea have followed this path. However, with the rise of newly industrialized countries and even into developed countries, its original comparative advantage in terms of factors of production will be lost, and its currency will appreciate. At this time, it must also follow the path of developed countries and become exporting countries in capital, science and technology to obtain new development. Japan used to be the cheapest labor force in the world, but now it has become one of the most expensive countries in the world. Fundamentally speaking, to solve this problem, we should gradually solve the problem of industrial upgrading in the process of economic growth, so that China's economy will gradually transform its external absorption energy into external radiation absorption energy.

Seventhly, education and technological development.

Education and technology are vital to the economic development of a country. Further development of education, especially higher education, is related to the quality of the entire nation and the improvement of China's overall international competitiveness. This is crucial for China's economic development in the next 20 years and should continue to be strengthened. It should be pointed out that the development of education and science and technology (especially the development of education) should of course mobilize resources from all quarters. But fundamentally speaking, it is still necessary for the government to invest, so that the people can have more opportunities in education. In 2002, the country's birth population was 16.47 million. After 20 years, the number of young people of 17 or 18 years old should be around 15 million. If half of them could attend university, the number of enrollments should reach 7.5 million. In 2002, the number of enrollments in general higher education in China was 3.21 million. If this goal is to be achieved, the growth in the enrollment of higher education can be lower than the growth of GDP. However, if the proportion of young people attending university is increased to 80% of the young people of 17 or 18 years old, the enrollment number should reach 12 million, which is quadrupled compared to the current enrollment. If we consider other education needs, then the growth rate of investment in education should be higher than the growth of GDP.

Chapter 5
The Characteristics of Economic Cycle and the Complexity of Macroeconomic Regulation and Control in the Institutional Transition

Economic cycle is an inherent phenomenon in market economy. It adjusts the economy through the self-improvement function of market to achieve the equilibrium of economic activities. The reallocation of resources in the process of adjustment may have a negative impact on economic growth. With the deepening of marketization, the law of economic cycle has begun to play a role in China's economy. An important task of macro-control is to reduce the negative impact of such economic cycle on economic growth through counter-cyclical operation. This chapter studies the performance, quantitative characteristics and formation mechanism of China's economic cycle, and points out how to ensure the sustained and stable growth of national economy through macro-control according to the characteristics of China's economic activities at the present stage.

5.1 The Periodicity of China's Economic Growth

Since the reform and opening up, China's economy has achieved sustained and high-speed growth. From 1978 to 2003, the average growth rate over the 25 years was 9.34%. For a large developing country like China, a period of sustained and rapid growth is very important. In the past quarter of a century, it is this sustained growth that has rapidly changed China's poverty and backwardness, and brought about an unprecedented rise in China's overall national strength, people's livelihood and international status. Long-term economic growth is made up of many short-term economic growths. Individual short-term increases are not difficult to achieve. The difficulty is to maintain the continuity of such growth over a long period of time.

The basic time reference for writing this chapter is 2004. The content of this chapter, titled "Economic Cycles and Macroeconomic Regulation", was published by Liu Wei and Cai Zhizhou in the second issue of *Journal of Peking University (Philosophy and Social Sciences)* in 2005.

W. Liu, *Research on China's Market Economy Development*,
https://doi.org/10.1007/978-981-97-1398-1_5

A typical example is China's "Great Leap Forward" in 1958, we achieved a 21.3% economic growth rate, while in 1961 the economic growth rate was −27.3%. There were obvious big ups and downs. Such a rapid economic growth is meaningless. Generally speaking, a good economic growth is to maximize the growth rate under certain constraints (such as time, resource allocation, etc.). However, due to different conditions in different countries and different guiding principles, the set of constraints may be different. Even if a set of constraints has been established, it may not be optimal in real life if the method is not correct. From the point of view of national economic accounting, the optimization target of economic growth can be analyzed from both supply and demand. On the supply side, it means to maximize the output and its continuity through the rational allocation of social and economic resources such as factors of production. On the demand side, the demand maximization and its continuity are expected to be realized on the basis of mutual coordination of investment, consumption and other demands. Due to the influence of various factors, it is difficult to fully realize this optimal state, but it can be approached through the implementation of various measures. Since the reform and opening up, China have pursued a state of economic growth, which is to use existing resources to achieve the fastest possible long-term economic growth. Overall, China's economic growth has been pretty good. It is mainly reflected in three aspects. Firstly, it has maintained sustained high-speed growth. From the perspective of the history of world economic development, few countries (especially big countries) have been able to maintain such a high average growth rate for such a long time, which is the greatest achievement of China's economic growth. Secondly, generally, market-oriented reform has promoted the optimization of resource allocation, especially institutional innovation, which has brought into full play the potential of the main body of economic activities, and this improves the efficiency of production factors. Thirdly, the demand for affordability is growing steadily, which promotes the continuous development of the whole national economy. In this sense, the overall state of China's economic growth is close to optimization. However, there are also some factors that move us away from this state from time to time. The greatest manifestation is the periodic fluctuation in the process of economic operation during the transition from planned economy to market economy. The fluctuation range is sometimes very large, which causes a certain waste of economic resources. There are many reasons for this kind of economic fluctuation, but the most important one is the impact of the economic cycle. Economic cycle is an inherent phenomenon under the condition of market economy, and it is a reflection of the inherent law of market economy. It reflects the self-perfection function of market economy, and constantly achieve the balance of economic activities through the cycle of economic cycles.

The economic cycle is an important subject in western economic theory. The American economist Simon Kuznets, Swedish economist Gunnar Myrdal, British economist Friedrich August Von Hayek and the American economist Robert Lucas won the Nobel Prize in economics, due to their studies of the economic cycle respectively from economic growth, monetary theory, rational expectations and other angles. Due to the various uncertainties in economic activities, the fluctuations in the process of self-adjustment may cost economic growth a lot. Therefore, it is necessary to smooth the fluctuations through the counter-cyclical operation of macro-control so as to alleviate the negative effects of cyclical factors. Therefore, to strengthen the study of economic cycle and countermeasures, is an important subject of economic theory research, but also the basic task of the government macro-control. However, due to the special background, China's economic cycle have their own characteristics in addition to the common places with the western developed market economy. After the reform and opening up, the economic cycle in the process of China's economic growth shows the following characteristics:

Firstly, with the deepening of the transition process and the improvement of marketization, the role of the law of business cycle in economic life is gradually strengthened.

Table 5.1 shows the economic growth rate as reflected by the GDP over a period of 26 years from 1978 to 2004. As can be seen from the table, in different years, the growth rate is different. The year with the fastest growth rate is 1992, when the economic growth rate was 14.2%, and the year with the lowest growth rate was 1990, when the economic growth rate was 3.8%. The growth rate that is too high or too low is not conducive to economic development.

Figure 5.1 shows the change in China's economic growth rate since 1978 according to the numerical values in Table 5.1. It reflects the undulating progress of China's economy since 1978. Before 1980s, China also had economic fluctuations, but that was mainly a matter of planning and execution under the condition of planned

Table 5.1 GDP index, 1978–2004 (at comparable prices)

Year	Index (last year = 100)	Year	Index (last year = 100)
1978	111.7	1992	114.2
1979	107.6	1993	113.5
1980	107.8	1994	112.6
1981	105.2	1995	110.5
1982	109.1	1996	109.6
1983	110.9	1997	108.8
1984	115.2	1998	107.8
1985	113.5	1999	107.1
1986	108.8	2000	108.0
1987	111.6	2001	107.5
1988	111.3	2002	108.0
1989	104.1	2003	109.3
1990	103.8	2004	109.0
1991	109.2	Average*	9.34

*Note** does not include the index comparing 1978 and 1977

Source China statistical yearbook, 2004. Data for 2004 was published by the National Bureau of Statistics

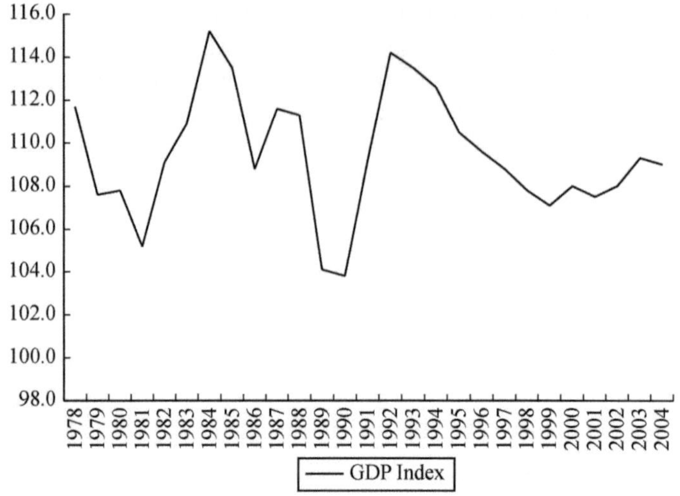

Fig. 5.1 Changes in GDP index, 1978–2004

economy. Since the 1980s, China's economic growth has gone through three major ups and downs.

The first one appeared in the early 1980s. It started around 1981, reached a high point in 1984, then gradually slowed down, and reached a low point in 1990, completing the first cycle after the reform and opening up.

The second one appeared in the early 1990s. It started in 1991, reached a high point in 1992, then gradually slowed down, and reached a low point around 1999, completing the second cycle after the reform and opening up.

The third is the beginning of the 20th century, the new period of economic development that we are now experiencing. It showed signs of acceleration around 2001 and is still operating in the ascender channel.

The ups and downs reflect the cyclical nature of China's economic growth, with cycles lasting about a decade. It is this cycle that causes China's economic growth to fluctuate. But the magnitude of the fluctuations is gradually diminishing. To some extent, it shows that with China's economic development, the government's macroeconomic regulation and control level is constantly improving, but the deeper reason lies in the subjects of various economic decisions are constantly decentralized, with the advancement of China's transition process and the deepening of marketization. This point and have a significant difference in the initial period of the reform and opening up. At that time, if the investment can not obtain benefit of state-owned enterprises, their countermeasures are mostly continue to expand investment, make the investment risks continue to spread. However, for today's private economy and joint-stock enterprises, most of them will be more to adjust investment activities through the risk assessment. In this case, the investment risk is gradually convergence in economic activity. This shows that the self-regulation function of the market economy is playing an increasingly important role.

Secondly, the cyclical fluctuations in economic growth have not affected the long-term trend of China's rapid economic growth.

It can be seen from Table 5.1 that since the reform and opening up, China's economy has maintained an average growth rate of over 9% for 26 years, which is rare in the history of world economic development. Although in this process, the impact of the economic cycle has led to large fluctuations in some periods, such fluctuations have not affected the long-term trend of China's economic growth. From a statistical point of view, the average index reflects the central trend of the observed objects, while in time series, it reflects the long-term trend of the observed objects. The realization of an average growth rate of over 9% proves that China has the potential for rapid growth, which has been stimulated by the reform and opening up. The cycle change or cycle fluctuation in the economic growth is reflected in the process of this high-speed growth.

Thirdly, in the cyclical changes of economic growth, the various components of the macro economy show some internal relations.

Although cyclical changes in the process of economic growth can affect all aspects of economic life, more needs to be done in terms of demand when observing such changes. In macroeconomic theory, the static analysis method explains the balance of supply and demand through a certain point, while in real life, this balance is often reflected by a series of points connected by a line. Because of the corresponding relationship between supply and demand, the dynamic investigation of aggregate demand and its components becomes an important tool for macroeconomic analysis. GDP, employment, investment, consumption and price movements are the most frequently used indicators in macroeconomic analysis of countries. Due to the problems in the definition and operation of China's employment statistics, the current employment statistics cannot meet the needs of macro analysis. Here we look at economic growth over the past 25 years through four economic variables: GDP index, total social fixed asset investment index, social retail commodity index and GDP deflator. The total social fixed asset investment index reflects the growth of investment, the social retail commodity index reflects the growth of consumption, and the GDP deflator[1] reflects the overall change of the general price level of the whole society. Strictly speaking, there is a difference between the total fixed asset investment of the whole society and the concept of total fixed capital formation reflected in the GDP. The total amount of social retail goods is not the same as the final consumption in the GDP.[2] However, since China only estimates the final demand component when it publishes the GDP according to the annual expenditure method, only the total fixed asset investment and total retail goods data are published in the quarterly progress statistics. Therefore, in the implementation of macroeconomic regulation, investment and consumption can only be analogized through these two indicators. Although there are differences in specific values, the trends reflected are still the same.

---

[1] The GDP deflator (the implicit GDP deflator) is the ratio of the GDP index at current prices to the GDP index at comparable prices to reflect the total price changes of the entire national economy.

[2] China Center for National Accounting and Economic Growth: *China Economic Growth Report*, 2004 and 2005.

Table 5.2 shows the changes of these four major macroeconomic variables over the past 20 years, while Fig. 5.2 visually reflects these changes.

By observing Fig. 5.2, we can find that:

(1) Fixed asset investment is a leading indicator of GDP. In every economic cycle, the fixed-asset investment index always accelerates before the GDP index, and then drives other economic variables.
(2) The acceleration of fixed assets in the early stages may affect the growth of consumption and thus reduce the growth rate of consumption, which was obvious in the mid-1990s and in this round of the economic cycle.
(3) Consumption is a lagging indicator of GDP. Generally speaking, the growth rate of consumption will increase after the growth of GDP and investment has entered a flat or even decelerated.
(4) The rise of the general price level is usually in sync with the acceleration of GDP growth. Therefore, in the early stage of economic acceleration, although the total consumption is likely to continue to maintain the past growth rate, due to the effect of inflation, the consumption growth of residents may be reduced. That is to say, in the early stage of economic acceleration, the welfare of residents, especially those of middle and low income, may be affected to some extent.
(5) After the economic boom passes a certain point, the overall price level becomes a leading indicator to some extent, indicating that the economic growth enters a process of slowdown.

Of course, due to different background of economic cycles, the performance of various macroeconomic components may also be different, such as the economic cycle in the 1980s, the consumption pulling is an important reason. As a result, its investment and consumption are launched in a different order than in subsequent years. However, on the whole, due to the internal connection of objective economic activities, in general, the order of changes of various variables in the economic cycle still has certain rules to follow.

After a general analysis of the long-term trends and cyclical changes in China's economic growth, we should further study the quantitative criteria for judging such cyclical changes. This is very important. In our current macroeconomic analysis, the criteria for whether the economy is overheated often rely on the intuitive feelings of the analysts rather than specific quantitative criteria. Scientific economic decisions should be based on more sophisticated quantitative analysis. In Table 5.2, we calculated the mean and standard deviation of four groups of macroeconomic variables (1981–2003).

In statistics, the average value reflects the central tendency of the random variable, while the standard deviation reflects the degree of dispersion of the variable. Economic growth cannot deviate too far from its underlying trend. It can be seen from the calculation results in the last four lines of Table 5.2 that since the 1980s, China's economic growth has been quite stable, basically fluctuating in the neighborhood

Table 5.2 Development trend of four major economic variables since the 1980s

Year	GDP index		Total Social fixed asset investment index*		Social retail commodity index*		GDP deflator	
	Value	Evaluation	Value	Evaluation	Value	Evaluation	Value	Evaluation
1981	105.2	Inactive	103.0	Normal	107.2	Normal	102.3	Normal
1982	109.1	Normal	125.6	Active	107.3	Normal	99.8	Normal
1983	110.9	Normal	114.5	Normal	109.2	Normal	101.1	Normal
1984	115.2	Active	124.7	Active	114.6	Active	104.9	Normal
1985	113.5	Active	127.6	Active	117.8	Active	110.1	Normal
1986	108.8	Normal	115.8	Normal	95.8	Inactive	104.6	Normal
1987	111.6	Normal	113.2	Normal	109.0	Normal	105.1	Normal
1988	111.3	Normal	105.8	Normal	107.8	Normal	112.1	Normal
1989	104.1	Inactive	78.8	Inactive	105.3	Normal	108.8	Normal
1990	103.8	Inactive	100.3	Inactive	100.3	Inactive	105.7	Normal
1991	109.2	Normal	113.2	Normal	110.2	Normal	106.7	Normal
1992	114.2	Active	125.2	Active	110.8	Normal	107.9	Normal
1993	113.5	Active	127.8	Active	100.1	Inactive	114.6	Active
1994	112.6	Active	118.1	Normal	107.2	Normal	119.9	Active
1995	110.5	Normal	111.0	Normal	110.4	Normal	113.2	Active
1996	109.6	Normal	110.4	Normal	113.2	Normal	105.9	Normal
1997	108.8	Normal	107.0	Normal	109.3	Normal	100.8	Normal
1998	107.8	Normal	114.1	Normal	109.6	Normal	97.6	Inactive
1999	107.1	Normal	105.5	Normal	110.1	Normal	97.8	Inactive
2000	108.0	Normal	109.1	Normal	111.4	Normal	100.9	Normal
2001	107.5	Normal	112.5	Normal	111.0	Normal	101.2	Normal
2002	108.0	Normal	116.7	Normal	112.2	Normal	99.8	Normal
2003	109.3	Normal	124.0	Normal	107.4	Normal	102.0	Normal
Average**	109.5		113.2		108.6		105.3	
Standard deviation	3.05		10.97		4.80		5.73	
Upper limit	112.55		124.19		113.37		111.07	
Lower limit	106.45		102.24		103.77		99.60	

Note * Price movements have been eliminated
** Starting from the need for statistical analysis, the mean here is calculated as an arithmetic average, while the usually calculated average development speed indicator is calculated by geometric mean
Source China Statistical Yearbook, 2004. Among them, the GDP index is directly quoted, and other indices are derived from relevant data

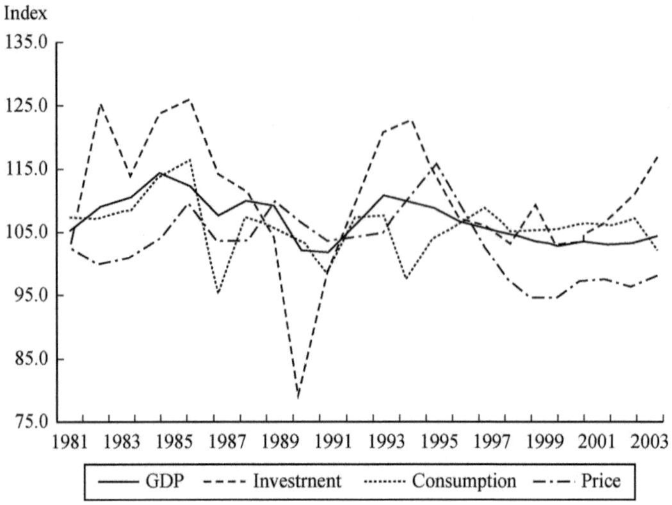

Fig. 5.2 Trends in the development of the four main economic variables since the 1980s

with an average growth rate of 9.5%. Under the assumption of normal distribution,[3] in 95% confidence, there is no growth rate outside the control area. Considering the requirement of economic growth stability, we reduce the control region to 1 standard deviation. According to China's experience over the past 20 years from 1981 to 2003, the one standard deviation of economic growth fluctuation is 3.05% (see Table 5.2), so the upper and lower limits of the confidence interval are 112.55 and 106.45%. By this measure, there were 3 years when the economy was relatively inactive and 5 years when the economy was overheated in the past 23 years from 1981 to 2003. And in this economic cycle, in terms of overall economic growth, there has been no overheating. A similar analysis can be made for other macroeconomic variables.

It can be seen from the comparison of several economic variables: From the comparison of several economic indicators, it can be seen that: in terms of long-term trends, after eliminating price changes, the growth rate of total fixed asset investment is the highest (13.21%) among GDP growth rate, growth rate of total social fixed asset investment, and growth rate of total retail commodity of consumer goods. The GDP growth rate is the second highest (9.54%), and the growth rate of total retail commodity of consumer goods is the lowest (8.6%); in terms of the volatility of growth rates, fixed asset investment is the highest (10.97%), followed by consumption (4.8%), and GDP is the lowest (3.05%). As the fluctuation of GDP is the result of the joint action of fixed asset investment and consumption fluctuation, since the fluctuation of fixed asset investment and consumption are not synchronized, they offset each other. The study of this numerical feature is significant. From the perspective of the growth of total social fixed asset investment in 2003, after the elimination of

[3] The data in Table 5.2 is 23, which is close to the number of large samples, and the analysis results are statistically based.

price changes, the growth rate has reached 24%, which is close to the upper limit of 24.19% calculated in Table 5.1. From this point of view, the fixed asset investment in that year has been too fast, need to take certain macroeconomic measures. This was later confirmed by events. This just shows the research on the quantitative characteristics of the economic cycle and the necessity of counter-cyclical regulation and control on macroeconomic operation according to these quantitative characteristics. The fluctuation range of GDP, investment and consumption is related to their own nature. This fluctuation can not be completely eliminated, but we can establish a series of control standards by observing and studying the total amount of GDP and its main components. We can take timely control measures when their trajectory deviates from the normal standard to reduce their fluctuation degree and the negative impact of unbalanced economic operation.

5.2 The Complexity of China's Economic Cycle at the Current Stage[4]

Due to the influence of developmental factors and institutional factors such as the historical process of China's industrialization and marketization, the imbalance in China's current economic growth has a series of new complexities. This complexity is manifested in the following three aspects.

5.2.1 The Overall Economic Growth Rate Marked by GDP Index is not Too Fast, but the Growth Rate of Fixed Asset Investment is Indeed Too Fast

After the economic growth reached 9.3% in 2003, China's economic growth rate will remain above 9% in 2004. Is the growth rate too fast? The criterion for judging whether the economy is growing too fast should be empirical, not mechanical. Based on the practice of China's economic growth from 1978 to 2004, China's average economic growth rate has been around 9.3% in the past 26 years. According to the above statistical analysis, one standard deviation of the fluctuation of China's economic growth is about 3% age points. Taking this as a unit, the normal fluctuation range of China's economic growth since the reform and opening up should be between 6.3 and 12.3%, that is, it fluctuates in the range of about 3% age points up or down the average. On this basis, China's economic growth at the current stage (2003–2004) has only reached the average level of the past 26 years of the reform and opening up, and is in the normal fluctuation range. It is estimated that the growth rate in 2005

[4] "Current" refers to the "10th Five-Year Plan" period.

will be between 8 and 9%, which is still in the normal fluctuation range, neither too fast nor too slow.

However, in contrast, China's fixed asset investment in the same period of growth is indeed too fast. From 1980s to 2003, the arithmetic average growth of investment in fixed assets in China was 13.2%, according to the above analysis, the volatility of investment in fixed assets since the reform and opening up to the outside of a standard deviation is about 11%, that is, starting from the Current reality (2004), China's fixed asset investment fluctuations range from 2.2 to 24%, belong to the normal range (China's fixed asset investment growth degree of volatility and ups and downs is obviously higher than that of economic growth degree of volatility and ups and downs). However, in fact, the growth rate of China's fixed asset investment in 2003 was close to 27%, and the growth rate of fixed asset investment from January to September 2004 reached 28%, both of which were significantly higher than the upper limit of the fluctuation range (24%). From 2001 to 2004, China's demand for steel and other important investment products and various types of development investment soared, and meanwhile, the demand for coal, electricity, transportation, oil and other energy, power and transportation capacity rose sharply, forming a relatively prominent contradiction between supply and demand. And fixed asset investment demand growth too fast, to a certain extent will reject the growth of the consumer demand, according to our calculations, when China's fixed asset investment growth in more than 23.5%, after each add 1%, accordingly, consumer demand growth will reduce the 0.8%, in turn, the structural contradiction of supply and demand at the same time in the field of stimulating investment, reducing aggregate demand.

Unlike previous growth cycles, the growth rate of fixed asset investment in the past was too fast (or too slow) basically in the same direction and synchronization. However, at this stage there is a significant difference between the two. The complexity of these contradictions cannot help but make it more difficult to choose a macro-control policy, or at least to adopt a policy of overall contraction or expansion, as was the case in previous economic fluctuations. If the economy expands in an all-round way, the contradiction that fixed asset investment grows too fast will become more acute and the whole national economy will run out of balance. If the economy were to shrink, growth would fall below its 26-year average and the contradictions of recession would worsen.

5.2.2 The Inflation Rate Marked by the Overall Price Level is not High, but the Pressure of Price Structural Rise and People's Expectation of Inflation Are Very Strong

Since 1993, taken to restrain aggregate demand, control inflation as the primary goal of tight macroeconomic policy, more than 50 consecutive months of macroeconomic tightening have made remarkable achievements to control inflation. Since November 1997, China's overall price level has begun to show negative values, and the price index has been negative for nearly 30 consecutive months. At the beginning of the 21st century, the price level only fluctuated in the empty index. As a result, some say China has gone from inflation to deflation. Since the second half of 1998 to take to stimulate aggregate demand pull economic growth as the primary goal of a proactive fiscal policy and prudent monetary policy, to get rid of the shadow of deflation in 2003, the overall price level of 3%, in 2004 is expected to be close to 5%, the price level is very low, according to our analysis, the present stage in the process of economic growth in China, the price index under 6%, the economic operation is completely can afford, or rather modest. Reasons summarized as the following three aspects: First, China's economic development is in the industrialization accelerating period, that is, from the middle income developing countries to progress, middle-income developing countries by 2010 will reach middle-income developing countries (GDP will exceed US$3,000 per person), by the year 2030 will reach high income levels in developing countries (per GDP will exceed US$8,000), the emerging industrialized countries. According to relevant statistics of the world bank, developing countries in low-income state of poor countries, low level of inflation, the average within single digits, but into the middle-income stage first to middle-income stage, due to the acceleration of industrialization, the inflation rate is quite high, in the middle income to middle-income stage of development, the average inflation rate in more than 30%; From the middle-income stage to the upper middle-income stage, the average inflation rate exceeded more than 60%. Only after the high-income stage did the inflation rate fall back into single digits. China's "10th Five-Year Plan" and the "11th Five-Year Plan" period can be said to be in the accelerated development of industrialization in the high inflation period.[5] Second, China's institutional transition is in a critical period, the process of marketization is accelerating, and the market system has become a fundamental force in allocating resources, but the construction of market order still needs to be strengthened. Market system has been formed, but it is important to seek market, including the progress of capital marketization and

[5] According to the criteria for the division of the industrialization phase of Chenery (1986), since 1985, China has truly entered the period of industrialization. Since 1998, China's industrialization process has accelerated the promotion of people to 1998. The industrial structure grew at an average annual rate of 0.5% between 1978 and 1998 percentage points, after 1998 into the accelerated period, an average annual increase of 3.5 percentage point. At this rate of growth, the industrial structure of the Chinese economy will reach 1 in 2024, that is, the completion of industrialization (Liu et al. 2008). Then we conservatively estimate that it would be more appropriate for our country to complete industrialization by 2030. At present, the "10th Five-Year Plan" and the "11th Five-Year Plan" period (2001–2010) are the stages in which China is moving from the middle income level to the middle income level in developing countries. According to the historical experience of the industrialized countries or regions in the world, the average inflation rate at this stage is generally about 30%, and the process of moving from the level of medium-income developing countries to that of high-income developing countries (corresponding to the stage of China's development in 2011–2030). The historical average inflation rate in the world is about 60%, so whether we are currently (before 2010). For a long period of time (2011–2030), it will be plagued by high inflation rates. See Liu Wei, Zhang Hui, Huang Zehua, "Investigation of the Height of China's Economic and Industrial Structure and Industrialization Process and Regional Differences", *Economic Dynamics*, 2008(11).

land marketization seriously lagged behind. In this process of institutional transformation, the inflationary pressure from institutional changes is quite large. Almost all the countries in transition have experienced serious inflation for a long period during the acceleration of marketization, which is a direct empirical explanation of the relationship between institutional change and inflation. Third, China is now in a period of rapid growth. Generally speaking, assuming other conditions remain unchanged, the higher the economic growth rate, the greater the pressure on the inflation rate. According to our analysis, during the 10 years from 2000 to 2010, the annual growth rate of China's economy averaged 8–9%. From 2010 to 2020, the average growth rate will be between 7 and 8%. From 2020 to 2030, the average annual growth rate will be 6–7% (China Center for National Accounting and Economic Growth, Peking University 2004). This kind of high-speed growth will naturally form a sustained high inflation pressure. Based on the above three reasons, China's economy is facing quite high inflationary pressure. If we can maintain inflation at around 6%, it will be both balanced and extremely difficult. In 2004, the general price level was only about 5%, which should be said to be a very low inflation rate. From the perspective of this inflation rate, the main contradiction in China's current macroeconomic operation is not inflation at all.

However, from a structural point of view, although the general price level is not high, or even just out of the deflation. On the one hand, however, the prices of important investment products, energy, power and transport capacity, which are associated with the excessively rapid growth of fixed asset investment, are under strong upward pressure, and their price indexes show an obvious upward trend. On the other hand, the prices of important agricultural and sideline products that are closely related to people's life have increased significantly. The prices of cereals, oils, meat, eggs, aquatic products and dairy products have all increased by more than double digits. In addition, the level of residential consumption expenditure (which is statistically included in the total social fixed asset investment) reflecting the content of residents' life is also on the rise. Moreover, due to the combined effect of demand pull and supply cost (especially land cost), there is no obvious room for housing prices to decline for a quite long period of time. As a result, both manufacturers and residents have very high expectations of future inflation, although the overall level of real prices is not high at present.

This has aggravated the difficulty of macro-control from another aspect. If an expansionary macroeconomic policy is adopted, the contradiction of a significant increase in structural prices is likely to quickly lead to a serious imbalance in the aggregate, leading to wild inflation. If the tightening macroeconomic policy is adopted, the overall price level is only out of the shadow of deflation, and further deflation is likely to fall into the trap of deflation.

5.2.3 *Economic Growth Has Picked up Obviously, but Unemployment Remains High*

Compared to the beginning of the expansionary macroeconomic policy in 1998, the current economic growth rate has shown significant rebound. In 1998, China's plan was to achieve a growth rate of no less than 8%, while the actual target was 7.8%. In the five years from 1998 to 2002, the average annual economic growth rate of China was 7.3%. Since 2003, the growth rate has rebounded significantly, and has exceeded 9% for two consecutive years in 2004. It can be said that the economic growth rate has returned to the average (normal) growth rate (9.34%) since the reform and opening up more than 20 years ago.[6]

However, the corresponding unemployment rate in China has not decreased significantly, but has increased. Marked by the registered unemployment rate, China's economic growth rate was 7.8% in 1998, corresponding to the registered unemployment rate of 3.8%, and the economic growth is 9.3% in 2003, the registered unemployment rate is more than 4%, 2004 is expected to continue to exceed 9% economic growth. The registered unemployment rate, however, is likely to be 4.5%.[7] The reason may be various, if other conditions remain unchanged, the economic growth rate should be increased corresponding to the decline in unemployment rate, China's reality of the existence of this contradiction, the root cause is the acceleration of economic industrialization and marketization of the dual transition. On the one hand, with the deepening of marketization, it is becoming increasingly impossible to improve the employment rate at the cost of enterprise efficiency. On the other hand, with the deepening of industrialization, the tendency of capital and technology to exclude labor will be more obvious. In the 1980s, China's economic growth was 1%, and the corresponding new job creation was more than 2.4 million, now it is only more than 900,000 (Zhu 2004).

This contradictory situation makes the choice of macroeconomic policy more difficult. If expansionary policies are adopted, the economic growth rate has obviously rebound, and has reached the average (normal) growth rate in the past 20 years, and continues to expand in terms of total output. Of course, it is possible to exceed the upper limit of normal fluctuations and form a serious imbalance characterized by hyperinflation. If the tightening policy is adopted, the unemployment rate will remain high, and China is a country with the largest amount of labor force and increment, so further tightening will naturally worsen the unemployment situation.

At least the above three aspects explain the complexity of macroeconomic operation contradictions, illustrates a series of unprecedented contradictions and difficulties of the current stage of China's macroeconomic policy choices and facts. Then require macroeconomic regulation and control to adapt to the particularity of the new economic reality.

---

6 *China Statistical Yearbook*, 2004–2005.

7 *China Statistical Yearbook*, 2005.

5.3 The Distinctiveness of China's Macroeconomic Regulatory Measures the Distinctiveness of China's Macroeconomic Regulatory Measures

In 2004, China took a series of macro-control measures, from the policy orientation to the implementation mode, from the transmission mechanism to the policy effect, summed up, there are the following aspects of the particularity.

5.3.1 Combining Aggregate Control with Structural Control, We Will Highlight the Objectives and Effects of Structural Control

According to the complexity of the current economic imbalance, the policy objectives and basic tendencies of macro-control do not adopt simple aggregate selection, nor do they simply judge whether the aggregate is too active or too inactive. Such structural differences are mainly reflected in the following aspects: First, there are differences between regions with different levels and speeds of development, such as the revitalization of the old industrial base in northeast China. Second, there are differences between different industries. While it is clearly pointed out that the development scale of some industries should be limited (such as steel, electrolytic aluminum, cement, real estate, various types of development zones and severely polluted industries, etc.), it is clearly proposed to encourage and actively support industries (such as electric power, oil, coal, railway and other infrastructure, agricultural infrastructure, etc.). Third, there are differences between different enterprises. According to the nature, driving force and competitiveness of enterprises, they have adopted different treatment for enterprises to enter different industrial markets.

Highlighting the differences in the policy structure, to some extent, slowed down the mechanical nature of the aggregate policy, but the questions raised are: First, whether the structure itself is "discriminatory"? Second, are structural differences administrative, or can they be made only by relying more on administrative power? Third, whether the structural "discriminatory" features pose a serious test to the "negotiation ability" between local governments and the central government, or between enterprises and the government, or whether this "negotiation ability" has a serious impact on macro-control? Fourth, structural policy itself more is not simple demand management, supply management from the industrial structure, regional structure, industry organization structure on the regulation and its effect is long-term rather than short-term, then, the structure of the macroeconomic regulation and control is the main amount or structural, mainly is the aggregate demand and aggregate supply, mainly short-term or long-term? In other words, can long-term structural problems be solved by short-term macroeconomic policies?

5.3.2 In the Process of Combined Application of Fiscal Policy and Monetary Policy, the Tightening Effect of Monetary Policy is More Significant

In this round of microstructural adjustment, in terms of tightening effect, monetary policy is prominent. Firstly, monetary policy started earlier. In fact, in the spring of 2003, there were already signals for monetary policy with tightening bias, but influenced by SARS; after September 2003, the tightening of monetary policy is the system. Secondly, the basic attitude of prudent, prudent and moderate monetary policy contraction is clear, and has been maintained since 2003, during which there is no wavering and repeated; Thirdly, the specific measures taken are continuous and steady. The strength of each measure is not big, but the austerity tendency is always maintained and the consistency is maintained; Fourthly, the policy tools used are diverse. Including the credit quantity control policy and the interest rate price policy and so on comprehensive utilization.

It even gives the illusion that China's economy relies mainly on fiscal policy when it expands and monetary policy when it contracts. In fact, both fiscal and monetary policies have the function of expansion and contraction.

On the one hand, fiscal and monetary policies, as two major macroeconomic policy instruments, have different characteristics in their policy functions. Under the condition that market economy or most of the resources are allocated by market mechanism, fiscal policies, whether expanding or contracting, can only act as an engine of macroeconomic regulation and control, that is, to trigger macroeconomic expansion or contraction, but could not rely on fiscal policy tightening or directly stimulate aggregate demand aggregate demand. Because both the proportion of fiscal revenue in the total GDP, or expenditure in aggregate demand share are few. The priming effect of fiscal policy must have the support of monetary policy and the echo to realize, because for the most part in national income into the hands of residents and businesses rather than into the government's financial conditions, a banking and financial system in the allocation of resources on the dominant role to obviously higher than that of finance, at the same time, the effect of the policy of any aggregate demand expansion and contraction, in which quantitative change into the first condition. Actually, since the second half of 1998, we began to adopt expansionary macro-policy. The strength of active fiscal policy can not be said to be small. But why did not the aggregate demand be obviously stimulated until 2002 and the total price level really get rid of the problem of deflation? The important reason is that the monetary policy was very stable at that time, the amount of money did not increase significantly, and the economic growth rate was obvious after 2003. Importantly, since 2002, especially in the first half of 2003, the money supply has increased rapidly. Therefore, the expansionary effect of proactive fiscal policies is actually supported by monetary expansion. Correspondingly, to tighten, it is important that the money supply contract first.

On the other hand, the tightening effect of this round of macro-control coincides with a new round of reform of the fiscal system. The basic tendency of this reform is to better adapt to the requirements of deepening the reform of the market economy. From the perspective of fiscal expenditure, the reform goal of public finance has become more and more clear, and the neutralization of fiscal policy has become more and more common. Therefore, in terms of the effect of fiscal expenditure policy, although the expansion is less than before, the positive direction of fiscal policy has not been reversed. From the perspective of fiscal revenue, China has implemented a tax-sharing system since 1994, which has merged and adjusted 33 types of taxes under the previous comprehensive tax system into 18 categories, and divided them into three major categories: national taxes, local taxes, and shared taxes. Most of the national and shared taxes are concentrated in the central finance. Compared with that, the tax burden on enterprises is relatively high. Meanwhile, the growth of fiscal revenue has always been significantly higher than that of economic growth in terms of the increment. Therefore, from 1994 to 2004, the increase in central fiscal revenue was quite large. In this context, promoting a new round of tax reform must have a clear tendency to reduce taxes. Since January 2004, the new export tax rebate system has been implemented. Although local governments have to bear part of the tax rebate instead of the separate tax rebate from the central finance, local governments have lost some benefits, but for export enterprises, it means tax reduction. In line with the principle of consistency between domestic and foreign enterprises, the corporate income tax has started to be adjusted. The corporate income tax in China will be greatly reduced from 33% in the past, gradually achieving equality between domestic and foreign enterprises. Value-added tax has been transformed from production-oriented to consumption-oriented, and has been piloted in northeastern region. The tendency to cut taxes is certainly an expansionary policy tendency.

Therefore, in this round of structural macro-control, in terms of tightening effect, the role of monetary policy is more prominent, and the relationship between fiscal and monetary policies starts to show a trend of combination of loose and tight to some extent. This is both normal and reasonable for macro-control under normal circumstances. In general, macro-control should try to avoid the "double tightening" or "double loosening" of monetary and fiscal policies at the same time, so as to slow down the degree of economic periodicity and drastic ups and downs.

5.3.3 Important Changes Have Taken Place in the Policy Objectives of Local Governments, Their Attitudes Towards the Ways of Conducting the Central Macroeconomic Policies

In the past practice, local governments have their local interests, so they have different understandings and attitudes toward the central macroeconomic policy. Generally speaking, local governments are only the implementers and implementers of the central macroeconomic policy. In this round of macroeconomic regulation and control, along with the 25-year system reform, local governments have different attitudes towards the interest's objectives and macroeconomic policies. In the transmission mechanism of macroeconomic policy, profound changes have taken place, which demonstrates the tendency of weakening the role of central macroeconomic policy.

Firstly, under the conditions of marketization, there is a growing difference between the goals of local governments' economic interests and those of the central government. At least compared with the planned economy, the deeper marketization is, the stronger the independence of local governments' interests will be. Balanced for the central government, the realization of the macro goal of economic stability and growth balance has no direct relationship with the interests of local governments and developing the local economy, increase the local employment, promote the local welfare more and become a local government behavior on the system rule, this makes the macroeconomic regulation and control policy target and local economic interests' conflict. Secondly, develop the local economy is the most effective also the most direct way to develop the local economy is investment, according to our analysis, at the present stage of China, the local level and the growth of investment in fixed assets, with the local economic development level, GDP and growth were highly unrelated, that is to say, the local investment growth, basically is not directly dependent on local economic development and accumulation, but more rely on the absorption of foreign capital to enter, namely, investment promotion and capital introduction. In this way, even in regions with completely different levels of economic development, strong investment impulses can be realized. Macroeconomic policies will have an important impact on the investment behavior of various regions, but when attracting investment, especially when a large amount of foreign capital is introduced to drive investment growth, the effect of macroeconomic policies will be significantly diluted. Thirdly, along with the deepening of the reform, especially the deepening of enterprise reform and marketization, lower and lower proportion of state-owned enterprises and state-owned holding enterprises, and mostly controlled by the central, local government control of state-owned enterprises is very few, even if it does, it generally have low competitiveness development and management issues, such as severe as a result, local governments rely more and more on non-state-owned enterprises. In the process of implementation of macro policy, the central government to local governments, for the control of central belongs to state-owned enterprises, can come up with policy into effect, carrying out direct administrative requirements, and local governments to rely on non-state enterprises cannot be directly administrative to carry out the government macro policy goals, can only be indirect guidance. Fourthly, in terms of local economic development, the central government and local governments are faced with different entry and exit barriers. In other words, the relationship between the central government and local governments is administrative, while the relationship between local governments and local economic development is largely market-oriented. Therefore, when enterprises are required to enter the market, the central government should give macro-policy signals to the local government, while the local government should not only give clear policy signals to investors, but also directly pay the price to create a series of economic conditions for investors to enter the local economy, such as infrastructure, land, tax preferences, energy power supply, labor supply and so on. The creation of these conditions is as follows: Much depends on the local government expenditure, or local financial expenditure, or government loan payment, in the local fixed assets investment mainly depends on attracting investment. Under the increasingly fierce competition among local governments around attracting investment, local governments pay more and more costs in this respect. Therefore, when the central macro-policy requires tightening and requires all regions to implement the tightening requirements, local governments often have to pay the economic cost of withdrawal at the same time when they withdraw from economic projects. Because the central and local governments face different direct exit costs, the local governments will naturally have different reflection and transmission effects on the central macro-policies.

The existence of differences in policy behavior between the central government and local governments is beneficial for improving the effectiveness of macroeconomic regulation under market economy conditions. The important purpose of macroeconomic regulation is to weaken the economic cycle itself and reduce the ups and downs of economic growth. In this process, if there is complete consistency in behavior from the central government to local governments and from various levels of government to various types of enterprises (of course, this is based on consistent interests), regardless of whether it is possible under market economy conditions, it will inevitably be very harmful for the policy effects of macroeconomic regulation because the high level of consistency will inevitably lack mutual game-playing, thereby promoting the large ups and downs of macroeconomic policies themselves and causing a sharp increase in the fluctuation degree of the effectiveness of macroeconomic policies. This lesson is quite profound under the highly centralized system of planned economy.

5.4 Changing the Growth Pattern and Continuing to Improve the Quality of Macroeconomic Regulation and Control

If 2004 is the year of macroeconomic regulation, which focuses on macroeconomic regulation, then a series of deep-seated problems exposed in macroeconomic regulation cannot be solved by the short-term aggregate policy. That is to say, short-term macroeconomic regulation and control policies have solved some of the imbalance in economic growth, or alleviated the degree of imbalance. How to promote aggregate supply management effectively while implementing aggregate demand management? How do short-term policy effects translate into long-term cumulative effects? The further solution of these problems cannot rely only on short-term aggregate macro policies, especially on direct administrative government intervention policies. We must deepen institutional reform to create conditions for balanced, effective and sustained high-speed growth. From the complexity of the contradictions in the current macroeconomic operation, and from the particularity of the current macroeconomic regulation and control policy measures, it is extremely urgent to innovate in the following areas to improve the quality of China's macroeconomic regulation and control and promote sustained and balanced economic growth.

5.4.1 We Must Actively and Prudently Advance China's Capital Marketization Process

Since the reform and opening up, China's capital marketization has made certain progress, mainly including the following three aspects. First, the reform of the enterprise property right system has created basic conditions for capital marketization. On the one hand, the reform of state-owned enterprises' property right and the reform of corporate governance structure have been gradually carried out. Second, the direct financing market has developed rapidly from scratch since the 1990s. Third, the reform of financial system has created institutional conditions for the cultivation of indirect financing market, including the independence of central bank since the reform and opening up, the construction of state-owned specialized banking system, the separation of policy banks, the development of various joint-stock banks, the reform of state-owned professional (commercial) banks and so on. But generally speaking, the progress of China's capital marketization is lagging behind that of commodity marketization and labor force marketization. On the one hand, the direct financing market accounts for only 4% of the total capital of Chinese enterprises. On the other hand, the price (interest rate) in the indirect financing market is still under the administrative control of the government. Although the flexible interest rate has been adopted step by step, it is still directly priced by the government in the indirect financing market. Moreover, China's banks are overwhelmingly state-owned and monopolistic.

The lag of capital market, have at least two aspects. On the one hand, from the microcosmic point of view, the enterprise is low, the proportion of direct financing mainly rely on bank loans, the bank credit resources is subject to the government administrative or policy requirements, at least a truly, in accordance with requirements of the capital market competition, natural at the same time of produce trade power, corporate rent-seeking, cause, the allocation of capital is divorced from market competition. The Asian financial crisis exposed under the excessive government intervention of financial corruption, is the most direct evidence of the problem. On the other hand, from a macro point of view, low level of capital market and capital configuration can not through the capital market, the government administrative intervention must be serious, especially under the condition of the bank itself to state-owned monopoly, which makes use of monetary policy in macroeconomic regulation and control has the serious administrative, it is also the current macroeconomic regulation and control the outstanding problem in the process of implementing monetary policy. Therefore, no matter from improving the micro benefits of enterprises, or from improving the overall benefits of macro-control, the acceleration of China's capital market process and the corresponding strengthening of order construction, are extremely urgent tasks of deepening reform in China.

5.4.2 Strive to Promote the Marketization of Land Elements in China

At present, the macro-control plays a key role in land clearing. The reason why the government can carry out top-down administrative cleaning indicates that the allocation of land elements in China is far from marketization, thus preserving the institutional basis for the government's administrative allocation and the administrative change of allocation. From the perspective of the operational elements of market economy, the allocation of resources, including land resources, should be carried out directly through the market. The government should establish and maintain the order, and influence the allocation of resources indirectly through guiding the market. In fact, if we say that since China's Reform and Opening-up, the marketization of factors lags behind the marketization of commodities and the marketization of capital lags behind the marketization of labor force, then the marketization degree of land elements still lags behind the marketization of capital, which is the most sluggish aspect in the marketization process of commodities and factors in China at the present stage. The two elements of capital and land have no or little market-oriented economy, and it is difficult to call it a real market economy.

From the perspective of macro-control, the allocation of land as a factor has not been marketized, and even mainly through the allocation of government administrative power. It means that the government always retains the possibility of comprehensive and direct administrative intervention in the economy from the allocation of land elements, and it is difficult to make the macro-control truly based on respect and use of the market mechanism. In fact, the allocation of land elements is a micro problem, not a macro proposition. In the current macro regulation and control, the government intervention as a micro land element allocation problem can play a crucial role in macroeconomic regulation and control. Because land is not market-oriented. Therefore, in order to make China's economy truly become a market economy and make the macro-control truly adapt to the requirements of market economy, the problem of land market allocation must be actively and orderly promoted.

5.4.3 Coordination Between the Central and Local Governments in Terms of Mechanisms

Of course, the institutional innovation discussed here is mainly about the cultivation of market system in the process of marketization, but the government system has not been discussed. For effective macro-control, the science and effectiveness of the government system is extremely important. The more developed the market mechanism is, the more efficient the government mechanism is required. The development of the market economy mechanism cannot simply replace the government. At present, the development of the market economy mechanism can not simply replace the government. In macro-control, as far as the government mechanism is concerned, the prominent problem is how to coordinate the mechanism between central and local governments.

Under the conditions of a market economy, there must be differences between local and central government interests and between local and local interests, the central government behavior should be focused on the control of macroeconomic goals, as far as possible not to, at least in the direct intervention system should not be too much of the local economic life, and the local economic choice should be mainly from taxpayers or local resident's democratic demands, should not be mainly comes from the administrative supervisor's instructions. The main reason for the difference between the local government's behavior and the central macro policy requirement in the current macro control is the difference in the target. Simply using the central macro policy target to negate the local government's behavior target will not only seriously damage the local enthusiasm, but also cause high cost. If the decentralization of local governments is not restrained, the macroeconomic imbalance will be more serious. The point is that there must be a strict institutional distinction between the central and local goals and the corresponding powers and responsibility, for economic life, it is important to promote the transformation of public finance system in terms of system. Public finance not only means that fiscal expenditure should be used to provide public goods as far as possible, but also means that fiscal revenue and expenditure must be an open, procedural and democratic process of public choice in the system. If the local financial revenue and expenditure are basically localized, and the local taxpayers make democratic and open choices, then the central government need not and should not intervene more in the local government's financial behavior. At the same time, the more the central government concentrates on the implementation of macro-target management and guides the local government behavior through macroeconomic policies, the more likely the local government behavior is to converge to the macro-target in the system. Of course, the coordination between the central and local governments is not only a financial issue, or even an economic issue, but also an extremely rich and profound social, political and cultural issue.

Chapter 6
Supply Regulation and China's Macroeconomic Regulation and Control at the Current Stage

Under the historical background of China's current[1] economic development and system reform, macroeconomic imbalances have emerged a series of new features, and corresponding macroeconomic policies have also emerged a series of new features. The limitations of demand management are increasingly apparent, and the requirements for supply management are becoming more apparent.

6.1 The Particular Complexity Disequilibrium in China's Macro Economy and the Major Limitations of Supply Regulation Policy

From the perspective of economic development, China's economic development level is now close to that of middle-income developing countries. In 2005, the World Bank classified countries in the world according to the per capita income by exchange rate method, among which the average national per capita income of low-middle income countries was US$1,746, and China had reached US$1,740 in 2005. According to the evolutionary law of the normal economic history, a country's entering or approaching the level of middle-income developing countries means the production of two aspects of economic characteristics: on the one hand, entering the high-speed sustained growth period of the total amount, once after the developing countries cross the low income "poverty trap", if without a special crisis, the economy will generally form an internal driving force for sustained growth, forming a relatively long-term

[1] "Current" refers to 2003—2006.

The basic time frame for the writing of this chapter is 2006. The main content of this chapter is based on the research paper "Supply Management and Macro-control in China's Current Stage" by Liu Wei and Su Jian, which was published in the first issue of *Economic Research Journal* in 2007.

W. Liu, *Research on China's Market Economy Development*,
https://doi.org/10.1007/978-981-97-1398-1_6

high-speed growth, as evidenced by the experience of the post-war emerging industrial economies in East Asia and Japan. In the 18 years from 1955 to 1973, Japan's annual GDP growth rate reached 9.2%. In the past 20 years from 1965 to 1984, Singapore's annual GDP growth rate reached up to 9.9%. In the past 30 years from 1963 to 1991, Republic of Korea's annual GDP growth rate reached 8.5% (Liu et al. 2004). China's economy has grown at an average annual rate of 9.63% from 1978 to 2005, and it is entirely economically possible to continue its rapid growth for 10 to 20 years. On the other hand, the entry of the economy into this period also means that the economic structure has entered a period of profound and rapid change, because entering or approaching the average level of middle-income developing countries, that is, entering the period of industrialization acceleration, the acceleration of industrialization itself drives the entire national economic structure to rapid changes, and industrial structure, regional structure, departmental structure, employment structure, and total product structure will all undergo profound evolution. In the history of developed countries, such as the United States, UK, France, Germany, Japan, etc., when entering the period of industrialization acceleration, the structural change speed in the national economy is significantly higher than other development periods. Structural change should be a function of technological innovation and institutional innovation. Due to the long-term nature of technological and institutional innovation, the significant changes in structure have long-term nature, but in the period of industrialization acceleration, the long-term nature of this structural change will be greatly weakened. As a result, the imbalance of the national economy is not only aggravated by the instability of sustained high-speed growth in total growth, but also intensified by the contradictions generated by the rapid structural transformation (Liu 1995). Under these historical conditions of economic development, the imbalances in China's economic growth has engendered new characteristics and new complexities, and they have their development inevitabilities.

Judging from the transition of China's economic system at the present stage, after nearly 30 years of the reform and opening up, although the order structure of the market mechanism still needs to be improved, the market mechanism has replaced the traditional planning mechanism as the basic force for allocating resources. Although the marketization of factors needs to be further deepened, the marketization of commodities has been basically completed; although the government reform adapted to the market economy are still relatively lagging behind, the reform of enterprises has made significant and profound progress; although most of the major developed countries of the international community have still not recognized China's market economy status, but after all, more than 50 countries have recognized China's market economy status, and this number is still increasing. It is precisely because of the historical friction of this system transition period that not only makes China's macroeconomic imbalances have institutional characteristics, but also causes macroeconomic policy effects to produce institutional characteristics (Liu 2006).

This special stage of economic development and the process of economic system transformation have made China's macroeconomic imbalances have a range of contradictory peculiarities. At least the following five major contradictions are prominent.

(1) The demand for investment in fixed assets has grown too fast, but at the same time the growth in consumer demand has been weak. According to the experience of 30 years of the reform and opening up from 1978 to 2008, the average annual growth rate of fixed asset investment in China is about 13.5%. If there is no major institutional and technological change, the fluctuation of fixed asset investment demand that China's national economy can withstand is 9 percentage points, that is, between 4.5 and 22.5% (plus or minus 9 percentage points around 13.5%). However, from 2003 to 2006, China's fixed asset investment demand has exceeded the upper limit of 22.5% prominently for four consecutive years, while the growth of consumer demand has become more and more significant. Not only the inventory level of consumer goods manufacturers continues to increase, but also the contribution rate of consumer demand growth to economic growth is only about 60%, which is significantly lower than the 80% level of contemporary international.

(2) The overall price level is very low, but people's expectations for future inflation are high. According to statistics, from November 1997 to the end of 1999, China's total price level showed a negative growth. Until 2002, the price level was generally zero growth. From 2003 to 2004, the price level began to increase positively, but only 3 and 3.9% of low-level growth, the price rise level began to fall again from 2005 to 2006 (*China Statistical Yearbook 2005*), and the National Bureau of Statistics announcement on major economic data for 2006). Under these conditions, people should not worry about serious inflation, and the threat of deflation is greater than inflation. But in fact, people have high expectations for inflation just in the face of the reality of serious deflationary threats. Judging from the manufacturers, the prices of upstream products such as raw materials, fuels, and power have risen sharply. The price increase of fixed assets investment products was 4.8% in 2003, 11.4% in 2004, and 8.3% in 2005,[2] both significantly higher than the rising level of consumer prices during same period. The significant increase in the price of upstream investment products indicates that the production costs of the downstream general consumer goods industry have increased substantially, which has created pressure on the future rise in the price of consumer goods. Judging from consumers, there is a significant difference between the feelings of rising consumer prices and the statistics of the consumer price index (CPI) in China's statistical departments, especially the drastic increase in the price level of food expenditures, which account for 1/3 of the CPI weight. Since 2004, despite continuous harvests, food prices have continued to rise at double-digit levels, coupled with the rapid rise in the price of urban housing expenditures and the uncertainty of expectations for future medical services and education expenditure prices, making consumers to have high expectations for future inflation.

[2] *China Statistical Yearbook*, 2004–2006.

(3) The rate of economic growth has rebounded remarkably, but the unemployment rate continues to rise. From 1998 to 2002, China's GDP growth rate was about 7.3% per year. Over the same period, the number of urban registered unemployed population was about 5 million, and the registered unemployment rate was around 2.3%. Since 2003, China's average annual economic growth rate has exceeded 10%. It is about 3 percentage points higher than the previous 7.3%, however the urban unemployment rate has not decreased but doubled correspondingly. In June 2006, the number of unemployed has reached 10 million, and the registered unemployment rate has reached 4.2%.[3]
(4) The momentum of economic growth is strong, but the contradiction of overcapacity is sharp. Since 2004, China's economic growth rate has exceeded 10% for four consecutive years, and reached 10.5% in 2006. At the same time, the contradiction between overcapacity and potential overcapacity has become increasingly serious. Judging from consumer goods, according to a 2006 survey by the Ministry of Commerce, among the 600 major consumer goods in China, 430 are oversupply, accounting for 71.7% of the total. There are 170 kinds of commodities with a general balance between supply and demand, accounting for 28.3% of the total. There are no commodities that are in short supply.[4] This shows that the relatively common surplus of consumer goods has become a reality. If we consider that a large number of consumer goods manufacturers in China are under-employed and their production capacity is relatively idle, it can be said that the overcapacity of consumer goods has become more common. Judging from investment products, according to a survey conducted by the Ministry of Commerce on 300 major production materials markets in 2006, there were 69 kinds of oversupply, accounting for 23% of the total, and 218 kinds of basic balance between supply and demand, accounting for 72.7%. Only 13 kinds, which account for 4.3%, are in short supply, and are mainly concentrated in resource investment products such as energy, non-ferrous metals and wood.[5] It shows that the demand for investment products of the national economy has generally begun to weaken, while at the same time the output capacity is still expanding, which has led to the formation of overcapacity of investment products. According to statistics, the contradiction of overcapacity in China's steel, electrolytic aluminum, aluminum alloy, coke, calcium carbide, automobile, copper smelting and other industries has been prominent at present, and there are also potential overcapacity problems in the cement, power, coal and textile industries.
(5) The degree of export-oriented economy has increased abnormally, but the problem of insufficient domestic demand has become increasingly serious. The

[3] "Officials from the National Bureau of Statistics answer questions from journalists on current economic hot topics-why has high economic growth not brought high employment", *China Information News*, September 4, 2006.

[4] Ministry of Commerce of the People's Republic of China, "70% of the 600 major consumer goods are oversupply", *Xinhua net*, February 13, 2006.

[5] Ministry of Commerce of the People's Republic of China, "A Survey of Supply and Demand Status of 300 Major Production Materials", *Xinhua net*, February 14, 2006.

price level is sluggish, the products are generally over-extended, the contradiction of overcapacity is increasingly apparent, and the unemployment rate continues to build. Both indicate that China's domestic demand is weak, so that economic growth has to rely more on the expansion of external demand, resulting in a significant shift between domestic demand and external demand growth. Since the reform and opening up, China's import and export growth rate has remained at double-digit annual average. In fact, as long as China's economic growth rate reaches 10%, the corresponding import and export growth will exceed 20%. By 2006, China's total import and export volume has exceeded US$1.7 trillion, and foreign trade dependence has reached more than 70%, far higher than the United States and Japan (about 20%). At the same time, the trade surplus has continued to expand, foreign exchange reserves have exceeded US$1 trillion, and the imbalance in the balance of payments has further intensified, which has brought about a series of new contradictions.

It is precisely because of the particularity of the above five aspects of economic imbalance that the macroeconomic policies starting from aggregate demand management have produced a series of limitations. The limitations of this demand management macroeconomic policy are mainly reflected in the following three aspects.

6.1.1 The Total Policy Effect of Demand is Reduced, and It is Even Difficult to Make Aggregate Policy Choices Regarding Demand Management

The basic direction of the choice of total policy in demand management is nothing more than expansion and austerity, and China's current macroeconomic imbalance is different from the past. Before 1998, whether it was under the planning system or entering the reform process, in general, in most years, China's economy is demand more than supply, and this imbalance is either a shortage (such as in the planning system) or inflation (such as during the reforms); from 1998 to 2002, China's economic imbalances showed a significant lack of prosperity. Under the condition that the direction of the total imbalance is clear, the direction of the total policy of demand management is easy to be clear and it can maintain its continuity for a certain period of time. For example, in the resolution of the 15th National Congress of the Communist Party of China in 1997, in view of the imbalance between aggregate demand and aggregate supply at that time. It was clearly stated that during the entire 9th Five-year Plan period (1996—2000), moderately tight macroeconomic policies with the primary goal of managing inflation remain unchanged. However, by the 16th National Congress of the Communist Party of China in 2002, in response to the imbalance of domestic demand at that time, it was particularly emphasized that during the entire 10th Five-year Plan period (2001—2005), the positive fiscal policy and the prudent monetary policy with the primary goal of expanding domestic demand remain unchanged, which is actually an expansionary macro policy choice. Although the direction of macroeconomic imbalances is different in different periods, it is clear in the direction of the overall macroeconomic policy choice, that is, either the total contraction or the total expansion. Then, at this stage, how should China's total macro policy for aggregate demand be selected? The demand for fixed assets is growing at a low rate while the demand for fixed assets is growing too fast, while the overall price level is low, but the society has high expectations for inflation. Under such contradictions if an expansionary policy is adopted on the total amount, it is beneficial to ease the unemployment and the active and depressed consumer demand. At the same time, it will inevitably aggravate the further expansion of fixed asset investment demand that has been growing too fast for a long time, and will further increase people's expectations for future inflation. A tightening macro policy on aggregate demand in aggregate will help to curb overheated fixed asset investment demand and reduce people's inflation expectations. However, under the contradiction that the rate of economic growth has recovered significantly while the unemployment rate has doubled, the tightening macro policy will curb aggregate demand and thus restrain the growth rate. It is likely to further worsen the unemployment situation, and it is difficult to decide whether to tighten or not. The expansion of aggregate demand cannot expand, and the tightening is difficult to tighten. This dilemma indicates that the complexity of macroeconomic imbalances in China at present has made the demand management on aggregate policies extremely limited.

6.1.2 *The Synchronization of Monetary and Fiscal Policies Has Decreased, and Even the Directional Differences in Policy Effects Have Arisen*

The directional difference between monetary policy and fiscal policy is mainly due to the particularity of current economic imbalances and the stage of institutional reform. In fact, at this stage, China's fiscal policy still maintains an expansionary trend in aggregate demand, while monetary policy adopts a tightening option. The directional differences in the choice of these two basic macroeconomic policy systems indicate that in the face of complex economic imbalances at the present stage, macroeconomic policy interventions from the perspective of demand management have more uncertainties and deeper contradictions. This is also an important manifestation of the limitations of the demand authority.

Let's first examine the direction of fiscal policy selection at this stage. As far as the fiscal expenditure policy is concerned, the fiscal deficit has not decreased. It was only slightly reduced after the deficit reached US$314.95 billion in 2002, but it has remained at a scale of more than RMB200 billion for many years. And in 2005, the fiscal deficit was expanded compared to 2004. In terms of national debt, the domestic debt issued by the state in 2002 was RMB322.877 billion. However, by 2005, it had increased to RMB692.287 billion, doubled. It can be seen that whether it is from the scale of the fiscal deficit or the expansion of the number of national debts, the fiscal expenditure policy still maintains the momentum of stimulating demand. As far as the fiscal revenue policy is concerned, China has entered a new round of tax adjustment since 2004. On the basis of the tax-sharing reform in 1994, the new round of tax adjustment is a norm for the emergence of new problems in the implementation of the tax-sharing system since 1994. The most prominent problem is that in the process of tax sharing, the central tax accounted for a large proportion and the growth rate was fast, while the local fiscal revenue was scattered and unstable in the tax system, and the collection cost was high. By 2005, central taxes accounted for 52.3% of all taxes, and total local taxes across the country accounted for only 47.7% of total taxes. At the same time as the problem of local tax revenue and financial resources arise, the local government's tax and fee requirements for enterprises will inevitably increase, thus increasing the tax burden of enterprises. Therefore, starting from 2004, a new round of tax adjustment has been proposed, which includes deep tax reduction requirements, especially to reduce the burden of corporate taxes and fees. Firstly, the implementation of the new export tax rebate method, although the local government may not be satisfied (because the original export tax rebate is refunded by the central government, the new method requires the local government to bear 25% of it). But for exporting enterprises, it is equal to speeding up and standardizing and serious export tax rebates. Secondly, the adjustment of income tax, including the increase of personal income tax threshold, and the reduction of corporate income tax rate for the majority of domestic enterprises. In particular, in the past, domestic enterprise income tax was 33%, while foreign corporate income tax was lower than this tax rate by about double. In order to truly embody fair competition, this trend is bound to gradually harmonize the tax rate between domestic and foreign capital. For domestic enterprises, the unification of the income tax rate of domestic and foreign-funded enterprises should be a process of sharply falling income tax. Finally, the trial transition from production-type value-added tax to consumption-type value-added tax on value-added tax means that fixed assets and technical equipment are also entering the VAT deduction as the intermediate inputs purchased. This is undoubtedly an important tax reduction measure for enterprises, especially for enterprises with high capital intensity, and this measure has already been implemented in the Northeast as one of the policies to revitalize the industrial hub of the Northeast. This series of tax reduction measures shows that China's current fiscal revenue policy is the same as the fiscal expenditure policy, and it adopts an expansionary fiscal revenue policy.

Let's then examine the direction of monetary policy. The basic tendency of monetary policy in recent years has been continued tightening. Due to the loosening of monetary policy in 2002, especially since the credit growth in the first half of 2003 was faster, the scale of credit released on June 30, 2003 was equivalent to 130% of the total annual lending in 2002. Moreover, the money supply in 2002 has significantly exceeded the average speed of previous years.[6] Thus, considering the time-lag characteristics of monetary policy (the United States and the European Union usually range from 6 to 18 months, and China is estimated to be roughly 7 months to 24

[6] *China Statistical Yearbook*, 2003–2004.

months), the central bank planned to adopt austerity measures in the spring of 2003. Although later it was not implemented due to the impact of SARS in the spring of 2003, since September 2003, until now, the Central Bank has successively introduced austerity measures with a one percentage point increase in the statutory reserve ratio. The characteristics are: Firstly, to maintain the austerity and persistence of a long period of time, from September 2003 to January 2007, the monetary policy has been tightened for nearly 40 consecutive months; secondly, the tightening of each specific measure is not large, usually in a small scope; at last, to use of various monetary policy tools comprehensively, from raising the statutory reserve ratio to strictly controlling the scale of credit, and then raising the interest rate of deposits and loans, etc., monetary policies are fully tightened.

Despite the fact that the direction of the imbalance of aggregate imbalances is still not very clear, the principle of "loose and tight match" between fiscal policy and monetary policy may be more conducive to the stability of economic growth. Perhaps it will be able to alleviate the economic shock caused by "double tightening" or "double loosening". However, the directional difference between China's current fiscal policy and monetary policy effect is not an active policy choice, but a passive helplessness. Because, on the one hand, the emergence of such differences is not based on the independence of the public finance system and monetary policy; on the other hand, it is not based on the premise of a clear judgment on the imbalance of macro-capacity. Therefore, this directional difference itself indicates the contradictory particularity of the total imbalance in China at this stage, making it difficult to coordinate between fiscal and monetary policies if only from the aggregate demand management. Especially under the condition that the "monetary liquidity trap" has begun to appear, the policy of tightening monetary policy such as raising interest rates will further increase people's propensity to save to a considerable extent. Commercial banks will face greater pressure on the difference between deposits and loans, and the situation of weak consumer demand growth may further intensify. This also shows that in the special total imbalance, the effectiveness of monetary policy in macroeconomic regulation and control with the aim of demand management begins to decrease. In fact, the simple short-term demand management on the total amount has been difficult to adapt to the requirements of China's macroeconomic regulation and control, but should combine demand management with supply management, so that the total policy and structural policy, short-term adjustment and long-term adjustment are coordinated.

6.1.3 The Central Government and Local Governments Have Produced Cyclical Differences in the Regulation and Control of Macroeconomic Imbalances, Which Has Profoundly Affected the Extent of the Government's Effect on the Implementation of Demand Management Policies on the Total Amount of Government

With the construction of the socialist market economic system, the mutual interest relationship between the central and local governments and the mutual mechanism has undergone profound changes. To a considerable extent, it can be said that the independence of the power, responsibility and profitability of local governments in the reform and opening up has greatly improved, and local governments themselves have increasingly become the masters of the residual claim and residual control the economic development of local society. As a result, the behaviors of the local government are significantly different from those of the central government. Firstly, the behavioral goals are different. The central government regulates the macro economy, and its goal is to achieve a balance in the macro sense, that is, to prevent hyperinflation and to prevent a serious recession; and the goal of local government economic behavior can only be to maximize local economic interests, especially maximize local government revenues (including fiscal revenues and non-financial local government income). Secondly, the ways and barriers to enter the economy are different. The contact between the central government and the local government is an administrative mechanism. Therefore, when the central government needs to implement its policy of expanding the policy of economic regulation through local governments, it can be arranged through administrative means and the local government as an administrative subordinate should also obey the administrative instructions of the central government. Here, for the decision-making of the central government, it is implemented through administrative methods. If there are mistakes, the first thing to pay is the price caused by administrative decisions. But the way local governments enter the economy and the barriers they face are different. Whether it is the impulse of the local government to maximize its income, or the need to implement the administrative instructions of the central government to accelerate the development of the economy, the development of the local economy must first accelerate investment, and the basic channels of investment are nothing more than two: Firstly, financial input. It should be said that the financial resources of most local governments are insufficient to support their investment requirements, and even the infrastructure, public goods production and public services that local finance should undertake are difficult to guarantee. Moreover, local governments cannot financially carry out "incremental reforms" by issuing bonds; the second is to convert bank savings into investment. However, due to the "verticality" of the monopoly financial system of state-owned professional banks in China, coupled with the underdevelopment of local small and medium-sized intermediary financial institutions, the investment growth of local governments in China is highly independent of the level of local economic development and the corresponding local residents' saving capacity (China Center for National Accounting and Economic Growth, Peking University 2004), which means that it is difficult for local governments to require banks and other financial institutions to support their local investments. Under the conditions that both finance and banking cannot or will not support their investment activities, the investment needed to develop the local economy can only rely on "inviting investment". The relationship between the local government and the business and investment that it relies on is not the relationship between the upper and lower levels of the administration. Unlike the previous relationship between the government and state-owned enterprises, local governments cannot rely on administrative means to direct them to enter the local economy. They can only be attracted through market negotiations. This requires not only a negotiation process, but also local governments' efforts to improve investment conditions, usually by improving these conditions as municipal infrastructure construction projects, secured by local finances, and financing loans to banks.

The changes in the relationship between the central government and local governments, local governments and enterprises, and the linkage mechanism have led to cyclical differences between the central government and local government in the regulation of macroeconomic demand. When the central government considers insufficient demand from the perspective of aggregate demand, the economy is in a downturn, and needs to prosper the economy and increase employment, the central government can use the administrative mechanism to require local governments to accelerate development and accelerate the stimulation of demand. However, at this time, local governments are unable to expand their investment in real time, whether through finance or through banks. Because local economic development relies mainly on attracting investment, this requires a process. When local governments have increased the intensity and speed of attracting investment, after a certain period of time, they have obtained the trust of the business and the capital they are recruiting. All localities have gathered a number of introduced businesses and capitals, which have formed a rapid growth in aggregate demand, especially investment demand, and the rapid expansion of aggregate demand has caused the economy to have an imbalance of excessive demand. Therefore, the central government must proceed from the macro-major balance of supply and demand, curb aggregate demand, and then require local governments to slow down investment impulses through administrative means, and even require them to withdraw from the already entered economy. However, local governments at this time have been difficult to withdraw because local governments have invested heavily in attracting investment, which constitutes an economic barrier for local governments to withdraw. Obviously, the changes in the system and the changes in the pattern of interests brought about by the reforms have also caused serious limitations in the macro-control of demand alone. At least as the main body of policy makers and implementers of macroeconomic policies, namely, the central government and local governments, there is a significant difference in the impulses of interest expansion or suppression of aggregate demand and the corresponding behavioral cycles. This kind of cycle staggering can even be said to be the difference in behavior between cycle and counter-cycle, and its effect on demand management will inevitably have a profound impact.

It can be seen from at least the above three aspects, that is, from the total directionality of macroeconomic policy effects, from the basic policy tools of macroeconomic policies, from the macroeconomic policy decisions and the subject of implementing behavior, the limitations of demand management policies becomes more and more obvious. The realization of China's current goal of regulating macroeconomic imbalances requires important adjustments to macroeconomic regulation and control, especially strengthen the application of supply management policies in the short-term adjustment of economic fluctuations.

6.2 Regulation and Control of Disequilibrium in China's Macro Economy and the Application of Supply Regulation Policy

The limitations of the demand management policy itself and the particularity of the dual transition of China's economic development and system reform indicate that it is necessary to introduce and attach importance to supply management. In general, changes in supply, including changes in production costs and economic structure, are often based on technological innovation and institutional innovation, that is, on the basis of efficiency changes. However, this change in growth pattern is only possible in the long run. Therefore, the policy effects of supply management are mostly more long-term. In the history of economic thought, supply management policies, as the integral part of macroeconomic policies, are far less important than demand management policies. The main reason is that Keynes emphasized on demand management policies and the success of post-war demand management policies which can promote balanced growth, leading to the neglect of supply management policies.

The impact of "stagflation" in the 1970s on Keynesian economics once led people to pay attention to supply management policies and form the so-called "supply-side economics", with particular emphasis on stimulating the economy and increasing employment by lowering tax rates to achieve equilibrium (as described in the Laffer Curve). The supply management policy at the time was proposed as a substitute for demand management policies, with the aim of coping with short-term economic fluctuations. In the view of supply-side economists, the reason why supply management policies can regulate the economy in the short term is that it can change the incentives faced by producers, including enterprises and laborers. The capital, labor, natural resources, technology, etc. of an economy may not change in the short term, but the incentives of producers can be changed at any time. As the representative of the supply-side school, Laffer said, once the incentives people face change, their behavior will change. Positive incentives attract people to do things, and negative incentives prevent people from doing something. The role of the government in this situation is to change the incentives people face and thus influence social behavior

(Laffer 1983). Therefore, regulating incentives for producers is at the heart of short-term supply management policies, and taxation is the most basic tool for regulating incentives. The supply-side school believes that for workers, the incentives are determined by two relative prices: the relative price of work and leisure, and the relative price of future consumption and current consumption (Bartlett and Roth 1983), the first relative price determines the worker's labor enthusiasm, and the second relative price determines the worker's enthusiasm for saving.

However, because the Reagan administration's policy of supplying schools to the school has not achieved the expected success, and people's understanding of "stagflation" has gradually deepened, the demand management policy has regained an important position in the macroeconomic policy system. The supply management policy has also gradually withdrawn from the mainstream macroeconomics. After the 1990s, with the industrial restructuring brought about by the technological revolution, and the profound changes in the regional economic layout caused by economic globalization, and the increasing attention to long-term economic growth propositions, making industrial policies, regional policies, and growth policies for long-term aggregate supply have become the main components of long-term supply management policies, which have renewed people's attention. It is precisely because of the long-term nature of supply management policies that people's emphasis on supply management policies is limited to their long-term effects on the economy, while the short-term adjustment effects of supply management policies are not fully recognized. In fact, supply management policies can not only be used, but are often used to regulate short-term economic fluctuations, but they are not taken care of, or are not regarded as supply management policies, and are taken for granted as demand management policies. The impact of supply management policy and demand management policy on equilibrium is different. The impact on price level and total output is different. Distinguishing the characteristics of these two policies directly affects the expectations of the macroeconomic situation and the judgment of macro policy effects. The contradiction complexity of China's current macroeconomic imbalance requires that even in the short-term adjustment, the demand management policy and supply management policy must be organically combined. Generally speaking, the supply management policies often used to regulate short-term economic fluctuations, mainly include monetary policy, fiscal policy, wage policy, raw materials and energy price policy.

6.2.1 *Characteristics of Monetary Policy Effects as a Means of Supply Management to Regulate Short-Term Economic Fluctuations*

In traditional macroeconomic theory, monetary policy is regarded as demand management policy. In fact, monetary policy is also a supply management policy, because it not only affects aggregate demand, but also affects aggregate supply. The main purpose of monetary policy is to adjust interest rates, and interest rates have two effects on the economy. It can affect both aggregate demand and aggregate supply. For example, lowering interest rates, on the one hand, can affect investment, increase investment demand, and thus increase aggregate demand. Monetary policy plays a role in demand management policy here; on the other hand, interest rates also affect the cost of capital use, the reduction in interest rates reduces the cost of production factors and thus the aggregate supply. In other words, the change in interest rates has both an aggregate demand effect and an aggregate supply effect. Both of these effects of interest rates contribute to an increase in equilibrium output, but the effect on price levels is different. The aggregate supply effect causes price levels to fall, while the aggregate demand effect causes price levels to rise. Whether the price level eventually declines or rises depends on the relative size of the two effects. From the perspective of the actual effect of monetary policy, the aggregate demand effect is generally greater than the aggregate supply effect, because in general, loose monetary policy of monetary policy generally drives the price level to rise. For China's macroeconomic regulation and control, which must pay attention to economic growth and prevent serious inflation, it is of special importance to pay attention to the aggregate supply effect of monetary policy.

Then, what are the factors that determine the aggregate supply effect of monetary policy[7]? The impact of monetary policy on aggregate supply can be divided into three links, that is, the change of currency first affects interest rate, and then the change of interest rate affects production cost, and after that the change in production costs affects the aggregate supply. Correspondingly, the extent of the aggregate supply effect of monetary policy depends on these three links. Firstly, how much influence does monetary policy have on interest rates? The other factors are the same, the greater the impact of monetary policy on interest rates is, the greater the aggregate supply effect of monetary policy will be, and the impact of monetary policy on interest rates depends on the sensitivity of monetary demand to interest rates. The more sensitive the money demand is to interest rates, the smaller the impact of monetary policy on interest rates will be, and thus the smaller the aggregate supply effect of monetary policy is. Secondly, how much influence does interest rate change have on production costs? This depends on the total capital stock in the economy. The larger the total capital stock is, the greater the impact of interest rate changes on production costs will be. With the continuous development of China's economy, ultra-high savings have led to rapid capital deepening, and thus the capital intensity of China's economy has been increasing, which will make the aggregate supply effect of monetary policy bigger and bigger. Thirdly, how much does the change in production costs affect the aggregate supply? This depends on the price elasticity of the aggregate supply. The greater the price elasticity of the aggregate supply is, the greater the impact of

[7] The channels through which monetary policy affects aggregate supply are not just interest rates, but also other channels, such as the uncertainty that monetary policy brings to the economy (refer to Tatom 1983, p. 12).

changes in the given production cost on the aggregate supply will be,[8] and thus the greater the aggregate supply effect of monetary policy will become. Then, under what circumstances is the price elasticity of the aggregate supply greater? Generally speaking, the greater the idle production capacity of an economy is, the greater the price elasticity of the aggregate supply will become. Therefore, when the economy is in a recession stage, the aggregate supply effect of monetary policy is greater.[9]

After taking the supply effect of monetary policy into account, we can better explain our experience since the outbreak of the Asian financial crisis in 1997. After the outbreak of the Asian financial crisis in 1997, China's central bank adopted an expansionary monetary policy. The growth rate of M2 is more than 20% per year. According to common sense, China should have higher inflation in the past few years, at least there will be no deflation. However, the situation in those years was exactly the opposite. For several consecutive years, the inflation rate was close to zero, and in some years there was even negative inflation. What is the reason for this? We know that during this period of time, the aggregate demand of China's economy is not sensitive to interest rates, so the demand effect of monetary policy is very small (Su Jian 1998). However, due to the large amount of idle production capacity in the economy, the supply effect of monetary policy is relatively large. In this way, under the condition that the supply effect of monetary policy is greater than the demand effect, there will be a situation of economic growth and falling prices.

In a certain sense, the greater the supply effect of monetary policy is, the greater the effect of monetary policy on promoting equilibrium will be. In particular, when economic growth is promoted through the supply effect of monetary policy, it is not necessary to pay more inflation as the demand effect of monetary policy drives economic growth. However, in the practice of macroeconomic policy, the demand effect of monetary policy usually exceeds its supply effect. Therefore, when a country's macroeconomic short-term regulation needs to introduce more supply management policies, the role of monetary policy is relatively weakened, especially when the national economy pays attention to economic growth and inflation targets at the same time. In other words, the macroeconomic imbalance is difficult to judge, and when it is difficult to expand or tighten from the aggregate demand management policy, it is necessary not only to focus on the long-term, but also to pay more attention to the combination of short-term demand management and supply management. Since the overall supply effect of monetary policy is relatively weak, its role in

[8] Reflected on the graph, the larger the amplitude of the aggregate supply curve is shifted to the right.

[9] The impact of monetary policy on total costs has been noted in China (but these studies view this effect from a demand perspective). The Macro Group of the China Center for Economic Research of Peking University (1998) made estimates based on the actual situation in China around 1997. According to their analysis, from 1996 to 1997, the loan interest rate fell by 5.17 percentage points. If the balance of various loans of financial institutions at the end of 1995 is more than RMB5 trillion, this will reduce the interest burden of enterprises by about RMB240 billion. They believe that "the role of interest rate cuts is equivalent to tax cuts in a certain sense, and the quantity must be greater than the tax cuts (mainly reductions)" (Macro Group of the China Center for Economic Research of Peking University 1998).

economic equilibrium is considerably limited. The monetary policy effect of China at this stage is undergoing the test of the complexity of this imbalance. Judging from the demand management policy effect, the continued tightening of monetary policy since September 2003 will definitely be limited by growth and employment goals. Therefore, while the inflation expectations have not been substantially reduced, the strength of monetary tightening is limited by growth and employment targets, and it cannot achieve effective control of inflation and suppression of excessive growth of structural demand. Judging from the effect of supply management policy, China's monetary policy at this stage, both from the long-term economic restructuring (including regional economic restructuring, industrial restructuring, etc.) or from the general impact of short-term interest rate changes on manufacturers' production costs, its role is still very limited. Therefore, in the complex macroeconomic imbalance environment that needs to focus on the combination of demand management policy and supply management policy, this limitation of monetary policy, especially its limitations on supply policy effects, should be given high priority.

6.2.2 Characteristics of Fiscal Policy Effects as a Means of Supply Management to Regulate Short-Term Economic Fluctuations

Tax policy is the most important policy tool in the eyes of the school. In fact, the policy prescriptions offered by the supply-side school to the Reagan administration in the 1980s were almost all tax policies.

Obviously, the supply-side management policy effect of fiscal policy is higher than that of monetary policy. For this reason, in the view of the supply-side school, the most effective way for the government to stimulate the economy and increase employment is to lower the tax rate. On the other hand, like monetary policy, fiscal policy is often seen as a demand management policy. In reality, however, fiscal policy also has a supply management policy effect. Whether a certain fiscal policy belongs to the supply management policy or the demand management policy depends mainly on whether it is aimed at producers or consumers. The fiscal policy for consumers generally belongs to the demand management policy, and the fiscal policy for producers mostly belongs to the supply management policy. The fiscal policy tool that serves as a management policy affects the cost of the manufacturer, including tax costs, wage costs, interest costs, and raw material costs.

Tax policies have an important impact on the actual cost of the manufacturer. Obviously, adjusting various taxes paid by enterprises, such as value-added tax, corporate income tax, business tax, import and export tax, etc., can affect the actual production cost of the enterprise, thereby increasing the aggregate supply. At the same time, the adjustment of personal income tax can also affect the aggregate supply, because, on the one hand, the adjustment of personal income tax can affect people's savings, and savings will affect interest rates, thus affecting the average cost change; On the other hand, personal income tax has an impact on workers' enthusiasm, which affects production efficiency and affects average cost. In addition, production subsidies to enterprises are equal to government support to enterprises and reduce production costs. The mechanism is the same as tax reduction. The problem is that taxation policies also affect aggregate demand. For example, tax cuts can affect both aggregate supply and aggregate demand. Then, does the tax reduction give a bigger stimulus to demand or supply? Further, is the tax reduction policy a demand management policy or a supply management policy? This issue has been a controversial issue that has not been fully resolved since the emergence of the supply-side school. Although there is a difference in the judgment of the magnitude of the impact of aggregate demand and aggregate supply, it is recognized that taxation policies affect the aggregate supply. China's economy has adopted an expansionary fiscal policy since 1998, including expansionary fiscal expenditures and fiscal revenue policies. This expansionary fiscal policy, on the one hand, plays an important role in stimulating aggregate demand (especially expanding domestic demand), but at the same time we cannot ignore its effect as a supply management policy. Since 1998, the tax rebate rate for textile exports has increased (from 9 to 11%), and the fees for 20 administrative enterprises have been cancelled. In 1999, the export tax rebate rate for garments was further increased successively (up to 17%). The relevant taxes and fees of the industry will be reduced or reduced. At the same time, 73 funds for enterprises were cancelled; in 2000, tax incentives were applied to high-tech industries such as software and integrated circuits (Macro Group of the China Center for Economic Research of Peking University 2005); In 2003, in response to the impact of SARS, phased tax cuts were implemented in aviation and tourism industries. Since 2004, a series of tax reduction and exemption policies have been introduced successively, including adopting new export tax rebates and eliminating rural agricultural taxes. Large-scale cancellation of payment projects for farmers, trial of corporate value-added tax from production to consumption, and so on. These measures have had an important impact on the actual production costs of enterprises and have played an important role in improving the competitiveness of enterprises. Therefore, from the perspective of aggregate supply, the balanced growth target of the Chinese economy has been promoted, and important contributions have been made in adjusting the total imbalance in the short term. The impact of fiscal policy on aggregate supply is usually more significant than the supply effect of monetary policy, because the supply management policy effect of monetary policy itself is lower than its demand policy management effect. At the same time, it is difficult for monetary policy to directly regulate the economy, so the extent and depth of the impact on supply is limited. Therefore, when the contradictions of macroeconomic imbalances are complicated, it is difficult to choose the total amount of regulation from the demand side. Therefore, when it is necessary to pay attention to the combination of supply management policies, this significant supply management policy effect of fiscal policy should be given special attention.

There may also be other short-term supply management policy tools, such as wage policies: including wage freezes, wage subsidies, and reducing the social security fees that enterprises should pay and so on, but these methods may be difficult to use because of the rigid wages and the difficulty in lowering wages; Or the government pays a certain subsidy to the enterprise workers, but the mechanism of this subsidy is similar to the fiscal policy; or it doesn't work very well, such as reducing or canceling the social security expenses of the enterprise, and has little effect on the current consumption of the workers. For example, although the raw material and energy price policies are related to the production costs of the manufacturers, the government's freezing or subsidies in this respect should not be excessive. Otherwise, long-term enterprises use resources at low cost, which is not conducive to efficiency improvement. Therefore, these aspects are not discussed specifically in detail here.

6.3 Principles of Demand and Supply Regulation Policy Combination in China's Macroeconomic Regulation and Control

As far as the adjustment of short-term fluctuations is concerned, if the overall direction of economic imbalances is clear, then which policy is mainly used in the process of combining demand management policies with supply management policies, it should also be chosen according to the direction of total imbalance and the primary objective of the corresponding macroeconomic policy. If the economy starts to be in the status of full employment, but due to negative demand shocks, resulting in a decline in equilibrium output and price levels, then a demand management policy can be adopted. At the same time, supply management policies can also be adopted to restore full employment status. However, the path and cost of restoring full employment using different types of management policies are different. The use of supply management policies, while promoting the restoration of full employment, will further reduce the price level, thereby increasing the pressure of deflation, which may have a negative impact on the aggregate demand of the national economy and prompt the economy to enter a vicious circle. The demand management policy is to promote the recovery of full employment, while raising the price level, thereby raising the level of inflation, so that it does not fall too fast, resulting in the expansion of the national economy's aggregate demand and speeding up economic recovery. Therefore, under these conditions, more demand management policies should be adopted. If the economy begins to be in full employment, but the negative supply shocks lead to economic imbalances, balanced output declines and price levels rise, it is also possible to adopt both a demand management policy and a supply management policy to bring the economy back to full employment. But with different types of policies, their impact on price levels is also different. The use of demand management policies will further increase the price level, which means that while alleviating unemployment, it will lead to higher inflation. The use of supply management policies will return the price level to its original state. That is to say, the use of supply management policies can enable the national economy to avoid or reduce inflation while promoting the recovery of full employment. Therefore, under these conditions, supply management policies should be adopted more in the combination of supply management and demand management policies. In short, in the short-term adjustment, in order to achieve the equilibrium goal, the demand management policy should be used to deal with the imbalance formed by the demand shock, and the supply management policy should be used to deal with the imbalance caused by the supply shock. Although the imbalance created by the use of demand management policies to deal with supply shocks, or the use of supply management policies to deal with the impact of demand shocks, can also promote the economy to return to full employment, but there is a price to pay, that is, a negative impact on the economy. This negative impact is mainly reflected in the instability of the price level. China's past macroeconomic imbalances are relatively clear in the direction of the total amount. For example, before 1998, demand was greater than supply, and from 1998 to 2002, demand was less than supply. Therefore, the short-term adjustment of macroeconomics was mainly to systematically apply demand management policies, or to tighten aggregate demand or expand aggregate demand. Although some supply management policies have been adopted in this process, they are far less than demand management policies in terms of systematicness and dependence. At present, China's macroeconomic imbalances have produced a series of new features, which have made the effectiveness of demand management policies have engendered significant limitations, while at the same time the price to pay is increasing, especially whether the aggregate demand is expanding or tightening, and it is difficult to choose. Therefore, there is a special need to emphasize the combination of demand management and supply management policies. According to different reasons for imbalance, different macro management policies are adopted from different aspects of demand and supply to promote balanced growth while avoiding or reducing the instability of prices.

In terms of long-term balanced growth, the use of supply management policies is of even greater significance. First, with the acceleration of technological progress, the industrial structure of the contemporary world economy is constantly changing. The speed of change and the degree of its deepness are unmatched in the past. However, China's current economic development is precisely in the period of accelerating industrialization. One of the prominent features of any country's accelerating period of industrialization in economic history is the dramatic change in industrial structure, in other words, the process of industrial structure upgrading has been unprecedentedly accelerated. Therefore, industrial policy is of great significance to the development of China at this stage, and industrial policy is of course a supply management policy. Second, regional economic policies are also an important part of supply management policies. As part of a sovereign state, a regional government cannot have macroeconomic instruments that are unique to the state. For example, an area cannot have an independent monetary policy. At the same time, a regional government uses fiscal policy to influence the aggregate demand of the region. Its role is very limited and extremely uncertain, because the regional government finance can only affect a small part of the aggregate demand of the residents in the region. To a greater extent, it is not affected by the fiscal policies of regional governments.

Moreover, even if local residents' needs are affected by the local government's fiscal policy, how much of their aggregate demand has formed demand for local products is even more limited and extremely uncertain, it may be that the government of this region has spent money, but it has affected the economy of other regions. Therefore, it is impossible for regional governments to use monetary policy to influence the local economy. At the same time, the use of local fiscal policies has little effect on local aggregate demand. Therefore, demand management policies are not applicable to the region. However, supply management has a prominent meaning. China is a country with significant regional differences. Therefore, changes in regional economic development and regional economic structure are important propositions for achieving long-term sustainable development in China. Especially under the condition that the aggregate demand management has formed the cyclical difference between the central government and local government policy regulation behavior, the supply management policy is of great significance to the coordinated development of China's regional economy. Third, the continuous improvement of economic openness and the deepening of economic globalization have also made the importance of China's long-term development of supply management policies constantly rising. Because the more open the market, including the gradual opening of commodity markets and capital markets, the effect of demand management policies will gradually decrease. The aggregate demand stimulated by a government's demand management policy is likely to not necessarily form a demand for domestic products. However, the supply management policy is different, the direct beneficiaries of the supply management policy are related enterprises within the scope of their sovereignty, those who have benefited the most are national companies. Residents or enterprises in other countries may also enjoy the benefits of their government's supply management policies, but it is, after all, a close second compared to the country's residents and businesses.

All in all, in regulating the economy, supply management policies have their own unique advantages and effects. Not only in the long-term regulation, the role of supply management policies is becoming more and more important, and in the regulation of short-term economic fluctuations, supply management policies are increasingly indispensable. Whether in the treatment of long-term propositions such as the evolution of the industrial structure and regional economic coordination in China's economic development or the enhancement of its opening to the outside world, or in the short-term adjustment under the background of the deeper complexity of China's macroeconomic imbalance, the role of supply management policies will become increasingly important. How to coordinate demand and supply management policies more effectively and scientifically in the long-term and short-term regulation of national economic development is an important issue for us.

Chapter 7
Supply Regulation and China's Market-oriented Reform Process

The purpose of this chapter is to discuss the short-term effects of supply management policy (hereinafter referred to as "supply management policy") and the necessity and particularity of introducing supply management policy into short-term macroeconomic regulation in China at present; the requirements of the application of supply management policy for economic system, especially for the process of marketization; and the market economy. Additionally, it will discuss what the main supply management policy instruments available under market economy conditions.

7.1 Why does China Need to Introduce Supply Regulation Policy

Demand management policy refers to those factors that can make changes to aggregate demand and can be controlled by the government, especially the central government; supply management policy refers to those factors that can make changes to aggregate supply and can be controlled by the government, also mainly by the central government.

As far as the adjustment of short-term economic fluctuations is concerned, the supply management policy is also of great significance in China at this stage. In fact, when the demand management policy overcomes the serious limitations of the current imbalance, the short-term effect of the supply policy must be particularly emphasized. On the one hand, in theory, short-term supply management policy

---

The basic time frame for writing this chapter is early 2007. The main content of this chapter is based on the article "Supply Management and the Marketization Reform Process in China" by Liu Wei and Su Jian, which was published in the *Journal of Peking University* (*Philosophy and Social Sciences*) in the fifth issue of 2007.

W. Liu, *Research on China's Market Economy Development*,
https://doi.org/10.1007/978-981-97-1398-1_7

has its own characteristics. In short-term regulation, the impact of supply management and demand management policy on the economy is different: (1) Different objects of action. Demand management policies are directed at consumers, including consumers of final consumer goods and enterprises that purchase investment products such as factories and equipment, while supply management policies are directed at producers, including producers, enterprises and workers. (2) The effect is different. The same nature of demand management and supply management policy, demand management policy makes the price level change in the same direction, and supply management policy makes the price level change in the opposite direction. In the face of certain economic imbalance, we can adopt demand management policy, supply management policy, or a combination of the two, so that the economy tends to be balanced. But the change of price level is different in this process. Take the economic recession as an example, we need to take expansionary measures. If we adopt demand management policy, with the increase of aggregate demand, the price level will generally rise, the profit of enterprises will rise under a given production cost and then increase production and employment. If we adopt supply management policy, with the increase of supply, the price level will generally decline, and then the aggregate demand will increase with the decrease of price. Additionally, balanced output rises, which will also increase employment. (3) Different ways of action. Demand management policy mainly regulates the purchasing power of buyers, while supply management policy mainly regulates the enthusiasm of producers. The important reason why supply management can regulate the economy in the short term is that it can change the enthusiasm of producers, including enterprises and workers. The objective endowment of factors in the economy, including capital, labor, resources and technology, is difficult to change significantly in the short term. Therefore, the object of supply management policy is difficult to target factor endowment, but the producer side. Facing incentives can change at any time, so they can be the object of short-term regulation of supply management policy. As Laffer, a representative of the supply-side school, said, once the incentives people face change, their behavior will change accordingly. Positive incentives attract people to do something, while negative incentives prevent people from doing something. The role of the government in this situation is to change the incentives people face, thus affecting social behavior. (Laffer 1983, p. XV) In fact, the incentive to regulate producers is the core of short-term supply policy (Liu and Su 2007).

On the other hand, from the perspective of macro-control practice, the introduction of supply management policy in short-term regulation can help overcome the limitations of China's current aggregate demand management policy: (1) In the case of reduced aggregate effect of demand management policy, or when the direction of aggregate policy is difficult to choose, supply management policy has actually become a necessary choice. The government can highlight the structural regulation and control characteristics of supply management policies, such as creating incentives and competitive conditions for structural differences among industries, regions, enterprises and sectors, so as to avoid the deterioration of contradictions caused by aggregate selection, make the government's macro-control more targeted, and reduce the cost of macro-control. (2) The government can directly control the effect of supply management policy. For example, the tax rate as a fiscal policy and the interest rate change as a monetary policy have both the demand effect and the supply effect. As a supply management policy, the government can clearly judge the extent of the impact on the production cost of enterprises, thus reducing the uncertainty of the role of macroeconomic control policy, and thus reducing the macroeconomic control risk. (3) The application of supply management policy is easier to coordinate the possible contradictions between policy effects. Especially when the effects of fiscal policy and monetary policy used as demand management policy have directional differences, the space of coordination is relatively narrow when there are contradictions between demand management policy tools, because the tools of demand management policy are relatively few and the objects of action are relatively general. There are many kinds of policy tools for supply management and their objects of action is also flexible and diverse, so it is easy to coordinate even if there are contradictions between policy instruments. (4) Supply management policy has not only the effect of total quantity control, but also various local characteristics. Therefore, it is more flexible under the condition that the behavior of central government and local government has periodic differences. Due to the differences of specific situations in different regions, the central government and local government form a game situation in the economic cycle movement. The difference between cyclical and counter-cyclical behavior is significant, which will weaken the total effect of demand management policy. In this case, because the total characteristics of demand management policies are strong, it is difficult to adapt to the uneven local economy, and the supply management policies with more local characteristics are more applicable and targeted accordingly. In fact, at present, most of the policy means of developing local economy in China are supply management policies in the form of fiscal policies, such as preferential tax policies, low land prices and so on. (5) Supply management policy can directly adjust the efficiency loss caused by the excessive income distribution gap. The imbalance in macroeconomic operation may be caused by unreasonable income distribution in terms of total amount. For example, the growth of consumption demand is weak. In addition to the fact that the growth of investment demand is too fast, which crowds out the growth space of consumption demand, the important reason is that the income distribution gap is too large, and the income of the high-income people (the stratum with relatively low savings tendency) grows faster and more widely. As low and middle-income people, although their consumption tendencies are relatively high, the income growth rate is slow. The excessive expansion of this distribution gap not only involves the rationality of income distribution, but also seriously affects the imbalance of the total operation. To overcome this imbalance, demand management policy has great limitations, because demand management involves the aggregate demand, and it is difficult to touch the income distribution structure among social strata. Supply management policy focuses on stimulating the enthusiasm of producers and adjusting the incentive conditions faced by producers. Therefore, it can make comprehensive use of policy tools such as taxation, from the total amount and structure. Income distribution should be adjusted.

7.2 Why has Supply Regulation Policy been Neglected for a Long Time

When it comes to macroeconomic policy, people tend to equate it with demand management policy. Although supply management policy is also an integral part of macroeconomic policy and is often adopted in economic practice, it is always ignored. The reasons are mainly from three aspects: First, institutional reason, that is, the application of supply management requires a more adequate and free competitive market mechanism as the institutional basis, otherwise, the systematic application of supply management policy will probably lead the economy to a planned mechanism, and the fear of planned economy will cause people to have doubts about supply management policy. Second, theoretical reason, that is, Keynesian preference. As the founder of modern macroeconomics, Keynes's preference and emphasis on demand management and the historic achievements of demand management policy in the post-war era have laid the foundation of demand management policy in macroeconomic management, and at the same time led to the neglect of supply management policy. Third, the reason for policy practice is the failure of the supply-side school policy practice in the early 1980s.

7.2.1 Fear of Planned Economy and Corresponding Doubts About Supply Management Policy

The role of supply management policy is the producer, so the government's policy can directly affect the micro-units of national economic production, so that the depth and specific degree of policy intervention may be higher than that of demand management policy. As a result, people have a doubt that the supply management of the system will eventually lead to the planned economy. Therefore, most of the theoretical and policy advocates of the supply-side school adhere to economic liberalism, and most of them emphasize that the application of supply management policy is based on a fully free market competition mechanism. Because, on the one hand, only the perfection and perfection of the market system can encourage competition in the system, thus speeding up technological innovation to stimulate efficiency; on the other hand, only by fully respecting the rights and responsibilities of producers in market competition, can we form sufficient competitive power and pressure on producers, and form sufficient stimulation and effective restraint on producers in the system. The core function of supply management policy lies in effectively stimulating and restraining producers to stimulate efficiency. Therefore, competitive market mechanism is the basic institutional prerequisite for supply management policy to be effective. Government policy intervention on producer's behavior, which is divorced from market mechanism, may lead to the administration of resource allocation, the substitution of government for market, the weakening of producer's competitive power and pressure, thus making the efficiency goal of supply management policy difficult to achieve. That is to say, supply management policy is based on the recognition and respect of market competition mechanism, so that the incentive and restraint conditions of market competition faced by real producers in market economy will change more conducive to the promotion of competitive efficiency, rather than the denial of market, let alone the denial of producers' rights and responsibilities in market competition. The more emphasis is placed on the realization of the efficiency goal of supply management policy, the more emphasis is placed on the freedom and adequacy of market competition.

But if we divorce from this system background, the planned economy is actually the supply management only in terms of the way and content of policy function. This is because: (1) The essence of planned economy is a policy system that directly promotes supply through government plan. The planned economy is aimed at social production, especially directly restraining producer's behavior. This is similar to the characteristics of supply management policy that takes producer as the object of policy. (2) Demand is neglected in the planned economy because, on the one hand, the subjectivity and complexity of demand, as well as the dispersion and diversity of demand, make it extremely difficult and costly for the government to grasp the demand situation and its changes; on the other hand, the planned economy negates the objectivity of the role of market mechanism, so it naturally does not need to pay attention to the market. Demand. In an economy that does not pay attention to and respect demand, when production and consumption, supply and demand are contradictory, the simplest and lowest-cost way is to use a variety of tickets, indicators and other quantitative signals to express the allocation system, that is, to achieve compulsory equilibrium under inefficiency by "queuing" of government administrative organizations. At the same time, taking supply rather than demand as the starting point of management policy is also the basic method of supply management, which further improves the similarity between planned economy and supply management. Therefore, in a sense, the planned economy is the extreme form of supply management, which can be used to the extreme, even on the basis of negating the system of market economy, the supply management policy, that is, the planned economy. The economic inefficiency of planned economy has been proved by history, and the political centralization is well known. Therefore, based on the fear of planned economy, especially the excessive introduction of supply management policy, which leads to the weakening and negation of free market competition, people have doubts and neglect of supply management.

7.2.2 Keynes's Preference for Demand Management and the Corresponding Disregard for Supply Management

Keynes, the founder of modern macroeconomics, gave more preference and emphasis to demand management policy in theory and policy. In the post-war practice of macroeconomic regulation and control in developed countries, Keynes' demand management policy has indeed achieved long-term success. In this way, while establishing the basic orthodox position of demand management policy in macroeconomic management, it also forms the tradition of neglecting supply management policy. Keynesian theory and policy are facing the Great Depression economy. How to manage the Great Depression? Keynes believes that the key is to reduce real wages. There are two ways to reduce real wages: one is to raise prices, the other is to reduce wages. Raising prices needs to stimulate aggregate demand, which belongs to demand management policy, while lowering wages is to reduce production costs, which belongs to supply management policy. In Keynes's view, wage cuts would be opposed by workers and unions, and social resistance was too great to be feasible. Keynes argues that it is foolish to choose a supply management policy with high social resistance to reduce wages, while it is wise and effective to stimulate aggregate demand directly through a flexible demand management policy, thereby reducing real wages and promoting economic recovery (Keynes 1983).

7.2.3 *The Failure of Supply-side School Policy in Practice in the 1980s Intensified People's Doubts About Supply Management*

By the 1970s, the emergence of "stagflation" made people doubt Keynesian economics, so supply management policy began to attract people's attention. That is the so-called "supply-side school economic revolution" in western economics (the re-revolution of Keynesian revolution). The supply-side school emphasizes the application of supply management policy, especially the role of tax policy, and the impact of tax on aggregate supply. The supply-side school believes that the change of tax rate will affect people's enthusiasm for work. When the tax rate increases, people's enthusiasm for work decreases gradually, thus the aggregate supply decreases. Therefore, the best way for the government to stimulate the economy and increase employment is to reduce the tax rate. The famous "Laffer Curve" in the theory of supply-side school is a systematic expression of the relationship between tax rate and government income.

Under the impact of "stagflation", the supply-side school became popular in the early 1980s. The Reagan Administration of the United States accepted the policy recommendations of the supply-side school. However, the Reagan Administration's policy experiment did not succeed. Subsequently, with the deepening of people's understanding of stagflation, under the background of both the failure of the experiment of supply management policy and the practice and theory of economic re-understanding of stagflation, demand management policy has again occupied a dominant position in the application of macroeconomic policy, and supply management has gradually withdrawn from people's vision. It is difficult to find the content of supply management policy in the mainstream textbooks of macroeconomics. In practice, some supply management policies have been adopted, but they are also mistaken for demand management policies.

7.3 What Conditions are Required for Systematically Implementing Supply Regulation Policy in China

The question is whether supply management policy can be introduced into macroeconomic management in China, or whether supply management can be carried out without leading to planned economy and adapting to market economy. The answer should be affirmative. In supply management, as long as we can respect the law of market economy and adapt to the characteristics of market economy, supply management can play a good role in macro-control, including long-term and short-term economic fluctuations. To this end, efforts must be made to create three basic conditions: On the one hand, the supply management policy should be systematically reformed to adapt to the characteristics of market economy; on the other hand, the competitive market economy system should be improved and perfected to create a solid institutional basis for the effective use of supply management; on the other hand, the government must have a strong ability to judge the macroeconomic imbalance.

7.3.1 Systematic Transformation of Supply Management Policies to Meet the Requirements of Market Economy

The so-called system reform mainly refers to the systematic correction of factors that are similar to or likely to lead to the planned economy in the supply management policy, which includes at least four aspects: (1) Indirect regulation instead of direct regulation. That is to say, the supply management policy is used to regulate the conditions of stimulating and restraining producers, and this regulation is carried out in the market order of fair competition and in the norms of legalization and democratization of government behavior, rather than directly intervening and denying producers' own behavior. (2) Price regulation instead of quantity regulation. Under planned economy, the role of price signal, that is, market, is negated. Quantity signal and quota index become the main regulation signals and basic ways of economy. In market economy, market is fundamental for resource allocation and price signal is basic. Therefore, price regulation should be the main means in supply management. Of course, this kind of price regulation cannot be a direct price control, but an indirect way of price regulation that affects production costs in the form of taxes and subsidies. In market economy, enterprises have the right to price products. Generally, the government should not directly regulate the price of products, but indirectly regulate the price of products. Enterprises should have the power and ability to find the right price signal in the system, especially in the property right system. They should also face the rigidity of competitive market price. (3) Substituting macro-control for micro-control. In the market economy, when using supply management policy to regulate enterprises (producers), we should not directly and specifically interfere with the operation of an enterprise. On the one hand, we should try our best to make the policy aimed at a certain type of enterprise, such as an industry, an industry, a region, or a similar enterprise with the same characteristics; on the other hand, we should try our best to influence the competition conditions faced by such enterprises. Environment, not directly affect the enterprise behavior itself. That is to say, although supply management policy is aimed at enterprises, it should be "macroscopic" and "universal" as far as possible. (4) Replacing administrative means with legal means. The advantage of legal means is that it includes the interaction mechanism between policy executors and policy actors. That is to say, it includes not only the legal constraints on policy actors (enterprises), but also the legal norms on policy executors (governments). One of the important conditions for applying supply management policy under market economy is to standardize government behavior and make it standardized, legalized and procedural. Otherwise, supply management may lead to administrative centralization of government. Moreover, there may be loopholes in any policy. On the one hand, the government may not understand the economy or lack sufficient information on some aspects of the economy. On the other hand, individual enterprises may indeed face special circumstances. Therefore, the existence of interaction mechanism between them is extremely important. If market economy is an economy governed by law, the key to deepening the rule of law lies not only in establishing and perfecting legal restrictions on private acts in the general market economy, but also in forming effective legal restrictions on the acts of public actors. Otherwise, the implementation of supply management policy may lead to the administration of the management system.

7.3.2 Deepening System Reform to Create Necessary Market System Foundation on for Effective Use of Supply Management Policy

A prominent institutional feature of applying supply management policy in China at present is that we are not introducing supply management in a relatively mature and complete market economy system, but gradually introducing supply management in the process of cultivating the reform of market economy system, that is, while systematically reforming and applying supply management policy, we are effectively applying supply management under market economy conditions. The institutional basis for policy creation. This requires us to realize that the more we emphasize supply management, the more we emphasize system reform, and that the systematicness of supply management policy application must be adapted to the depth of market-oriented process. Otherwise, the application of supply management policy may be seriously opposed to the market-oriented economic reform, which not only increases the cost of system transition, but also reduces the effectiveness of supply management policy.

Therefore, we must clearly grasp the historical process of China's economic reform and the historical characteristics of China's market economy cultivation at this stage. At present, at least three characteristics are outstanding. (1) Has the core proposition of reform changed from enterprise reform, especially the reform of state-owned enterprises, to government reform, especially the transformation of the functions of the central government? At the beginning of the reform and opening up, we emphasized that taking enterprise (state-owned) reform as the core has great revolutionary significance, but after nearly 30 years of reform from 1978 to 2007, the key proposition that really determines the depth of China's marketization has actually changed from enterprise reform to government reform. Government reform includes the transformation of government functions towards market economy, the transformation of government economic regulation and control mode, the transformation of economic policy making and transmission mechanism, and the process of legalization and standardization of government behavior. Without these fundamental changes, the application of supply management policy will be difficult to achieve market competitiveness efficiency. (2) Is the main difficulty of the reform transformed from building a socialist market economy system to improving the market economy order? The purpose of the reform is to replace the planned economy system with the market economy system and make it the basic force for allocating resources, and to replace the quantity signal with the price signal as the main signal for allocating resources. After nearly 30 years of reform from 1978 to 2007, as far as the mode of resource allocation is concerned, the market has replaced the dominant position of the planned mechanism in the scope of market mechanism. The marketization process in China has shifted from expanding the market space, mainly through the construction of market mechanisms in quantity, to improving the quality of market mechanisms and continuously enhancing the order of the market. This includes the main order of market competition, such as enterprise property rights and the quasi-personnel system of the market, as well as the transaction order of market competition, such as the market price system and other arrangements to ensure fair competition. The main order answers "who is competing", while the transaction order answers "how to compete". The unification of these two systems constitutes the internal competition mechanism of market economy. Corresponding to the internal competition mechanism, the unity of the legal order and the moral order of the market economy in the market economy society constitutes the order of the social environment outside the market economy. That is to say, the recognition and promotion of the internal competitive order of the market in terms of the rule of law and morality. Obviously, the construction of the internal and external order of the market economy is a long and in-depth historical process. But without the construction and perfection of market order, there is no way to improve the effectiveness and fairness of the market. Under the condition that the market economy order is chaotic and the effectiveness and fairness of market competition are seriously destroyed, it is difficult for the government to implement its supply management policy by using market mechanism, because the supply management adapted to the requirements of market economy is actually to adjust the market competition conditions faced by producers through policies so as to improve the producers' enthusiasm under the premise of fair competition, and then improve efficiency. (3) Has the basic task of reform changed from product marketization to factor marketization? After 30 years of reform, the marketization of commodities, including consumer goods and investment goods, has made rapid progress. In terms of pricing, at least 90% of commodity prices have been priced by the market, rather than by the government's administrative pricing. The fundamental problem is that the more important proposition of marketization is to realize the marketization of factors, including labor, capital, land, technology and other resources. Compared with commodity marketization, factor marketization in China lags behind seriously, especially capital market and land resource marketization, which makes the systematic application of supply management policy face serious institutional limitations, because supply management policy is to the producers without directly affecting factor endowment, or on the premise that the market fully dominates factor allocation. To adjust the incentive conditions faced by the manufacturer and the laborer who use the essential factors, so as to achieve the goal of supply management policy under the condition of market economy. Obviously, the above three historical characteristics of China's marketization process not only create the possibility of market economy system for us to use supply management, but also form important constraints. In order to apply supply management policy systematically in China and achieve its policy objectives in line with the requirements of market economy, we must take reform as the driving force of institutional change, take the depth of marketization as the institutional basis for effective application of supply management policy, and prevent the government supply management from being separated from the institutional premise of deep marketization. Otherwise, it may lead to the administrative return of the system.

7.3.3 Continuously Improve the Government's Judgment on the Direction and Extent of Macroeconomic Imbalances, and Create the Basis of Macroeconomic Analysis and Effective Decision-making Mechanism to Improve the Scientificity of Supply Management Policies

Improving the effectiveness and scientificity of supply management policy is based on accurate judgment of macroeconomic imbalance. In the face of certain macroeconomic imbalances, the government can adopt either demand management policy or supply management policy, and combine them into an organic whole. But when and for what problems should we choose demand management policies? When and for what problems should we choose supply management policies? Its basic principles should be based on the causes of economic imbalances, using demand management policies to deal with the imbalances caused by demand shocks, and using supply management policies to deal with the imbalances caused by supply shocks. This can minimize economic fluctuations while paying policy costs to a lesser extent.

Firstly, assume that the economy is in full employment at the beginning, but due to negative demand shocks, equilibrium output and price levels decline. At this time, both demand management policy and supply management policy can restore the economy to a balanced state, but the consequences of the two are different. If we adopt supply management policy at this time, we can restore balanced output and full employment, but at the same time, the price level will further decline, which means that deflation may have a negative impact on the aggregate demand of the market (private sector), thus making the economy face a vicious circle of depression. If demand management policy is adopted at this time, while promoting the recovery of balanced output and full employment, the expansion of demand will also restore the price to the level of the original equilibrium state, so that before and after the policy function, that is, from the previous equilibrium to the imbalance and then to the recovery of equilibrium, the price level has not changed before and after, which can avoid the risk of the economy entering deflation. Therefore, in this case, it is more effective and less risky to choose more demand management policies.

Secondly, it is assumed that the economy is in equilibrium at the beginning, but due to negative supply shocks, the equilibrium output falls and the price level rises, that is stagflation. Similarly, we can adopt either expansionary demand management policy or expansive supply management policy to restore the economy to full employment. But the consequences are also different. In this case, the expansionary demand management policy will further increase the price level, which means that while unemployment is gradually alleviated, inflation will increase; and if the expansionary supply management policy is applied, unemployment will be gradually alleviated, while prices will return to the original equilibrium level, so that the economy can recover fully without or less inflationary pressure. Obtain employment. Therefore, under such conditions, it is more effective and less risky to choose more supply management policies (Liu and Su 2007).

7.4 What are the Alternative Supply Regulation Policies that are Suitable for Market Economy[1]

7.4.1 Government Regulation as Supply Management Policy

(1) Government regulation of prices

The way of price regulation includes the regulation of price level and rising rate. Generally, it includes the supervision of the prices of raw materials, energy, land,

[1] What is discussed here is the main supply management policy for the short-term adjustment of the economy.

capital, labor and other important commodities and elements. This kind of supervision is extremely common and severe under the traditional planned economy system of China. Since the reform and opening up, the price of most commodities has been determined by the market, but there are still some commodities, especially important elements, including capital (interest rate), land (rent) and energy, electricity and other important raw materials, of which the price is largely controlled by the government. With the deepening of factor marketization, the situation that the government directly controls factor prices needs to be fundamentally changed.

In terms of price control, the most extreme measure is the wage-price freeze, which means that the government requires enterprises not to adjust wages and prices by mandatory order. This kind of policy has been applied even in the reality of market economy, but the effect is often contrary to the original intention. For example, under the impact of the 1970s oil crisis in the United States, stagflation occurred. At this time, if the economy adjusts itself through the market, wages should fall, so that aggregate supply returns to its original state. Therefore, if we want to restore full employment through wage adjustment, the US government should have promoted wage adjustment, but the US government chose to freeze wages at that time, resulting in increased economic volatility and prolonged recession.

The wage freeze policy generally applies to situations where Trade Union forces or other non-economic factors cause wages to grow too fast. If other factors remain unchanged, excessive wage growth will lead to stagflation in the short run. In the long run, with the decline of corporate profits and investment, competitiveness will weaken, and ultimately slow down economic growth. At this time, if the government comes forward to freeze wages, thus restraining the rise of production costs, protecting and maintaining the production enthusiasm of enterprises, unemployment rate and inflation rate can be controlled.

In the modern economy, in addition to wages, enterprises often pay workers certain remuneration in other forms, such as housing provident fund, social security fees and so on. If these expenditures are abolished or reduced in legal form, the actual burden of enterprises can be reduced and the aggregate supply curve can be shifted to the right. For workers, the way or direction of using these incomes is often limited, so the reduction of these incomes has little impact on the current consumption of workers. During the Asian financial crisis in 1997, the Singapore government adopted such a policy. In Singapore, besides paying workers' wages, enterprises have to pay 10% of their wages to their provident fund accounts. During the Asian financial crisis, the Singapore government announced the temporary abolition of this requirement, thus reducing the real wage cost of enterprises from a year ago.

(2) The government regulates the allocation of resources and other economic regulations

In addition to price (including wages) regulation, the government has other aspects of economic regulation, including: Firstly, the direction of the use of resources, that is, the government to regulate the direction of the use of resources. For example, the government's special loans, special funds, land use direction and conditions, as well as the government's industrial policies, regional economic policies stipulated by the direction of the use of other resources regulation. In China, these policies are often used, for example, the direction of land use in China is very strict. Regulatory measures on the direction of resource use are often based on long-term and global considerations, but in the short term, they often have a negative impact on aggregate supply. Secondly, the regulation of enterprise market behavior, the government's anti-unfair competition measures, will produce supply effect. The economic policies that regulate the operation of enterprises will affect supply. The government can improve efficiency by supervising the monopoly of enterprises on resources or product markets. This regulatory policy can also achieve faster output growth by restraining firms from restricting competition, development and innovation (Tatom 1983). Thirdly, the regulation of factor mobility and its relaxation. In theory, in a market economy, any regulation of factor mobility will lead to a reduction in the efficiency of resource allocation, thus shifting the production possibility boundary of the economy inward. Worldwide, the most common restrictions are on capital flows and on labor flows. These regulations are extremely strict in China. Even after nearly 30 years of reform, the regulation has been relaxed to a great extent, but due to the serious lag of factor marketization in China, especially the capital market marketization (including the progress of indirect financing marketization and the degree of direct financing marketization); although the labor market has made great progress, it contains profound institutional discrimination and administrative restrictions. All these restrictions have seriously affected the efficiency of factor allocation in China. Relaxation of these controls is clearly conducive to expanding the production possibilities of our economy. Fourthly, the supply effect of other regulatory measures that Chinese government may take in the future. China is an economic developing country and a transitional country. In this process, various regulatory measures will gradually develop and improve with the further improvement of the market economic system and the gradual improvement of the level of social and economic development. For example, with the improvement of people's living standards, the requirements of product quality, environmental quality, production safety, national economic security and quality of life will also be improved. The improvement of these requirements will often increase the production costs of enterprises, and the increase of production costs of such enterprises, to a large extent, needs the help of compulsory measures of the government.

7.4.2 Fiscal Policy as the Application of Supply Management Policy

Fiscal policy is usually regarded as demand management policy. In fact, most fiscal policies are also supply management policies, at least affecting aggregate supply. Generally speaking, whether a fiscal policy is a demand management policy or a supply management policy depends on whether it is aimed at consumers or producers. The fiscal policy for consumers is generally a demand management policy, while the fiscal policy for producers (enterprises) is generally a supply management policy. As a financial policy tool of supply management policy, it aims at the actual production cost (or effective production cost) of enterprises, and the actual production cost of enterprises generally includes four aspects, namely, tax, wage cost, interest cost and raw material cost.

The main tools for fiscal policy as supply management include: (1) Tax policy. Adjusting various taxes paid by enterprises, such as VAT, enterprise income tax and business tax, can affect the actual production cost of enterprises. Export rebate is also a commonly used tax reduction means for export enterprises. At the same price level, the actual production cost of enterprises decreases, so the aggregate supply curve moves to the right. The adjustment of individual income tax can also have an impact on the aggregate supply. There are two ways to influence it. Taking tax reduction as an example, firstly, the reduction of personal income tax will lead to an increase in private savings and a decrease in the interest rate, which will reduce the average cost of producers; secondly, the reduction of personal income tax will lead to an increase in workers' labor enthusiasm and production efficiency, thus reducing the average cost of producers. It can be seen that tax policies for enterprises and individuals have not only demand management policy effects, such as tax reduction can stimulate investment and consumption expenditure, but also supply management policy effects, such as tax reduction can also reduce production costs of enterprises. The question is whether fiscal and taxation policies, such as tax cuts, stimulate demand more or supply more? This problem has not been completely solved since the emergence of the supply-side school. Although there are theoretical divergences on the level of demand effect and supply effect of tax policy, it is generally acknowledged that tax policy has both supply effect and demand effect. (2) Production subsidy policy. Including subsidies for the output produced by enterprises, or for the input of specific factors of production used by enterprises. For example, wage subsidy, interest subsidy, research and development subsidy, export subsidy and so on. Subsidies are equivalent to reducing the production costs of enterprises, and their mechanism is the same as the tax reduction as a supply management policy. Among them, export subsidies and R&D subsidies are more common policies. (3) Redistribution policy. For example, transfer payments, food stamps, social security and welfare policies will affect workers' enthusiasm and savings rate, thus affecting the aggregate supply.

The above-mentioned fiscal policy instruments as supply management policies have been adopted by Chinese government to varying degrees. For example, from 1998 to 2003, in order to expand domestic demand, a series of fiscal policies have been adopted, including both demand effect and supply effect. For example, in February 1998, the textile export rebate rate was raised from 9 to 11% in order to reduce taxes and promote the growth of textile exports; In July 1998, the value-added tax rebate rate for seven categories of mechanical and electrical products, such as telecommunications equipment, and five categories of light industrial products was increased from 9 to 11% in order to reduce taxes to support the development of related industries and promote economic growth; In October 1998, 20 administrative fees were abolished in order to reduce the burden of enterprises and reduce costs; Further increase export rebate rate (annual tax rebate of RMB62.2 billion), reduce the cost of export enterprises and promote export; In August 1999, some reduction and exemption of business tax, deed tax and land value-added tax related to real estate were given to support the growth of real estate industry; In November 1999, 732 fund charges were abolished to alleviate the burden of enterprises and reduce the cost of enterprises; In June 2000, preferential tax was applied to industries such as software and integrated circuits. Policies should be adopted to encourage the development of high and new technology and the upgrading of industrial structure. In February 2003, phased tax cuts were implemented in aviation, tourism and other industries to eliminate the negative impact of SARS on these industries, etc. (Macro Group of the China Center for Economic Research of Peking University 2005).

Since entering a new round of macro-control in 2004, the fiscal revenue policy based on tax reduction and reducing production costs of enterprises has never been interrupted, and the effect of its supply management policy is also significant. For example, since January 2004, a new method of export tax rebate has been implemented, which has increased and accelerated the level and speed of tax rebate for export enterprises and further supported the development of export enterprises. In the new round of tax system adjustment since 2004, a trial value-added tax transformation has been carried out in Northeast China since August 2005, with the transformation from production-based value-added tax to consumption-based value-added tax, increasing the amount of enterprise value-added tax deduction and reducing the burden of enterprises. We should adjust the personal income tax threshold, reduce the level of individual income tax and stimulate the enthusiasm of workers; we should reduce the income tax of domestic enterprises and strive to unify the income tax of domestic and foreign enterprises so as to reduce the income tax rate of domestic enterprises from 33 to 24%, and gradually implement it after a certain transition period; especially since 2006, the national agricultural tax has been abolished universally, and the majority of agricultural producers have been popularized throughout the country. In addition, in view of the momentum of the rapid development of some industries, tax policies have also taken some restraints, such as the imposition of land value-added tax on the real estate industry in 2007.

7.4.3 Monetary Policy as Supply Management Policy

In traditional macroeconomic theory, monetary policy is regarded as demand management policy. In fact, monetary policy is also a supply management policy, because it affects not only the aggregate demand, but also the aggregate supply. Therefore, monetary policy tools are not only the policy tools of demand management, but also the policy tools of supply management. So, what is the demand effect and supply effect of monetary policy? We know that interest rate is the main channel for monetary policy to play a role. Therefore, the demand effect and supply effect of monetary policy depends on which is more sensitive to interest rate. In developed market economy countries such as the United States, investors and consumers are in a sound, large and convenient financial system, and their credit system is also complete, so their investment and consumption needs are more dependent on the financial system, so their aggregate demand is more sensitive to interest rates. In developing countries like China, the financial system is not perfect, and the credit system is not perfect, the financial service procedures are cumbersome and the cost is high; in addition, there are still some ambiguous boundaries in the property rights system of enterprises to a certain extent, so the interest rate of enterprises is not sufficient; thus, investors and consumers are less sensitive to interest rates than developed countries, and the need for monetary policy. The effect should be smaller in developing countries. Therefore, for developed countries, the demand effect of monetary policy is likely to be greater than the supply effect; for developing countries like China, the demand effect of monetary policy is likely to be smaller than the supply effect. From 1997 to 2003, especially from 2002 to the first half of 2003 in China, the money supply increased significantly, but the price level did not rise or fall, or nearly zero inflation, and the economy continued to grow at a high speed. The phenomenon of growth is a clear evidence.

As a supply management policy, monetary policy plays an important role in three ways. First, monetary policy affects the cost of capital usage; second, monetary policy affects the actual tax burden of enterprises and workers; and third, monetary policy affects enterprises' judgment of economic situation.

(1) The impact of monetary policy on the cost of capital usage

The important means of monetary policy is to adjust interest rates, and the change of interest rates has two effects on the economy, namely, demand effect and supply effect. Take reducing interest rate as an example. On the one hand, lowering interest rate can increase investment demand and thus expand aggregate demand, which belongs to demand management policy. The corresponding effect is the aggregate demand effect caused by the change of interest rate. On the other hand, interest rate is also the main factor determining the cost of capital usage, so the reduction of interest rate also reduces the factor cost of production, thus shifting the aggregate supply curve to the right, which belongs to the supply management policy. This effect is the aggregate supply effect of interest rate changes. Because the reduction of interest rate affects the cost of using existing capital, and the existing capital is the stock accumulated over many years, the reduction of interest rate has a great effect on the reduction of cost.

The aggregate demand effect and the aggregate supply effect of interest rate fluctuation increase the equilibrium output, However, in this process, the impact on price level is different. The aggregate supply effect increases output while lowering price level, while the aggregate demand effect increases price level. In practice, whether the price level eventually rises or falls depends on the relative magnitude of the two effects. From the actual effect of monetary policy, the effect of aggregate demand is generally greater than that of aggregate supply. Therefore, generally speaking, loose monetary policy usually leads to higher price levels.

Then, what factors determine the aggregate supply effect of monetary policy? The impact of monetary policy on aggregate supply can be divided into three parts: the change in money affects interest rate → the change in interest rate affects production cost → the change in production cost makes the aggregate supply increase. Therefore, the aggregate supply effect of monetary policy depends on three links. Firstly, how much impact monetary policy has on interest rates? The greater the impact of monetary policy on interest rates, the greater the aggregate supply effect of monetary policy. The impact of monetary policy on interest rate depends on the sensitivity of money demand to interest rate. The more sensitive money demand is to interest rate, the less the impact of monetary policy on interest rate, and the smaller the aggregate supply effect of monetary policy. Secondly, how much impact does the change of interest rate have on the production cost? It depends on the total capital stock in the national economy. The cost of capital usage is equal to the total capital multiplied by the interest rate.[2] As a result, the greater the total capital stock in the national economy, the greater the impact of interest rate changes on production costs. Thirdly, how much impact does the change of production cost have on aggregate supply? It depends on the price elasticity of aggregate supply. The greater the price elasticity of aggregate supply (the flatter the aggregate supply curve), the greater the impact of the given change of production cost on aggregate supply. Therefore, the greater the aggregate supply effect of monetary policy (Liu and Su 2007).

(2) The impact on monetary policy on the tax burden of enterprises and workers

First of all, currency issuance itself is a tax. Secondly, because the tax rates in most countries are progressive, and the tax is levied on the basis of nominal income. Therefore, when the monetary policy is loose, the nominal income of enterprises and workers will generally increase. With the increase in nominal income, the nominal income of enterprises and workers will be more likely to enter higher income areas, thus increasing their marginal tax rate. This will affect the production enthusiasm for enterprises and workers, thus affecting the aggregate supply. On the contrary, when tight monetary policy is adopted, it will also affect the actual tax burden of enterprises and workers, and then affect the aggregate supply (Tatom 1983).

(3) The influence of monetary policy on enterprises' judgment on economic situation and their corresponding decision

When the money supply increases, the price of enterprise products will rise. Because the information about enterprises is not as good as that of the government, they do not know whether the rising price of their products is due to the rising market demand for their own products or to the rising total price level, so it is difficult to make decisions. In this way, when the growth rate of money rises, the uncertainty faced by enterprises rises, which increases the complexity of extracting price signals. In order to mitigate the impact on the rising uncertainty, enterprises may take conservative measures to reduce the aggregate supply.

[2] For the sake of discussion, this chapter ignores the impact of depreciation and capital price changes on the cost of capital usage.

Part III
Structural Changes and Growth Efficiency in China's Socialist Market-Oriented Process

This part consists of four chapters (Chaps. 8 to 11). The core proposition of this part is based on the discussion of the relationship between system reform and economic growth and aggregate quantity in the previous one. It further discusses whether institutional change has brought about the improvement of factor efficiency, and whether economic aggregate expansion has achieved substantial economic development at the same time. That is, whether the economic structure has undergone profound changes, and whether the structural changes are based on technological innovation and institutional innovation, which has led to the improvement of the efficiency of growth. In fact, there is not much doubt about the quantitative growth of China's economy since the reform and opening up. The main question is whether this quantitative expansion is accompanied by the improvement of the quality of the national economy, whether there is real development, rather than simple growth. In addition, the more important thing is whether or to what extent this growth depends on efficiency improvement, rather than simply on the expansion of factor input. In a word, what is the efficiency basis of achieving high-speed growth in the process of institutional change? What is the cost of growth? This part first analyses the characteristics and constraints of industrial structure evolution since the reform and opening up (Chap. 8). Then, it discusses the altitude of China's industrial structure at this stage (Chap. 9). Then, from the structural changes and interactions of industrial structure, ownership structure and regional structure, the effects of structural changes on China's economic growth are investigated (Chap. 10). On this basis, we focus on the role of structural change in the improvement of total factor efficiency (Chap. 11). It demonstrates the historical necessity and value of socialist marketization in China from the aspects of institutional change, economic growth, economic structural evolution and economic efficiency improvement.

Chapter 8
Structure Supererogation in Market-oriented Process, Economic Efficiency and Economic Growth

As a country in the process of industrialization, China's essential feature of economic growth is the deepening of industrialization. The basic connotation of industrialization refers to the change in industrial structure and the accompanying increase in economic efficiency. This includes two aspects: Firstly, the change in the proportional relationship between various industries, mainly the rapid increase in the output value of the industrial sector, which is a change in the level of quantity; Secondly, the improvement of economic efficiency, which means the overall improvement of labor productivity and total factor productivity in all industrial sectors, is a qualitative change. Only the simultaneous advancement of quantity and quality is the economic development in the true sense.

If the "industry structural height" is used to measure the changes in the two levels of economic development, it should be a measure of the share and proportional relationship of various industries, and also a measure of the economic efficiency of each industry. If it is only a measure of the relationship between shares and proportional relationship, it is possible that the phenomenon of "spurious height" will occur in a certain period of time. That is to say, by surpassing the objective constraints of economic development in a way that is contrary to the logic of economic growth, the so-called industrial structural altitude (spurious height) is raised at the cost of seriously damaging the efficiency of resource allocation. Therefore, the measure of the height of the industrial structure should essentially be attributed to the measurement of labor productivity. Only when the proportion of industries with higher labor productivity in a country or region is large can it indicate the authenticity of the promotion of the industrial structure in this country or region.

The transformation of industrial structure can be divided into two basic types: market orientation and government orientation. For backward developing countries, the key to realizing the upgrading of industrial structure lies in promoting marketization while unifying the Changes in industrial structure changes through the organic combination of market orientation and government orientation. For China, which transforms from a traditional planned economy to a socialist market economic

W. Liu, *Research on China's Market Economy Development*,
https://doi.org/10.1007/978-981-97-1398-1_8

system, the level of industrial structure is highly advanced, and the key is how to make the government's macro-control effectively implement its industrial structure development goals through market mechanisms on the basis of in-depth reform and improvement of competitive market mechanisms. In other words, only through the organic combination of market mechanism and government macro-control, can the industrial structure produce both quantitative changes and qualitative changes, realizing economic development in the true sense.

8.1 Historical Trajectory of the Transformation in China's Industrial Structure Since the Reform and Opening up

According to the stage characteristics of the system reform and the cyclical characteristics of economic growth, China's high-speed economic growth from 1978 to 2007 can be divided into four stages: The first stage was from 1978 to 1983 is the start-up stage of China's economic reform and rapid growth. The convening of the Third Plenary Session of the 11th CPC Central Committee made economic construction as the focus of China's development, and the development and deepening of rural economic system reform laid the foundation for China's later reform and economic construction; The second stage of economic growth was from 1984 to 1991. At the Third Plenary Session of the 12th CPC Central Committee, the focus of China's economic system reform shifted from rural to urban areas, which drove China's economic growth into the second development cycle after the reform and opening up; The third stage of economic growth was from 1992 to 2002. China clearly defined the establishment of a market economy as the goal of economic system reform, which means China to entered the third cycle of economic growth; The fourth stage of economic growth was from 2003 to 2008. This is the fourth cycle of China's economic growth characterized by accelerating industrialization.

On the whole, after the reform and opening up, China's economy has been growing at a high rate for a long time, and the average annual GDP growth rate has reached 9.8%. Although the growth rate of each year has a certain fluctuation, the average growth rate for each stage is very eminent, and there is a gradual acceleration. The average growth rates for the four phases were: 8.7, 9.6, 10.2, and 10.8%. Long-term high-speed economic growth has significantly expanded China's economic aggregate. The total economic output in 2007 reached 14.96 times as much as in 1978, which reflected by GDP in comparable prices. There are 3.65 times for the primary industry, 23.15 times for the secondary industry, and 18.96 times for the tertiary industry.[1] China created more GDP in one month in 2008 than in all of 1978.

In the first stage, due to the reform of the rural economic system, China's agricultural production was first started and promote related industries. The production efficiency of China's primary industry, especially labor productivity, was low among various industries, but in the context of the time, the system of the people's

[1] *China Statistical Yearbook, 2008.*.

communes greatly hampered the enthusiasm of farmers, institutional innovation rapidly increased agricultural labor productivity, which is the basic reason why the rural economy has became the most active part of China's productivity at the time. From 1981 to 1984, the primary industry maintained a rapid growth of more than 7% for four consecutive years, which led to a rapid increase in the proportion of the primary industry in the national economy, from 28.2% in 1978 to 33.2% in 1983, increased by 5%. Since entering the second phase of economic growth, the growth rate of the primary industry has started to decline, and has maintained a relatively low growth rate since then. From the 30 years of the reform and opening up from 1978 to 2008, the average annual growth rate of the primary industry was 4.6%, which was significantly lower than the overall growth rate of the Chinese economy and the growth rate of the secondary and tertiary industries[2]. This low growth rate is determined by the characteristics of agricultural production itself, but the average annual growth rate of 4.6% is quite high, both in terms of the general growth rate of world agriculture and the agricultural growth rate in Chinese history. In this sense, the development of China's agriculture before the economic take-off made a significant contribution to China's subsequent economic growth.

In the second growth cycle after the reform and opening up, the growth rate of the secondary industry began to increase. From 1984 to 1991, the average annual growth rate of the added value of the secondary industry was 11.4%, much higher than the 2.4% in the start-up phase[3]. At this stage, light industry and textile industry, which are closely related to people's lives, have developed rapidly. The development of new home appliance industry represented by televisions, washing machines and refrigerators has significantly upgraded China's consumption structure. The development of the light and textile industries have expanded China's foreign trade and increased the country's foreign exchange earnings, which in turn have promoted investment and economic development. From the perspective of industrial upgrading during the accelerated industrialization period, in the second phase of economic growth after the reform and opening up, China began the basic industrial structural upgrade, that is, switching from agricultural-led economic growth to economic growth dominated by the light and textile industries.

In the third economic growth cycle after the reform and opening up, this expansion trend of the secondary and tertiary industries continued. The growth rate of the secondary industry continued to increase, with an average annual growth rate of 12.7%. The tertiary industry still maintained high growth, with an average annual growth rate of 10.3%, while the growth rate of the primary industry fell back to 3.8%. The second economic growth cycle is China's transition from the first industrial upgrade to the second industrial upgrade. At the beginning of this stage, light industry was still the mainstream of industrialization, but the leading specific industries have changed. The upgrading of consumer products has led to the upgrading of industrial products, and industrial products with high technological content have developed, such as computers, communication products, electronic products, and air

[2] *China Statistical Yearbook, 2008.*

[3] *China Statistical Yearbook, 2008.*

conditioners. The development of the tertiary industry has also had new characteristics. At the same time as the development of the traditional tertiary industry, the modern tertiary industry (finance, communications, real estate, aviation and highway transportation, etc.) has also developed. By the end of this period, before and after the turn of the century, due to factors such as macroeconomic regulation and control, the Asian financial crisis and industrial adjustment, China's economic growth began to slow down, from more than 10% (before 1996) to below 10%. Inflation, which began in 1992, has also turned into deflation. Under this circumstance, China has adjusted the economic structure by increasing the investment in intensity of infrastructure and strengthening the shareholding system reform of state-owned enterprises which promoted a new round of industrial upgrading in other words, which promoted the second industrial upgrading that is, the leading industry has begun to transform from a light textile industry to a heavy chemical industry. There was the new round of transformation in the context of new consumption upgrades, which was higher demand for automobiles and housing, and the expanding demand for Chinese industrial products in the international market. These requirements played a major role in the development of China's heavy chemical industry. The comprehensive national strength caused by China's 20 years of economic growth after the reform and opening up also provided a solid material foundation for this industrial upgrading.

Since the second half of 2002, the Chinese economy has entered a fourth growth cycle. Not only is the growth rate accelerating, but its leading industries are also completely different from the beginning of the previous cycle. The output of raw materials such as steel, cement and building materials, and technical equipment has risen rapidly, and the output of many products has leapt to the forefront of the world. The heavy chemical industry has achieved unprecedented development, and China's status as a new international manufacturing center has begun to be established, which indicates that China has achieved the second industrial structure upgrade. From the perspective of demand, the reason for this upgrade is the continuous pull of investment and consumption at home and abroad. From the supply side, it is because of the long-term growth of accumulated production capacity and the constant improvement of technological level that has enabled China to develop its own industry at a higher level. The upgrading of the secondary industrial structure has rapidly increased China's overall national strength, people's living standards and international status. China has truly become a big country which can influence international economic in the true sense.

8.2 Evolution of the Height of Industrial Structure in China Since the Reform and Opening up

In 1978, the ratio of China's primary, secondary and tertiary industries was 28.2:47.9:23.9. In terms of numbers, the secondary industry which is dominated by industry seems to have accounted for a large proportion of the national economy, but in a sense, it can be said that the degree of progress in China's industrialization is not large. It can be seen that the secondary industry has reached the standard of completion of industrialization in the proportional relationship of China's industrial structure before the reform and opening up, but in fact, China's economic development level and labor productivity were still very backward. This shows that the change in the amount of industrial structure is only a representation, which did not represent economic efficiency and real economic development.

If we use the "height of industrial structure" to measure changes in industrial structure, this indicator not only should be a measure of the share and proportional relationship of each industry, but also a measure of the economic efficiency of each industry. The high height of industrial structure of an economy indicates that the industry with higher labor productivity in this economy has a larger share. Only when the evolution of the industrial structure can increase the labor productivity of various industries to a higher level, at the same time, the industries and sectors with higher labor productivity and faster growth rate, account for the greater the proportion in the national economy and the faster the proportion of the increase, this evolution of industrial structure is meaningful, and it is also the called "structural benefit" improvement. Otherwise, we should only call it the industrial structure backwards or "spurious height." The highly evolved industrial structure that has long-term implications for economic development should be such a process: The original elements and resources are transferred from the industrial sector with low labor productivity to higher ones, and the newly added elements and resources are also allocated to the industrial sectors with higher labor productivity, resulting in an increasing share of the industrial sector with higher labor productivity, which leads to a common increase in labor productivity in different industrial sectors. Therefore, the height of the evolution of the industrial structure actually contains two connotations: Firstly, the evolution of proportional relations; Secondly, the improvement of the labor productivity. The former is the meaning of the quantity of the evolution of industrial structural height, and the latter is the qualitative connotation of the evolution of industrial structural height.

The connotation of the quantity of industrial structure height is subject to the connotation of quality. In the long run, the connotation of quantity will never violate the connotation of quality. However, in the short term, even if we artificially violate the quality requirements, and raised the height of the industrial structure height in a "spurious height" manner, this will eventually be forcibly corrected by economic development and this correction is bound to be accompanied by huge costs.

To do this, we have established an industrial structural height indicator that can be used for both cross-sectional data comparison and time series comparison. The closer the value of this indicator is to 1, the closer it is to the end of industrialization. By measuring the indicators of the height of the industrial structure and comparing the horizontal and vertical data, we have the following meaningful conclusions (Liu et al. 2008).

First of all, an international comparison of the height of the industrial structure reveals that there is a clear correlation between the evolution of the industrial structural height and the improvement of the level of economic development. The industrial structural height of the developed economies is significantly larger than 1, while the industrial structural height of developing countries is significantly lower than 1. From the perspective of the height of industrial structure, by 2006, China's industrialization process has already completed more than a third. However, there is no equilibrium between industries. The modernization process of the tertiary industry is obviously faster than the primary and secondary industries. The distances between the primary industry and the secondary and tertiary industry industries are widening.

Secondly, a sequence comparison of the altitudes of the industrial structure reveals that since 1985, China has truly entered the industrialization period. In addition to the short-term fluctuations during the period 1989–1991, the industrial structure height has been steadily advancing. Since 1998, the industrial structure height has entered a stage of accelerated lifting, and the Chinese economy has gradually entered a benign development track of optimizing industrial structure and transforming growth patterns. With 1998 as the dividing line, the industrial structure height grew at an average annual rate of 0.5 percentage points during the period from 1978 to 1998. After 1998, it entered the period of accelerated industrialization, with an average annual growth rate of 3.5 percentage points. At this rate, the industrial structural height of the Chinese economy will reach 1 in 2024, which means China complete industrialization. Correspondingly, during the period from 1978 to 1998, China's urbanization rate increased from 17.9 to 30.4%, with an average annual increase of 0.625 percentage points, and in 2007 it increased to 44.9%. During the period from 1998 to 2007, China's urbanization entered the accelerated growth stage of the Northam urbanization curve, with an average annual increase of 1.61 percentage points.[4] According to this progress, the accelerated phase of urbanization in China will end in 2023. It can be seen that according to the current development situation, both industrialization and urbanization in China, it will be completed around 2024, and the overall national strategic goal is locked in 2030, which further indicates that the equation of the national development strategy is fully taken into account of various unfavorable factors.

Finally, the study on the industrial structural height of various regions in China found that, based on the level value of industrial structural height, each province and city can be divided into three echelons: the industrial structural height of Shanghai, Beijing and Tianjin, three municipalities directly under the central government, is greater than 1, so these three cities are in the first echelon; The industrial structural altitudes of the eastern coastal areas such as Guangdong, Jiangsu, Zhejiang, Shandong, and Liaoning are between 0.5 and 1, and are in the second echelon; The industrial structure altitudes of Hebei, Henan, Hubei, Shaanxi, Sichuan, Guizhou and other central and western regions in China are between 0 and 0.5 in the third echelon. From an average perspective, Shanghai, Beijing, and Tianjin have completed industrialization, but this is mainly due to urbanization and the unbalanced growth of the

[4] By 2008, it has increased to 45.7%. During the period from 1998 to 2008, China's urbanization entered the accelerated growth stage of the Northam urbanization curve, with an average annual increase of 1.53 percentage points. Refer to *China Statistical Yearbook, 2008* and http://news.sohu.com/20090615/n264533280.shtml.

tertiary industry. Except for Shanghai, which is relatively close to industrialization, Beijing and Tianjin are still some distance away from industrialization. Data from various provinces in China generally show that the growth of the tertiary industry has greatly promoted the altitudes of the industrial structure. The primary and secondary industries are still quite far from the completion of industrialization.

8.3 Influential Factors for Structural Transition of China's Industry Since the Reform and Opening up

Then, what factors have contributed to the optimization of China's industrial structure after the reform and opening up, and created conditions for China's long-term sustained high-speed growth? In a nutshell, at least it can be summarized as follows:

Firstly, institutional innovation and technological innovation aimed at improving efficiency have encouraged sectors and enterprises with higher production efficiency or faster improvement to develop faster and thus affect the industrial structure of the national economy.

The basis of economic development is the improvement of efficiency. Efficiency reflects the input–output relationship in the production process, which is, using smaller inputs to achieve larger output. We can divide the input in national economic activities into three major categories, namely, time input, labor input, and inputs from other production factors (such as capital, land, and natural resources). Then, the efficiency of the national economy is divided into time efficiency, labor efficiency and technical efficiency of economic activities according to different levels. In the early stages of economic take-off or economic acceleration, (1) We should emphasize time efficiency, that is, to achieve a higher growth rate per unit time, while also ensuring sustained growth in each successive unit time. (2) It is necessary to improve labor efficiency, that is, to increase labor productivity. Without the increase in labor productivity, it is impossible to guarantee the time efficiency of economic growth. The results of economic growth are also shared by the workers who created them and the people around them. The labor productivity of the entire national economy can be measured by per capita GDP, and the increase of per capita GDP can be achieved in two ways. One way is to increase the added value created by the unit labor of various departments and enterprises, another way is to increase the production share of sectors and enterprises with higher labor productivity in the national economy. This requires institutional innovation and technological innovation. Between the two above, institutional innovation is more fundamental, because technological innovation ultimately depends on institutional innovation to provide security; On the other hand, like institutional innovation, technological innovation also should go through a gradual process, which requires a certain degree of system, economic development level and accumulation of scientific and technological development as the basis. The higher the labor productivity, the more emphasis should be placed on the promotion of technological progress to economic growth. (3) Improve technical efficiency, that is, the efficiency of capital, land and energy, and natural resources. In the initial stage of economic development, people pay more attention to the time efficiency and labor efficiency of economic activities. However, with the improvement of economic development level and the expansion of economic scale, the contradiction of scarcity of resources will be more prominent, and technical efficiency will attract more attention. So, how to improve the efficiency of these three aspects of the Chinese economy? In the case that the traditional system hampers the development of China's productive forces, it is necessary to carry out institutional innovation and drive reforms in a series of related fields, including technological innovation and management innovation which is also the reason why China's economic restructuring has such a huge boost to economic growth.

Secondly, the marketization process has strengthened the leading role of the market in the allocation of resources, thus making the evolution of the industrial structure more reasonable and more in line with the principle of efficiency.

Before the reform and opening up, China had a long-standing policy of price control. The prices of goods, services, and production factors did not reflect the relationship between supply and demand in reality. The reform of the economic system after the reform and opening up has greatly improved the degree of marketization in China. The impact of price factors on the industrial structure actually reflects in the process of marketization, which means the regulating effect of the market economy on the development and the profit distribution of various departments.

From 1978 to 2007, the average annual price increase reflected by the GDP deflator was 5.39%, which is relatively high for a country whose economy is in normal operation. For example, in developed market economies, the GDP deflator is often kept below 3%. But for a newly industrialized country in the process of transition, this increase is not high. In the early days of industrialization in most countries, double-digit price increases are common. As institutional reforms tend to stabilize, fluctuations in economic growth decrease, and price volatility also decreases. The situation in China is similar (The World Bank 1989). By sector, the average annual price increase of the primary industry from 1978 to 2007 was the highest, which was 7.14%, followed by the third industry, which was 6.30%, both exceeding the overall economic price increase level, which was 1.76% higher and 0.91% higher respectively. In contrast, the secondary industry is 1.52% lower than the price increase of the entire economy.[5] We can find that the long-term changes in prices in various sectors are inversely proportional to their growth rates and labor productivity. In other words, the higher the growth rate, the smaller the long-term fluctuation of the price, and vice versa. Under the modern economic conditions, the main driving force for the rapid growth of an industrial sector is the increase in productivity. In the production sector where productivity is increasing faster, the unit price increase of its products is inevitably lower than that of the lower productivity sector, which is proved in the practice of China's economic growth in the past 30 years. This phenomenon also exists in the long-term growth of other countries. This shows that once the market economy is established, price leverage will play a role. If there is a distortion between

[5] *China Statistical Yearbook, 2008.*

China's industrial and agricultural product prices before the reform and opening up, then due to the role of the market economy, this distortion has been effectively improved in the long-term growth after the reform and opening up. Therefore, from a dynamic point of view, the industrial structure reflected at the current price is the result of the combined effect of total growth and price changes in various sectors. Under the combined effect of quantity and price, there is the development trend of China's GDP sector which is the proportion of the primary industry has dropped significantly, the secondary industry has remained stable, and the tertiary industry has developed considerably. This is consistent with the common trend in the process of industrialization in all countries of the world.

8.4 The Impact of Industrial Structural Transformation on Economic Efficiency

As mentioned earlier, changes in the proportional relationship between industries do not necessarily mean an increase in economic efficiency. Since 1998, the industrial structural height has entered a stage of accelerating growth, and the Chinese economy has gradually entered a benign development track of optimizing the industrial structure and transforming the growth mode. This indicates that the changes in industrial structure have different contributions to economic efficiency and economic growth at different stages of development.

8.4.1 The Impact of Industrial Structure Changes on Economic Efficiency from the Perspective of Input–output Analysis

The direct consumption coefficient matrix studies the technical relationship between the intermediate input and the total input, while the intermediate demand coefficient measures the proportional relationship between the intermediate demand in the aggregate demand and the final demand of each department. Both of these indicate to some extent the changes in economic efficiency. The direct consumption coefficient matrix mainly reflects the technical relationship in the national economy. Its changes need to be gradually reflected through long-term technological progress. The intermediate demand coefficient matrix reflects the economic relationship between various departments in the production activities, and its timeliness of improvement is relatively strong.

We use the input–output data over the years to analyze the trends of China's direct consumption coefficient and intermediate demand coefficient since 1992. Through the direct consumption coefficient matrix and the intermediate demand consumption matrix time series of the three major industrial sectors, we studied the impact of technological progress, industrial structural changes and price changes on the overall intermediate consumption level of the national economy (Liu and Cai 2008).

Studies have shown that during this period, technological progress has contributed to reducing the level of intermediate consumption of the national economy and improving the efficiency of economic growth during this period. However, due to the change in the price relationship and the increase in the proportion of sectors with higher intermediate consumption levels, the intermediate consumption rate of the entire national economy reflected by the current price has increased. In order to change this trend and maintain China's sustainable development, it is necessary to combine the improvement of the input and output efficiency in various departments and the upgrading of industrial structure.

(1) If we use the input–output table compiled by the current price for dynamic analysis and comparison, the intermediate consumption level of the national economy from 1992 to 2005 is generally rising. The intermediate consumption rate increased from 0.6060 to 0.6223, of which the intermediate consumption factor increased by 0.38% due to technical factors, and it increased by 1.25% due to sectoral factors. The result of the combined effect of the two increased the intermediate consumption coefficient of the entire national economy by 1.63%. This shows that in the analysis of the value of input and output of the national economy including price changes, the impact of structural changes on intermediate consumption levels is greater than technical factors.
(2) Calculated by using comparable prices, the median consumption rate of the entire national economy from 1992 to 2005, that is, the direct consumption coefficient decreased from 0.6060 to 0.5745. This reflects the contribution of technological advancement to reducing intermediate consumption in the process of economic growth after the elimination of price changes. Among them, technological progress has reduced the intermediate consumption level of the national economy by 4.56%, and the impact of industrial structural changes is −1.41% (it makes the intermediate consumption level has increased by 1.41%). As a result of the combined effect of the two, the intermediate consumption rate of the entire national economy has been reduced by 3.15%. This shows that technological progress has contributed to improving the efficiency of China's economic growth at this stage.
(3) Comparing the analysis according to the constant price and the current price, we see that for technological progress, we should not only examine the input–output relationship from a technical perspective, but also inspect the relationship between product price and cost from an economic perspective. Even under the conditions of technological advancement, due to market reasons, it is possible to find an increase in the ratio of the intermediate consumption of a unit product. This has been reflected in the development of China in recent years, which requires a greater technological advancement to offset this increase in intermediate consumption due to changes in market conditions.
(4) The secondary industry is the largest production sector in the national economy since the reform and opening up, and at the same time the fastest growing

production sector. Due to the features of production of the secondary industry itself, its intermediate consumption rate is the highest among all sectors of the national economy, both in terms of current prices and comparable prices. From the experience of newly industrialized countries and regions, in the process of industrialization, the intermediate consumption level of the national economy will increase as the first industrial upgrade that the textile industry replaced agriculture as the leading industry, the second industrial upgrade that the manufacturing industry replaced the textile industry as the leading industry. However, with the third industrial upgrading, that is, the high-tech industries with low intermediate consumption levels and the tertiary industry gradually become the leading industries for economic growth, the intermediate consumption level of the entire national economy will gradually decline. China is now entering this stage. While improving the intermediate consumption level of various departments, focusing on the development of emerging industries and the optimization of departmental structure which is an important way to reduce the intermediate consumption level of the entire national economy and achieve sustainable development.

8.4.2 Viewing the Contribution of Industrial Structural Change to Economic Efficiency from the Decomposition of Factor Productivity

If technological progress and industrial structural change are decomposed from factor productivity, we can compare the contribution of industrial structural change to China's economic efficiency with the contribution of technological progress. Studies have shown that since the reform and opening up, the impact of industrial structural changes on China's economic growth has been very significant. However, as China's marketization has increased, the role of industrial structural structure changes in economic growth is constantly weakened (Liu and Zhang 2008). In the 1980s, the contribution rate of structural change effects was always greater than 50%, and the contribution of industrial structural changes to economic growth even exceeded the contribution of technological progress; In the early and mid-1990s, the contribution of industrial restructuring to economic growth and the contribution of technological progress were basically the same; After 1998, the contribution of industrial restructuring to economic growth has become less and less significant, gradually giving way to technological progress, that is, the power of marketization represented by the changes in industrial structure has gradually given way to the power of technological progress. Thus, Krugman (1994) pointed out that the unsustainable East Asian growth model is similar to China's economic growth model before 1998. However, in the process of China's economic growth after 1998, on the one hand, the contribution rate of factor input growth gradually reduced and the contribution rate of total factor productivity growth is continuously increasing; On the other hand, within the total factor productivity, the effect of industrial structural change effect and the net technological progress effect also show a trade-off relationship. It can be seen that after 1998, China's economic growth model has increasingly reflected its own sustainability.

8.4.2.1 Decomposition of Labor Productivity

We use the empirical study of decomposition of labor productivity to show the trend of structural effects (the contribution of industrial structure changes to factor productivity improvement is called structural effect) since the reform and opening up and the contribution of structural effects to labor productivity growth and its trend. These studies have led to the following conclusions:

(1) In the course of the reform and opening up in 28 years (1978–2006), the cumulative contribution of the structural effects of the three industries to the overall labor productivity growth was 38.5%. The structural effect of the primary industry is negative, but the intra-industry growth effect of the primary industry is more significant because of endogenous technological advancement and technological efficiency in the primary industry. The structural change of the secondary industry had a positive effect, but it was lower than the intra-industry growth effect of the secondary industry, which indicates that the increase in labor productivity of the secondary industry depends to a greater extent on technological efficiency and technological progress within the industry. Among the three industries, the structural effect of the tertiary industry is the most significant. The tertiary industry has greatly liberated the labor productivity of the rural surplus labor force, and it increased the overall labor productivity of the economy. However, the structural effect of the tertiary industry is greater than the growth effect within the industry, indicating that the growth of labor productivity in the tertiary industry mainly depends on the improvement of resource allocation efficiency caused by structural effects, rather than technological efficiency changes and technological progress.
(2) Due to the impact of macroeconomic and effective demand, structural effects are volatile. When the economy is in a period of prosperity, the structural effect further amplifies the growth of labor productivity when the economy is in a downturn, the structural effect is negative. The volatility of structural effects indicates that the change of industrial structure is driven by the change of demand structure, which is especially obvious for developing countries with obvious dual economic characteristics.
(3) From 1978 to 2006, the contribution of the structural effects of the secondary and tertiary industries gradually reduced. Before 1991, the contribution of the structural effects of the secondary and tertiary industries was greater than 50%. Since 1991, the growth of labor productivity in the secondary industry has begun to shake off the state of relying on structural effects. While the growth effect in the industry caused by the improvement of capital accumulation, technological

progress and organizational efficiency has begun to dominate the labor productivity growth of the secondary industry. Before 1998, the tertiary industry relied on extensive growth. However, the deflation from 1998 to 2002 was a profit from a misfortune to the tertiary industry. The shrinking of effective demand and the situation of oversupply promote the survival of the fittest, and force companies to reduce production costs, improve technical efficiency, and accelerate technological progress in the fierce market competition. Therefore, there is the starting point for China's tertiary industry to improve technical efficiency within the industry, accelerate technological progress, and transform economic growth in 1998.

(4) The contribution of structural effects declines mainly because the gap between resource inefficient allocation and resource efficient allocation (the gap in labor productivity of different industries) is decreasing. However, the structural effect will not tend to zero, it will continue to exist and will remain an indispensable factor in China's economic growth in the future.

8.4.2.2 Decomposition of Total Factor Productivity

Through the decomposition of total factor productivity, we decompose technological progress and industrial structural change from total factor productivity, and conduct horizontal and vertical comparative analysis of industrial structural changes and technological progress in promoting economic growth. Through the decomposition of total factor productivity, we not only measure the role of structural change and its relative importance in economic growth, but also analyze the structural changes of capital and labor factors among the three industries, and can draw the following conclusions:

(1) Since the reform and opening up, the impact of industrial structural changes on China's economic growth has been very significant, and the contribution of structural changes to total factor productivity is 43.5%. However, as China's marketization level increases, the role of industrial structural changes in promoting economic growth is waning. After 1998, the contribution of industrial restructuring to economic growth has become less and less significant, gradually giving way to technological progress. That is, the power of marketization represented by the changes in industrial structure has gradually given way to the power of technological progress.

(2) The analysis of the structural changes in capital elements shows that the Chinese economy appears the phenomenon of capital deepening too fast, that is, capital labor ratio is growing faster than capital output ratio, and even more deadly is that the marginal return of capital shows a downward trend, which is a dangerous signal for the Chinese economy that relies on investment to promote economic growth, because once the growth rate of investment declines, economic growth will slow down. An analysis of the structural changes in labor factors shows that the labor that can be driven by unit capital is decreasing, which explains from another perspective that capital is rapidly replacing labor. On the one hand, it

is possible to lead to a decline in the marginal remuneration of capital. On the other hand, it limits the further expansion of the scale of employment and the transfer of rural surplus labor. It also increases the labor income gap between the secondary and tertiary industries in the city and the primary industry in the rural areas.

(3) A comparative study of the three industries find that the capital and labor marginal returns of the primary industry rise very slowly, and the progress towards industrialization and urbanization in China is still very long. The accumulation of high-speed capital stocks in the secondary industry is the main reason for the adverse consequences of excessive capital deepening and diminishing marginal returns to capital. The capitalization of the industrial sector (the main body of the secondary industry) is too fast. On the one hand, it makes the marginal returns of capital decline too fast and the growth of investment demand slow down, and the output growth rate will decline. On the other hand, the growth rate of labor and employment that can be driven by industrialization is declining, which is not conducive to the improvement of labor wages and per capita income. Compared with the secondary industry, the capital deepening speed of the tertiary industry is relatively reasonable, and the combination ratio of capital and labor factors is also within a reasonable range. Moreover, the ability of the tertiary industry to create employment is much greater than that of the secondary industry, about four times that of the secondary industry. However, the technical efficiency of the tertiary industry is not high, and it is still dominated by extensional growth. The task of improving economic efficiency still has a long way to go.

Chapter 9
Measuring the Height of Industrial Structure in China

9.1 Introduction: Implications of the Height of Industrial Structure

If the economic structural change is the basic connotation of industrialization, then the industrial structure supererogation is the basic element of the transformation of supply structure in the process of industrialization.[1] Before analyzing the relationship between the industrialization and economic growth, we must construct an accurate and appropriate index system to measure the industrialization process and the height of the industrial structure. The task of this chapter is to consolidate the basic connotation of the industrial structural height and build on it. The indicator that can be used for the comparison between horizontal cross-sectional data and for the comparison between longitudinal time series data.

The history of studying industrial structure is as old as the history of development economics. From Fisher's three industry classifications, Clark's "Petty-Clark Theorem", to Kuznets's industrial connection theory, Hoffman's empirical rule of industrialization, and the standard model of Chenery's structural transformation and Rostow's leading industry theory. These theories explore the history and regularity of the industrial structural transformation in the process of long-term economic development from the perspective of economic history. They reveal the same consensus: in the process of industrialization, the structure of the three industries has shown a historical and regular transformation with the development of the economy.

[1] Correspondingly, the structural transformation of industrialization also includes changes in the structure of demand.

The basic time frame for the writing of this chapter is 2006. The main content of this chapter is based on the interim results of the project titled "An Investigation into the High Degree of Industrial Structure in China's Economic Development and Regional Differences in Industrialization Process" by Liu Wei, Zhang Hui, and Huang Zehua, which was published in the 11th issue of *Economic Perspectives* in 2008.

W. Liu, *Research on China's Market Economy Development*,
https://doi.org/10.1007/978-981-97-1398-1_9

This historical and regularity is roughly shown as: the output value and the employment share of the primary industry have dropped significantly, the output value and employment share of the tertiary industry have increased significantly, while the changes in the output value and employment share of the secondary industry have been unstable. When the industrialization in a country enters the acceleration phase from the primary stage (from the underdeveloped stage to the middle income stage), the output value and the employment share of the secondary industry rise rapidly and obviously, when industrialization enters a mature stage (from upper middle income to developed stage), the proportion of the output value of the secondary industry fluctuated, while the employment share of the secondary industry increased slowly.

The further research found that the industrial structure supererogation is a consequent process of gradual evolution based on the history and logical sequence of economic development, which includes three aspects: (1) In the entire industrial structure, the leading role of the primary industry gradually evolves toward the secondary industry and the tertiary industry; (2) The dominant position of the labor-intensive industry gradually evolves toward the capital-intensive and technological (knowledge)-intensive industries; (3) The industry that manufactures primary products dominates and gradually evolves toward the industry that manufactures intermediate products and final products.[2] Gua (1990) believes that the industrial structure supererogation includes at least four aspects: the output value structure supererogation, the asset structure supererogation, the technical structure supererogation and the employment structure supererogation.

Unfortunately, the existing research has deepened the connotation and external representation of "the industrial structure supererogation", but did not properly answer what is "the height of industrial structure." The industrial structure supererogation is a change of directed and regular share change in the process of industrialization. So is the height of the industrial structure a measure of its share? Most of the relevant researches in China used several kinds of shares, such as the employment share, the capital share, the Hoffmann ratio, etc., as a measure of the height of the industrial structure according to some subjectively set weights. It is undeniable that such indicators have certain reference value, but such they are not very applicable, and they are not applicable to the agricultural economy and the urban economy in the process of industrialization. Taking New Zealand as an example, the proportion of industrial output of the agricultural economy has not increased significantly in the course of its economic development, because agriculture has always occupied a significant proportion in its economy. Taking the urban economy of Hong Kong as an example in the process of economic development, the tertiary industry has always occupied an absolute proportion.[3] These two economies are not showing significant and directional share changes. If we only use the share to measure the height of the industrial structure and simulate the industrial structure supererogation

[2] Zhou et al. (1987).

[3] China's big cities such as Beijing and Shanghai also exhibit such characteristics, and the proportion of the tertiary industry has remained high, but this does not indicate the completion of industrialization.

with the change of share, we will find that the industrial structural height of these economies has hardly increased significantly and even declined in the process from developing to the developed economy. Obviously, the transformation in the share of the three industries is not the essence of the industrial structure supererogation.

We believe that the evolution of the industrial structure is meaningful only when the evolution of the industrial structure can increase the labor productivity of various industries to a higher level. Otherwise, we can only refer to the evolution of such an industrial structure as a retrogression of the industrial structure. Industrial structure supererogation is a process in which the original elements and resources are transferred from the industrial sector with low labor productivity to the industrial sector with high labor productivity, and the newly added elements and resources are also allocated to the industrial sectors with higher labor productivity, resulting in an increasing share of the industrial sector with higher labor productivity, leading to a common increase of labor productivity in different industrial sectors. Therefore, the industrial structure supererogation actually contains two connotations: one is the evolution of proportional relationship, and the other is the improvement of labor productivity. The former is the connotation of the quantity of industrial structure supererogation, and the latter is the qualitative connotation of industrial structure supererogation. Economists' exploration and research on economic history has shown such an iron law: the proportional relationship between industries presents a regular change, which is actually accompanied by the common improvement of labor productivity in different industries. Therefore, the connotation of the quantity of industrial structure supererogation is subject to the connotation of quality. In the long run, the connotation of quantity will never violate the connotation of quality.

After defining the connotation of the industrial structure supererogation, the meaning of the height of the industrial structure is very clear. Industrial structural height is apparently a measure of the share and proportional relationship of different industries, but it is essentially a measure of labor productivity. Therefore, a relatively high industrial structural height of an economy indicates that the industry with higher labor productivity in this economy has a larger share. Some people may wonder whether labor productivity covers the full connotation of the height of industrial structure and whether the height of industrial structure should also include the height of capital accumulation (per capita capital) and the height of technological progress. Research on technological progress using the new growth theory shows[4] that the achievements of capital accumulation and technological progress can be fully reflected in the growth of labor productivity. The height of the industrial structure is the embodiment of the evolution of the industrial structure, and it is only necessary to abstract the indicators of such achievements.

Based on an in-depth discussion of the basic connotation of industrial structural height, this chapter establishes an industrial structural height index that can be used for cross-sectional data comparison and time series comparison. The author

[4] Kumar and Russell (2002) argue that the growth of labor productivity can be decomposed into the growth of technological efficiency, the growth of technological progress and the growth of capital accumulation.

believes that the industrial structural height is apparently a measure of the share and proportional relationship of different industries, but essentially a measure of labor productivity. The industry with high labor productivity has a larger share in a country or region, indicating that the industrial structural height of this country or region is higher. After using the indicators in this chapter for empirical research, we found that: (1) From the perspective of industrial structural height, China's industrialization process in 2005 was about one-third completed; (2) The industrial structural height of each province and region is highly hierarchical, and the industrial structural height of the eastern coastal areas is significantly higher than that of the central and western regions; (3) Since 1998, the industrial structural height has shown an extraordinary high-speed growth, and the Chinese economy is entering a benign track of optimizing the industrial structure and transforming the growth mode.

In the following, based on the connotation of this industrial structural height, an index that can be used for both comparison in various regions of China and for cross-country comparison will be constructed, which can also be used for both cross-sectional data comparison and industrial structural height indicators for time series data comparison.

9.2 Indices of the Height of Industrial Structure

9.2.1 Standard Structure Method and Similarity Discrimination Method

There are three main methods for measuring the height of the industrial structure:

(1) Static and intuitive comparison method. This method refers to comparing the industrial proportional relationship of the economy under investigation with the industrial structure of the developed countries or the industrial proportional relationship of the so-called "standard structure", and determines the height of the industrial structure of the economy under investigation. By studying the empirical facts of the evolution of multinational industrial structures, Kuznets, Chenery, Syrquin and others used the input–output analysis method and the econometric empirical method to summarize the typical characteristics of the industrial structural height at different stages of the industrialization process. They all put forward the criteria for the height of industrial structure under different per capita incomes. These "standards" are often used to measure the height of the industrial structure of the economy under investigation.

(2) Dynamic comparison discrimination method.[5] This method discriminates the industrial structural height of the economy under investigation by constructing certain quantitative indicators and using another economic industrial structure system as a frame of reference. This method is similar to the first method, and the comparative method is still used to measure the height of the industrial structure of the economy examined. The difference is that the dynamic comparison discriminant method can use the statistical method to dynamically determine the similarity of the industrial structural altitudes of the two economies (deviation). This type of method is most typical of structural similarity coefficient and structural change value, which represent two types of dynamic comparison discrimination methods: One is the similarity discrimination method, which compares the degree of similarity between the two industrial structure systems, and measures the industrial structural height of the examined economy according to the "proximity degree" of the two, including structural similarity coefficient (also called angle cosine method), correlation coefficient method[6]; The other is the distance discrimination method, which measures the gap between the two industrial structures, and determines the height of the industrial structure of the economy under consideration according to the "degree of dispersion" of the two, including structural change values (Hamming distance method), Euclidean distance method and Lance and Williams distance method.

(3) Indicator method. This type of method determines the height of an economic industrial structure by constructing one or more indicators. The first two methods are comparative (relative), qualitative, and discrete, and can only be used for qualitative and discrete judgments. The indicator method corrects the shortcomings of the first two, which can be used for continuous, quantitative analysis of cross-sectional data and time series.[7] Pan and Chen (1994) used the reciprocal of the largest eigenvalue of the structure-associated economic technology matrix as the measure of the height of the industrial structure. Bai and Zhao (1995) used the revised norm to construct an index describing the height of the regional industrial structure. Chen and Lu (2001), Song (2000) began to try to establish an index system for measuring the industrial structure supererogation. However, they only proposed a number of theoretically measurable indicators, and no actual estimates were made. Lun (2005) constructed a set of industrial structural height index system with three aspects and 16 indicators, and carried out calculations, which is a useful attempt in related research. Zhou and Wei (2007)

[5] For the first two methods to measure the height of the industrial structure, Gong (2002) made a good overview. He divided the existing measurement methods of industrial structure height into two categories: one is the "standard structure" method, and the other is the relative comparison method. This book has improved its classification.

[6] Correlation coefficient in statistics.

[7] The Hoffmann ratio can also be classified as this category because it provides an indicator for measuring the internal structure of the industry—the ratio of the output value of the consumer goods industry to the industrial value of the capital goods, which has a time series of extensions, (from 5 to less than 1) and can also be used for horizontal comparison.

used the weighted average of the square root of labor productivity of various industries as an indicator to measure the level of industrial structure.

The index method has strong applicability and can be used for continuous analysis of cross-section data and time series, as well as basic data for measurement empirical research, so it is the direction of future research.

9.2.2 Industrial Structural Height Indicators

In order to be consistent with the connotation of the industrial structural height explained in the previous section, the industrial structural height index of this chapter must include at least two parts: proportional relationship and labor productivity. Therefore, we use the product of proportional relationship and labor productivity as a measure of the height of the industrial structure, that is, the height of the industrial structure H is:

$$H = \sum v_{it} \times LP_{it} \tag{9.1}$$

Here i is in an open collection, it can be 1, 2, 3, representing the first, second, and third industries, or it can be 1, 2, ..., m, that is, as the industry categories are continuously subdivided (subdivision to m industries), the collection of i can continue to increase. Among them, v_{it} is the proportion of the output value of industry i in GDP in t time, LP_{it} is the labor productivity of industry i in t time. Obviously, this equation is in line with the connotation of the industrial structural height explained in the previous article: if an industry with high labor productivity in an economy has a large share, then its industrial structural height value H is large.

However, in general, labor productivity is a qualitative value, while the industrial output value is a dimensionless value. Therefore, we must standardize the "labor productivity" indicator. In order to make our industrial structural height indicators not only can be used to judge the progress of industrialization, but also for international comparison, the standardized equation of labor productivity is:

$$LP_{it}^{N} = \frac{LP_{it} - LP_{ib}}{LP_{if} - LP_{ib}} \tag{9.2}$$

Among them, LP_{it}^{N} is the labor productivity of the standardized industry i, LP_{if} is the labor productivity of the industry i at the completion of industrialization, LP_{ib} is the labor productivity of the industry i at the beginning of industrialization, and LP_{it} is the labor productivity of the original, directly calculated industry i, The equation is $LP_{it} = VA_i/L_i$, which is the ratio of the added value of industry i to the number of employed people.

Here, we use the per capita income of US $706 in the standard structural model of Chenery et al. (1986) as the starting point for industrialization, and the per capita

Table 9.1 Standards of labor productivity in China's industrialization process

Item	Labor productivity (1970 US dollar)	Labor productivity (2005 US dollar)	Labor productivity[a] (2005 renminbi)
Industrialization starting point (per capita income is US $706)			
Primary industry	70	352	2570
Secondary industry	292	1473	10,755
Tertiary industry	340	1714	12,509
Industrialization end point (per capita income is US $10,584)			
Primary industry	1442	7268	53,058
Secondary industry	3833	19,320	141,036
Tertiary industry	1344	6773	49,441

Note aBased on the current exchange rate (US $1 = RMB7.3)

income of US $10,584[8] as the end of industrialization, after this point in time, the economy will enter the stage of developed economies,[9] see Table 9.1.

The standardized labor productivity of industry *i* indicates the closeness of the labor productivity of industry *i* and the labor productivity of developed economic industry *i*, The industrial structural height obtained by weighted average summation of the standardized labor productivity of each industry indicates the dispersion of the industrial structure and the industrial structural height in the state of industrialization completion, which becomes an indicator that can be used for both horizontal and vertical comparisons. If the industrial base data of developed countries are substituted into Eq. (9.1), because the United States is already in the post-industrial era, the labor productivity of each industry is significantly higher than the labor productivity of various industries when industrialization is completed. We will find that the industrial structural height value H of the developed economy is significantly greater than 1.

[8] The book by Chenery et al. (1986) is based on the 1970 US dollar. The starting point for the original text is US $140, and the end point is US $2100. It is converted into the 2005 US dollar here. According to the US CPI data, the conversion factor for the US dollar in 2005 was 5.04, and all other US dollar data in this chapter was calculated in 2005 dollars.

[9] The per capita income of the developed and underdeveloped countries divided by the World Bank in 2005 is US $10,725, which is negligible from the US $10,584.

9.3 Comparison of the Height of Industrial Structure Using Cross Sectional Data: International and Domestic Comparison

9.3.1 International Comparison

We use Eqs. (9.1) and (9.2) to calculate the industrial structural altitudes of countries in the world in 2005. The results are shown in Table 9.2:

Table 9.2 shows that developed countries such as the UK, the US, Germany, and France, the height of industrial structure are significantly larger than 1, while the industrial structure of developing countries such as China, Thailand, Brazil, and Indonesia is significantly lower than 1. Table 9.2 measures the height of the industrial structure of each country to verify the consistency of industrial structural height and economic development stage and development level in the sense of efficiency. From the perspective of the height of industrial structure, China's industrialization process has gone through about one-third. However, the industries are not balanced, the process of modernization of the tertiary industry is faster than that of the secondary industry, even faster than the primary industry, and the distance between the primary industry and the secondary and tertiary industries is widening.

Table 9.2 Industrial structural altitudes of countries in the world in 2005

Country	LP_{1t}^{N} of the primary industry	LP_{2t}^{N} of the secondary industry	LP_{3t}^{N} of the tertiary industry	Industrial structural altitude H
China	0.084	0.288	0.498	0.346
Germany	0.202	3.905	16.094	12.372
France	0.578	4.171	16.922	13.746
UK	0.180	4.827	14.661	11.929
US	0.265	5.092	17.480	14.511
Singapore	−0.036	3.954	8.565	6.944
Japan	0.222	4.142	14.291	11.013
Republic of Korea	0.330	2.810	5.693	4.318
Thailand	0.096	0.529	0.946	0.679
Brazil	0.168	0.658	0.860	0.707
Indonesia	0.088	0.486	0.274	0.343

Table 9.3 Industrial structural altitudes in various regions of China in 2005

Region	LP_{1t}^N of the primary industry	LP_{2t}^N of the secondary industry	LP_{3t}^N of the tertiary industry	Industrial structural height H
Shanghai	0.210	0.949	2.361	1.655
Beijing	0.261	0.605	1.702	1.359
Tianjin	0.226	0.826	2.062	1.320
Guangdong	0.132	0.521	1.181	0.779
Jiangsu	0.218	0.450	1.005	0.628
Zhejiang	0.173	0.328	1.020	0.595
Liaoning	0.192	0.519	0.799	0.594
Fujian	0.186	0.339	0.834	0.510
Shandong	0.138	0.441	0.734	0.503
Hebei	0.140	0.301	0.724	0.417
Hubei	0.138	0.331	0.359	0.310
Qinghai	0.047	0.354	0.306	0.299
Shaanxi	0.039	0.325	0.313	0.286
Henan	0.068	0.256	0.339	0.247
Sichuan	0.075	0.196	0.199	0.173
Guizhou	0.007	0.195	−0.042	0.066

9.3.2 Domestic Comparison

We Substituted the industrial data of various regions in China in 2005 into Eqs. (9.1) and (9.2). The results are shown in Table 9.3[10]:

The results in Table 9.3 show that the industrial structural altitudes of each region are apparently hierarchical. The industrial structural altitudes in all regions of China are basically consistent with the level of economic development. It is not completely consistent with the GDP level, and has a high correlation with the level of per capita GDP. The industrial structural altitudes in the eastern region are significantly higher than that in the central and western regions. The industrial structural altitudes of the three municipalities directly under the central government, Shanghai, Beijing, and Tianjin, are greater than 1. The industrial structural altitudes of the eastern coastal areas such as Guangdong, Jiangsu, Zhejiang, Shandong, and Liaoning are between 0.5 and 1. The industrial structural altitudes of the central and western regions such as Hebei, Henan, Hubei, Shaanxi, Sichuan, and Guizhou are between 0 and 0.5. According to the above definition of the height of the industrial structure, the closer the height value of an economic industrial structure is to 1, the closer it is to the industrial structural height of the industrialization completion period. From an average perspective of view, Shanghai, Beijing and Tianjin have completed industrialization, but this is mainly due to the unbalanced growth of urbanization

[10] We have selected results for some typical regions.

and tertiary industry. In addition to Shanghai, the secondary industry of Beijing and Tianjin (Beijing: 0.605, Tianjin: 0.826). There is still a long way to go before industrialization is completed, and the labor productivity of the primary industry is far from the completion of industrialization. Therefore, it is necessary to be cautious to say that Beijing, Shanghai and Tianjin have completed industrialization.[11] The data of various provinces and autonomous regions in China generally show that the growth of the tertiary industry has greatly promoted the height of the industrial structure. In addition to the individual regions, the efficiency of the primary and secondary industries is still quite a long distance to the completion of industrialization.

9.4 Comparison of the Height of Industrial Structure Using Time Series

We substitute the national macro data from 1978 to 2005 into Eqs. (9.1) and (9.2). The results are shown in Table 9.4[12]:

It is very meaningful to examine the process of China's reform and opening up and the process of industrialization from the perspective of industrial structural height. The last column of Table 9.4 shows that before 1985, China's industrial structural height has been wandering. Although the labor productivity of the secondary industry has been significantly improved, the overall economy has clearly characterized the industrial flight state. We can think that since 1985, China has really entered a period of accelerated industrialization. In addition to the short-term fluctuations during the period 1989–1991, the industrial structural height has been steadily advancing. Since 1998, the industrial structural height has experienced a high growth rate (average annual average of 0.03, previously average annual growth of about 0.003), indicating that the Chinese economy has entered a healthy and steady state of development. However, this growth is mainly driven by the increase in the labor productivity in the tertiary industry. The tertiary industry not only has a significant increase in labor productivity, but its share in total output continues to grow, and this trend continues.

9.5 Conclusion

Based on the in-depth discussion of the basic connotation of industrial structural height, this chapter establishes an industrial structural height index that can be used to compare between cross-sectional dataand between time series data. The author believes that the industrial structural height is a measure of the share and proportional

[11] Chen (2007) and others believe that in 2005, Beijing and Shanghai have entered the post-industrialization stage, while Tianjin and Guangdong have reached the second half of industrialization.

[12] Calculated at constant price in 2005.

Table 9.4 Evolution of China's industrial structure from 1978 to 2005

Year	LP^N_{1t} of the primary industry	LP^N_{2t} of the secondary industry	LP^N_{3t} of the tertiary industry	Industrial structural height H
1978	−0.015	0.015	−0.095	−0.020
1979	−0.007	0.018	−0.112	−0.018
1980	−0.008	0.018	−0.118	−0.019
1981	−0.004	0.014	−0.119	−0.021
1982	−0.001	0.014	−0.111	−0.018
1983	0.003	0.018	−0.102	−0.014
1984	0.011	0.022	−0.076	−0.006
1985	0.010	0.025	−0.025	0.006
1986	0.011	0.025	−0.016	0.009
1987	0.014	0.028	−0.007	0.014
1988	0.012	0.029	−0.005	0.014
1989	0.007	0.025	−0.004	0.011
1990	0.007	0.014	−0.037	−0.004
1991	0.007	0.025	0.007	0.015
1992	0.009	0.042	0.045	0.036
1993	0.012	0.062	0.051	0.048
1994	0.020	0.071	0.048	0.053
1995	0.028	0.082	0.037	0.056
1996	0.035	0.090	0.041	0.063
1997	0.035	0.099	0.075	0.079
1998	0.037	0.107	0.122	0.100
1999	0.036	0.122	0.170	0.126
2000	0.036	0.145	0.220	0.158
2001	0.039	0.162	0.284	0.194
2002	0.043	0.195	0.340	0.234
2003	0.048	0.230	0.391	0.273
2004	0.071	0.258	0.433	0.304
2005	0.084	0.288	0.498	0.346

relation- ship of different industries on the surface, which is essentially a measure of labor productivity. The share of industries with higher labor productivity in a country or region is larger, indicating that the industrial structural height of this country or region is higher. Through the international comparison, the domestic comparison of various regions, and the national data sequence comparison, this chapter finds that:

(1) The international comparison of industrial structural altitudes shows that the high degree of industrial structure evolution and the improvement of economic development level are obviously correlated. The industrial structural height of

the developed economy is significantly higher than 1, and the industrial structural height of developing countries is significantly lower than 1. The closer the industrial structural height value of an economy is to 1, the closer it is to the destination of industrialization. From the perspective of industrial structural height, by 2005, China's industrialization process was about one-third. However, the industries are not balanced. The modernization process of the tertiary industry is obviously faster than the primary and the secondary industries. The distance between the primary industry and the secondary and tertiary industries is widening.

(2) Research on the industrial structural altitudes of various regions in China found that according to the height of industrial structure, each province can be divided into three levels. The industrial structural altitudes of three municipalities directly under the central government, Shanghai, Beijing and Tianjin are greater than 1, in the first echelon. The industrial structural altitudes of the eastern coastal areas such as Guangdong, Jiangsu, Zhejiang, Shandong, and Liaoning are between 0.5 and 1, and is in the second echelon; The industrial structural altitudes of Hebei, Henan, Hubei, Shaanxi, Sichuan, Guizhou and other central and western regions are between 0 and 0.5, and is in the third echelon. From an average perspective, Shanghai, Beijing, and Tianjin have completed industrialization, but this is mainly due to the unbalanced growth of urbanization and the tertiary industry. In addition to Shanghai, Beijing and Tianjin are still some distance away from industrialization. Data from various provinces of China generally show that the growth of the tertiary industry has greatly promoted the development of the industrial structural height. The first and second industries are still quite far from the destination of industrialization.

(3) A time series comparison of industrial structural altitudes shown that since 1985, China has truly entered the period of industrialization acceleration. In addition to the short-term fluctuations during 1989–1991, the industrial structural height has been steadily advancing. Since 1998, the industrial structural height has experienced an extraordinary high-speed growth, and the Chinese economy is entering a benign development track of optimizing the industrial structure and transforming the growth mode. In this process, the tertiary industry has the greatest driving force.

Chapter 10
Industrial Structure, Ownership Structure and China's Economic Growth

This chapter uses the empirical data since China's reform and opening up to examine empirically how the reform with market system as the goal of institutional change has played a role in resource allocation. Trying to explain, under the existing production technology conditions, the market system should reflect what kind of value orientation, can adjust the reasonable economic structure through the market. Through the empirical analysis carried out through the model of the industrial structure, ownership structure and the interaction between the industrial structure and ownership structure of China's economy, it is found that the economic structure cannot reach a reasonable state by unilaterally adjusting the economic structure from the industrial structure or ownership structure. And when adjusting economic structure through the market, the value orientation of the market system will play a key role. Comparing and analyzing the adjustment of market to economic structure under different value orientation of market system, we can find that only when the state-owned economy forms an institutional environment that does not compete with the people (capital and labor), and the value orientation of the system lays particular emphasis on protecting capital interests, while at the same time, taking into account labor interests, can the market adjust out a reasonable economic structure.

The basic time frame for writing this chapter is 2003. The main content of this chapter is based on the interim results of a project titled "Value Orientation of Market System and Market Adjustment of Economic Structure" by Liu Wei and Li Shaorong, which was published in the 6th issue of *China Industrial Economics* in 2004.

W. Liu, *Research on China's Market Economy Development*,
https://doi.org/10.1007/978-981-97-1398-1_10

10.1 Introduction: Methodology and Data Description

Economic structure mainly refers to the ownership structure and industrial structure in an economy entity. Under certain technological conditions, the owners of production factors put the factors into different industries through the profit seeking behavior in the market, thus forming a certain industrial structure. Due to the different owners of factors, such as state-owned or private ownership, these profit seeking behaviors, investment directions of factors and organizational forms of factors are different. This from another angle shows that ownership structure has a strong influence on industrial structure. In addition, the industrial structure determines the mode of production of the economy in a certain sense. Different modes of production will affect the production efficiency of factors and the market exchange of factors, so the industrial structure also affects the ownership structure of the economy to a certain extent. When people study the adjustment of economic structure, they often discuss whether it should be led by the government or driven by the market. The theorists generally hold that the adjustment of economic structure should be driven by the market. However, in the real economy, is it more inclined to efficiency or more inclined to fairness? and so on. The value orientation of the market system is also different, so the different economic structure of the market system is also different. Based on the existing production technology conditions, this chapter tries to explain what kind of market system value orientation can make the market adjust out the reasonable economic structure.

Market development degree of the value orientation of different market system performance will be different, such as in the primary market economy, the market system almost only provide security for capital to pursues profits in the market. The entire capital market system around how to make capital get maximum benefit to arrange. Labor becomes the employment of capital. The whole market system rarely considers the interests of labor. In such a market system, the value orientation of the system is fully inclined to protect the interests of capital. With the development of market economy, labor elements formed some organizations and groups to protect their own interests in the market economy, such as trade unions and so on. These organizations and groups as a part of the market system, will affect the exchange and configuration of elements. In such a market economy, the market system itself can't completely only to protect the interests of the capital, it also partially consider the interests of labor. Therefore, in this relatively high-level market economy, the market system not only protects the interests of capital, but also gives consideration to the interests of labor. Different value orientations of the market system will lead to different market operation mechanisms, and the economic structure selected by the market with different operation mechanisms will also be different. This chapter will discuss the adjustment of the market to the economic structure under different value orientations of the market system, and conduct a comparative study on the adjusted economic structure.

This chapter attempts to study the changes in the industrial structure, the changes in the ownership structure, and the interaction between the industrial structure and the ownership structure in the Chinese economy from a completely new perspective, and uses this interaction to explain that under different market systems, by optimizing the industrial structure and ownership structure, different economic structures will be formed, thus explaining the effect of the value orientation of the market system on the economic structure adjustment. The comparative analysis of the economic structure formed by market choices with different values shows that only the interests of capital and labor factors are protected, and only in the market system where the protection of capital interests is slightly higher than the protection of labor factors, the economic structure adjusted by the market mechanism is the ownership structure that meets the needs of industrial structure and high-level market economy.

10.1.1 Model Setting

In the process of calculating economic growth, Romer (2000) found that technological progress (including the change of economic system) determines the long-term economic growth, while the contribution of capital and labor and other essential productive factors only determines the short-term economic growth. The logical conclusion of this discovery is that a certain economic system organizes such elements as capital and labor to produce. In the short term, under the condition of constant economic system, the change of capital, labor and other factors will change the total output of the economy and lead to the short-term change of the economy. However, in the long run, the economic system will change with the change of technology. Therefore, in the long run, the economic system will inevitably change. Under the changed economic system, the production efficiency of capital, labor and other factors of production, such as output elasticity, will change. Economic structure, including ownership structure and industrial structure, represents a certain economic system, or in other words, is the feature of economic system, which indicates that the change of economic structure means the change of economic system, which also means that the production efficiency of capital, labor and other factors is different in different economic structures. This economic thinking is the economic basis supporting our analysis of the impact of economic structure on economic growth (Liu and Li 2001a, b, 2002; Liu et al. 2003a, b). Now consider the production function of the interaction of economic structure on the efficiency of production factors:

$$Y = k^{\alpha_0+\sum_{i=1}^{k}\alpha_i x_i+\sum_{j=1}^{k}\sum_{i=j}^{k}\alpha_{ji}x_j x_i} L^{\beta_0+\sum_{i=1}^{k}\beta_i x_i+\sum_{j=1}^{k}\sum_{i=j}^{k}\beta_{ji}x_j x_i} e^{\gamma_0+\sum_{i=1}^{k}\gamma_i x_i+\sum_{j=1}^{k}\sum_{i=j}^{k}\gamma_{ji}x_j x_i+\varepsilon} \tag{10.1}$$

where Y is the total economic output; K is the amount of capital input used; L represents the input amount of labor, x_i ($i = 1, 2, \ldots, k$) represents the proportion of various economic structures. Equation (10.1) take logarithms at both ends to get the econometric model that the interaction of econometric structure has an impact on the production scale and factor efficiency, thus:

$$\log(Y) = \left(\alpha_0 + \sum_{i=1}^{k} \alpha_i x_i + \sum_{j=1}^{k} \sum_{i=j+1}^{k} \alpha_{ji} x_j x_i\right) \log(K) +$$
$$\left(\beta_0 + \sum_{i=1}^{k} \beta_i x_i + \sum_{j=1}^{k} \sum_{i=j+1}^{k} \beta_{ji} x_j x_i\right) \log(L) +$$
$$\gamma_0 + \sum_{i=1}^{k} \gamma_i x_i + \sum_{j=1}^{k} \sum_{i=j+1}^{k} \gamma_{ji} x_j x_i + \varepsilon \tag{10.2}$$

The rest of the paper will be based on China's economic aggregate datas to do an econometric analysis of Eq. (10.2). The empirical results show that the interaction between ownership structure, industrial structure, ownership structure and industrial structure has an impact on economic aggregate. And then, according to that impact relationship, it makes a comparative analysis of adjustment made by market for economic structure under the different value orientation of the market system. And then it puts forward some policy suggestions on the adjustment of industrial structure and the reform of ownership structure in China.

10.1.2 Data Description

This chapter studies the main impact of China's economic structure on economic growth under the market economy system, so the research object is mainly the Chinese economy after the 1990s. It mainly studies China's economy after 1992. According to these tables like "gross domestic product of each region", "gross domestic product by expenditure approach of each region", "total capital formation and composition of each region", "employees of each region according to three industrial sectors", "employees of state-owned units at year-end of each industry", "employees of private enterprises at year-end of each region" and "individual employees at year-end of each region" of the *China Statistical Yearbook*. We can get the sample observation values of gross domestic product (measured by expenditure method) Y, fixed capital formation K, employees L, output X_1 of primary industry, output X_2 of secondary industry, output X_3 of tertiary industry, number L_1 of employees of state-owned units, number L_2 of employees of private enterprises and number L_3 of employees of individual enterprises from 1993 to 2001.

Regional sample observation value was used to study the interaction between economic structure and economic growth, the reason for this is the same reason we used to study the relationship between industrial structure and economic growth, mainly because of the formation time of the market economy in China is not long. If we use these sample observation values of national aggregate to study, there will be a problem that the sample size and freedom are too small, and we will ignore the influence of economic structure difference on economic growth. While using sample observation values from different regions, it is possible to consider not only the effects of a given economic structure on economic growth over time, but also the effects of other economic structures on economic growth over time in the same population. Based on these reasons, we use sample observation datas from different regions to study the impact of interactive changes in China's economic structure on economic growth.

10.2 Empirical Analysis of the Economic Impact of the Interaction Between Industrial Structure, Ownership Structure and Economic Structure

10.2.1 Impact of Interaction of Industrial Structure on Economy

In this part, we only consider the interactive influence of industrial structure on economic growth, but leave out the influence of ownership structure on economic growth. According to these regional gross domestic product (GDP), these sample observation data of the primary industry, the secondary industry and the tertiary industry from 1993 to 2001, using Eviews 4.0 econometric software do regression estimation of Eq. (10.2). After removing the collinearity phenomenon between interaction influences variables of the primary industry, the secondary industry and the tertiary industry and other influence variables. Then, the modified regression estimation model is obtained[1]:

$$\begin{aligned}\log(Y) = {} & \underset{(8.41)}{1.99x_1 \log K} - \underset{(-2.95)}{1.14x_2 \log K} - \underset{(-4.19)}{2.20x_3 \log k} + \underset{(5.95)}{11.36x_2x_3 \log K} + \underset{(5.43)}{2.06x_3 \log L} \\ & - \underset{(-3.99)}{3.41x_2x_3 \log L} - \underset{(-4.30)}{7.59x_1} + \underset{(6.04)}{18.06x_2} + \underset{(4.61)}{10.46x_3} - \underset{(-5.83)}{63.44x_2x_3}\end{aligned} \tag{10.3}$$

The judgment coefficient R^2 of this equation is 0.983531, and the adjusted judgment coefficient $\overline{R}^2$ is 0.982808. The D-W statistic[2] is 1.48. The equation shows that these three industries all have an effect on the output elasticity of capital. From the perspective of a direct impact, the effect of the primary industry is positive, the effect of the secondary industry and the tertiary industry are negative. If only to see that, we seems to come to an absurd conclusion, that is, in China's economy, increasing the share of the primary industry reducing the shares of the secondary industry and

[1] The number in parentheses below the estimated parameter in the regression model is the t statistic of the corresponding parameter.

[2] See the Eq. (11) of Liu and Li (2002) for details. In this equation, the judgment coefficient $R^2 =$ 0.978460, and the corrected judgment system $\overline{R}^2 = 0.976686$, are lower than the above Eq. (10.3).

the tertiary industry at the same time will improve the output efficiency of capital. In other words, the non-agriculturalization of China's economy will reduce the output efficiency of capital. However, the fourth item of Eq. (10.3) shows that the interaction between the secondary industry and the tertiary industry has a positive effect on the output elasticity of capital, that is, the simultaneous increase of the secondary industry and the tertiary industry will produce a very large effect on the output elasticity of capital (relative to the impact of the secondary industry and the tertiary industry on the elasticity of capital output). Moreover, if the share of secondary and tertiary industries increases differently, then the effects of the two industries on the elasticity of capital output are also different. This leads to the main concern of this chapter, that is, non-agriculture in China's economy or, generally speaking, there is a problem of how to coordinate the secondary industry and the tertiary industry in the process of industrialization in China's economy. Later in this chapter, under the value orientation of different market systems, the choice made by the market to solve this problem will be explained. The elasticity of labour output is mainly affected by the tertiary industry, and this impact will be weakened by the increase of the share of the secondary industry. These three industries all have a direct impact on the scale of production. Among them, the primary industry has a negative impact, the secondary industry and the tertiary industry have a positive impact, but the interactive influence between the secondary industry and the primary industry is negative. This means that the simultaneous increase of the secondary industry and the tertiary industry will greatly weaken the positive impact of the two industries on the economic scale. It shows that under the condition of the current production technology, if we want to greatly improve production efficiency and expand the size of the economy, we must coordinate the development of these three industries.

10.2.2 The Impact of Interaction of Ownership Structure on Economy

Here we leave out the influence of industrial structure on economic growth and simply consider the interactive influence of ownership structure on economic growth. According to the sample observation datas of the number of employees in state-owned units, workers in private units and individual households from 1993 to 2001, we can calculate the proportion l_1, l_2 and l_3 of employment in the three ownership units. The sum of these three proportions is 1. However, because the denominator is not the number of employees L, the three proportions are only absorbed by the three ownership systems under the established industrial structure and employment scale. And use these three proportions to express the relative size of the three ownership economies. In addition, the sample observation values of GDP, total capital formation and total employment in various regions from 1993 to 2001 were used to make regression estimation of Eq. (10.2) with Eviews 4.0 econometric software, and some insignificant variables with collinearity phenomenon were omitted. The modified estimation model was obtained:

$$
\begin{aligned}
\log(Y) = & 0.85 l_1 \log K + 1.03 l_2 \log K + 0.82 l_3 \log K + 1.43 l_1 l_2 \log K + 0.33 l_1 \log L \\
& (20.66) \quad (18.41) \quad (6.79) \quad (4.8) \quad (7.15) \\
& - 0.34 l_3 \log L - 0.58 l_1 + 5.32 l_3 - 9.04 l_1 l_2 \\
& (-2.37) \quad (-2.2) \quad (6.86) \quad (-5.3)
\end{aligned} \tag{10.4}
$$

The judgment coefficient $R^2 = 0.985403$, the adjusted judgment coefficient $\overline{R}^2 = 0.984836$, and the D-W statistic is 1.72. It can be seen from the equation that the output elasticity of factors of production is affected by various forms of ownership economy, that is, by state-owned economy, private economy and individual economy. In terms of the capital-output elasticity, the increase of various economic shares will increase the capital-output elasticity regardless of the interaction effect of ownership. From the perspective of the interaction, the common development of state-owned economy and private economy have a positive effect on the output elasticity of capital, plus individual economic domino effect of capital output is less than the state-owned economy and private economy. Therefore in China's economy, reducing the share of individual economy in the ownership structure and increasing the share of state-owned economy and private economy at the same time will improve the output efficiency of capital in the economy.

For the output elasticity of labor, there is no interaction effect of ownership structure, but there is substitution effect between ownership structure. From the perspective of economic variable relationship reflected in the equation, increasing the share of state-owned economy and reducing the share of individual economy at the same time will improve the output elasticity of labor. However, in equation, if we replace l_3 with l_1 and l_2, we can see domino effect of state-owned economy of labor output elasticity is 0.67 (= 0.33 + 0.34), while the positive effect of private economy on labor output elasticity is 0.34, thus the domino effect of state-owned economy on the labor efficiency is double that of the private economy, that is to say, if the reduce of the individual economy is dominated by state-owned economy and private economy to absorb, then the increase of state-owned economy to improve the labor efficiency is nearly twice that of private economy. From this perspective, the positive impact of state-owned economy on the output elasticity of capital is 0.03 (= 0.85 − 0.82), while the positive impact of private economy on the output elasticity of capital is 0.21 (= 1.03 − 0.82), so the positive effect of the private economy on capital is seven times that of the state-owned economy. Under the condition of market economy, this means that the development of private economy makes the increase of capital income seven times that of state-owned economy, but the increase of labor income is only one half of that of state-owned economy. If the value orientation of market system focuses on capital interests, that is, market system guarantees that capital dominates the market and pursues profits, then capital, whether state-owned capital or private capital, from the perspective of its own interests, both will encourage the development of private economy, supplemented by a certain degree of coordinated development of state-owned economy. From this, we can see that in the future of China's economy, the best way to adjust the ownership system driven by the market from the interests of capital is the private ownership of state-owned capital, which not only vigorously develops the private economy, but also coordinates the development of the state-owned economy and maximizes the capital gains. However, this reform way will reduce the increase of the demand income nearly double, which will inevitably increase the income gap between the capital owner and the labor owner.

In terms of economic scale, the state-owned economy has a negative effect on the total size of the economy, while the individual economy has a positive effect. If we replace the individual economy with the state-owned economy and the private economy, then both the state-owned economy and the private economy will have negative effects on the economic scale, and the interaction between the state-owned economy and the private economy will also have a negative effect on the economic scale. That is, the joint development of the state-owned economy and the private economy will reduce the total scale of the economy. Therefore, from the perspective of expanding the total scale of the economy, there is an alternative relationship between the state-owned economy and the private economy. That is, only by increasing the share of the state-owned economy while reducing the share of the private economy at the same time, or increasing the share of the private economy while reducing the share of the state-owned economy, can the total scale of the economy be expanded.

10.2.3 The Effect of Interaction of Economic Structure on Economy

Here we will empirically analyze the interaction between economic structures on the impact of this relationship on economic growth. Using these shares of GDP by region, capital formation, employees and industries, and sample observations of economic share of each ownership system to do regression estimation of Eq. (10.2) and removing related variables with collinearity in the equation. Then, the modified regression model is obtained:

$$
\begin{aligned}
\log Y = {} & 0.67 l_1 \log K - 1.71 x_2 \log K - 2.89 x_3 \log K + 6.2 l_2 x_2 \log K - 1.65 l_3 x_2 \log K \\
& \quad (2.99) \qquad (-2.91) \qquad (-3.74) \qquad (9.22) \qquad (-4.59) \\
& + 5.48 l_1 l_3 \log K + 1.37 l_2 l_3 \log K + 8.84 x_2 x_3 \log K + 0.68 l_1 \log L - 1.76 l_2 \log L \\
& \quad (6.77) \qquad (4.30) \qquad (4.27) \qquad (4.17) \qquad (-3.91) \\
& + 1.55 l_3 \log L + 2.32 x_3 \log L - 5.44 l_1 l_3 \log L - 3.7 x_2 x_3 \log L + 18.59 x_2 + 10.78 x_3 \\
& \quad (8.74) \qquad (4.01) \qquad (-7) \qquad (-3.6) \qquad (4.14) \qquad (2.9) \\
& - 6.78 l_1 + 14.1 l_2 - 44.8 l_2 x_2 - 14.69 l_3 x_3 + 8.44 l_1 l_3 - 41.82 x_2 x_3 \\
& \quad (-4.56) \quad (5.75) \quad (-7.99) \quad (-3.94) \quad (2.11) \quad (-3.46)
\end{aligned}
\tag{10.5}
$$

The judgment coefficient $R^2 = 0.990129$, the modified judgment coefficient $\overline{R}^2 = 0.989055$, and the D-W statistic is 1.87. As can be seen from Eq. (10.5), the interaction between industrial structure and ownership structure, as well as the interaction between the two structures themselves, has a very high impact on the factor efficiency and the total scale of the economy, but the impact is different on the capital factor efficiency, labor factor efficiency and the economic scale. Look from the output elasticity of capital, the increase of the secondary industry and tertiary industry share the output elasticity of capital will have a negative impact, but the interaction between the secondary industry and the primary industry output elasticity of capital has a major positive effect, namely, the secondary industry and the primary industry at the same time will increase the output elasticity of capital produces a very large (relative to the secondary industry and tertiary industry respectively on the influence of the output elasticity of capital), and the increase shares of the secondary industry and the tertiary industry are different, then the effects of the two industries on the interaction of capital output elasticity will be different, because the interaction between the secondary industry and the private economy has a positive effect on the output efficiency of capital and a negative effect on the interaction with the individual economy. Therefore, from the perspective of increasing the capital output elasticity, the tendency to increase the share of the secondary industry is greater than that of the tertiary industry, and there is a tendency to increase the share of the private economy and reduce the share of the individual economy. While increasing the share of the state economy can directly improve the output elasticity of capital, but the interaction between the ownership structure shows that the state-owned economy and the interaction of the individual economy relative to the interaction between the private and individual economy output elasticity of capital has a great positive effect, thus reducing the share of the individual economy, from the point of view of the increasing capital output efficiency, and can reduce the state-owned share of the economy. According to the above analysis, in the process of market-oriented economic restructuring, the industrial structure will be inclined to increase the share of the secondary industry, and the ownership structure will be inclined to increase the share of the private economy.

For the output efficiency of labor factors, the tertiary industry has a positive effect on the output elasticity of labor, while the interaction between the secondary industry and the tertiary industry has a negative effect on the output elasticity of labor, which means that increasing the share of the tertiary industry while reducing the share of the secondary industry will improve the output elasticity of labor. In terms of ownership structure, the private economic effect of labor output elasticity is negative, therefore improve the efficiency of labor output and increase the labor income tend to reduce the share of private economy, state-owned economy and individual economy has at the same time improve labor output elasticity of positive effect, and the interaction of the two is to produce a negative effect, which is both to increase or decrease will lower the output elasticity of labor. Since the positive effect of the state-owned economy on labor efficiency (0.68) is far less than the positive effect of the individual economy on labor efficiency (1.55), the negative effect of the interaction between the state-owned economy and the individual economy will lead to the choice of reducing the share of the state-owned economy and increasing the share of the individual economy when increasing the labor output efficiency. Therefore, from the perspective of improving the elasticity of labor output, there is a tendency to increase the share of the tertiary industry and individual economy.

For the total scale of the economy, the secondary industry and the tertiary industry has a positive effect, but the interaction has a negative effect. Because of the positive effect of the secondary industry (18.59) is greater than the primary industry (10.78). Therefore, from the perspective of industrial interaction, increasing the total scale of economy will incline to improving the share of the secondary industry, at the same time reducing the share of the tertiary industry; from ownership interactive perspective, state-owned economy of scale to create a negative effect, and the private economy has a positive effects, state-owned economy and the interaction of the individual economy at the same time produce a positive effect. So the feasible choice is to increase the size of the new economy, the increase of the private economy share at the same time reduce the state-owned and the share of the individual economy; Look from the interaction between industrial structure and ownership structure, the interaction between the secondary industry and the private economy and the tertiary industry and the interaction of the individual economy are negative effects of economic scale. Therefore, interaction between structures doesn't support the structural choices of each structure's own interaction. Expanding the structural choice of economic scale needs to do further optimization analysis.

10.3 Comparative Analysis of the Optimized Economic Structure

Based on the previous empirical analysis of the interaction of economic structure on economic aggregate, we will compare and study the optimal economic structure selected by the market under various conditions on the basis of this empirical analysis. Comparative research is based on the following theoretical understanding: in a market economy where capital occupies an absolute position (relative to labor), the organization and determination of production are determined by capital, and the purpose of capital in the market is to chase profits and maximize the return of capital. Due to the income that element obtains in the market decided by the output efficiency of element, the mode of production and organizational form chosen by the market is the mode of production and organizational form to maximize the output efficiency of capital factors. In such a market economy, the market system is completely inclined to protect the interests of capital. Under the value orientation of such a market system, the optimal economic structure selected by the market is called the economic structure that maximizes the efficiency of capital output. The pursuit of profit by capital in the market is conditional, and the pursuit of profit without giving consideration to labor interests cannot last long. From the perspective of the long-term development of market economy, the market system not only protects the interests of capital, but also needs to protect labor interests. In a market system, if labor interests and capital interests are equally protected, the economic structure selected by the market is called the optimal economic structure that takes into account labor interests. Therefore, such optimal economic structure refers to the economic structure that maximizes the sum of capital factor efficiency and labor efficiency. The scale of the economy is determined by the specialization of factors and the division of labor in the society, which in turn depends on the scale and scope of the market. Therefore, the economic structure of the largest market scale refers to the economic structure that maximizes the scale of the total economy. After defining the above concepts, we will compare and analyze the optimal economic structure under the value orientation of different market systems.

10.3.1 The Optimal Industrial Structure with an Unchanged Ownership Structure

Equation (10.3) represents the impact of interaction of industrial structure on economic aggregate when ownership structure remains unchanged. Therefore, the market chooses the industrial structure that maximizes the capital output efficiency, which is determined by the following optimization problems:

$$\begin{aligned} &\max \alpha = 1.99x_1 - 1.14x_2 - 2.20x_3 + 11.36x_2x_3 \\ &s.t. \quad x_1 + x_2 + x_3 = 1 \end{aligned}$$

To solve the above problems, $x_1 = 35.57\%$, $x_2 = 36.88\%$ and $x_3 = 27.55\%$. It can be seen that under the condition that the current ownership structure remains unchanged, the optimal industrial structure is 35.57% of the primary industry share, 36.88% of the secondary industry share and 27.55% of the tertiary industry share for the market choice driven by the pursuit of profit by capital. However, in the long run, the optimal industrial structure selected by the market with both consideration of labor benefits should be determined by the following optimization problems:

$$\begin{aligned} &\max \alpha + \beta = 1.99x_1 - 1.14x_2 - 0.14x_3 + 7.95x_2x_3 \\ &s.t. \quad x_1 + x_2 + x_3 = 1 \end{aligned}$$

To solve the above problems, $x_1 = 33.84\%$, $x_2 = 26.79\%$ and $x_3 = 39.37\%$. It can be seen that under the condition that the existing ownership structure remains unchanged, the optimal industrial structure selected by the market through long-term consideration of the benefits of factors is the share of the primary industry 33.84%, the share of the secondary industry 26.79% and the share of the tertiary industry 39.37%. Therefore, under the current ownership structure, China's economy cannot achieve industrialization through market regulation in a long or short period of time. It is necessary to adjust the existing ownership structure in order to realize the industrial economy in harmony with the market.

From the perspective of market scale, the industrial structure with the largest market scale is the solution of the following equation:

$$\max \gamma = -7.59x_1 + 18.06x_2 + 10.46x_3 - 63.44x_2x_3$$
$$s.t.\quad x_1 + x_2 + x_3 = 1$$

The optimal solutions of the above optimization problems are $x_1 = 0, x_2 = 1$and $x_3 = 0$. This shows that only industrialization can expand the market scale of the economy. However, under the existing ownership structure, whether the value orientation of the market system protects only capital interests or at the same time takes into account labor interests. The economy can not make the total size of the economy or the scale of the market through the industrial structure chosen by the market. Therefore, there are only two options for expanding the market scale of the economy: First, expanding the share of the secondary industry under the existing ownership structure through non-market- based methods. The industrial structure thus formed will not be in harmony with the market; Second, adjusting the existing ownership structure and expanding the share of the secondary industry in the economy through market choices, in order to industrialize the economy and increase the market scale of the economy at the same time.

10.3.2 The Optimal Ownership Structure with an Unchanged Industrial Structure

Equation (10.4) describes the impact of interaction of ownership structure on economic aggregate when industrial structure remains unchanged. Therefore, under the condition of unchanged industrial structure, the market chooses the ownership structure with the maximum capital output efficiency, which is determined by the following optimization problems:

$$\max \alpha = 0.85l_1 + 1.03l_2 + 0.82l_3 + 1.43l_1l_2$$
$$s.t.\quad l_1 + l_2 + l_3 = 1$$

The solution of the problem is $l_1 = 43.71\%$, $l_2 = 56.29\%$ and $l_3 = 0$. Therefore, under the condition that the existing industrial structure remains unchanged, the optimal ownership structure selected by the market is the share of the state-owned economy is 43.71%, the share of the private economy is 56.29%, and the share of the individual economy is 0. However, in the long term, the optimal industrial structure selected by the market should be determined by the following optimization problems under the condition of giving consideration to labor interests:

$$\max \alpha + \beta = 1.19l_1 + 1.03l_2 + 0.48l_3 + 1.43l_1 l_2$$
$$s.t. \quad l_1 + l_2 + l_3 = 1$$

The solution of the problem is $l_1 = 55.59\%$, $l_2 = 44.41\%$ and $l_3 = 0$. Therefore, under the condition that the existing industrial structure remains unchanged, the optimal ownership structure selected by the market in a long period of time is the share of the state-owned economy is 55.59%, the share of the private economy is 44.41%, and the share of the individual economy is 0. It can be seen that under the existing industrial structure, if the value orientation of the market system only considers the interests of capital, through the pursuit of profits by capital, the ownership structure will be adjusted to a ownership structure in which the state-owned economy accounts for slightly more than 40%, the private economy accounts for more than 50%, and the individual economy has less than 10%. If in a long period of time, organizations or behaviors protecting labor interests appear in the market, that is, the capital pursues profits in the market and also considers the interests of workers, then the market will choose the state-owned economy accounting for slightly more than 50%, the private economy accounting for slightly more than 40%, and the individual economy accounting for about 10%.

From the perspective of expanding market scale, under the condition of unchanged industrial structure, the optimal ownership structure is the solution of the following equation:

$$\max \gamma = 0.58l_1 + 5.32l_3 - 9.04l_1 l_2$$
$$s.t. \quad x_1 + x_2 + x_3 = 1$$

The optimal solutions above are $l_1 = 0$, $l_2 = 0$ and $l_3 = 1$. It shows that under the condition of industrial structure now, regardless of the value orientation of the market system only to protect the interests of the capital or the profit of labor at the same time, the economy can not make the economic aggregate scale or market scale the largest through the ownership structure selected by the market. Therefore, it is necessary to adjust the ownership structure and industrial structure at the same time in order to achieve the optimal economic structure through the market.

10.3.3 Optimal Economic Structure

Equation (10.5) describes the impact of interaction between industrial structure, ownership structure and industrial structure and ownership structure on economic aggregate. Therefore, the economic structure with the maximum capital output efficiency selected by the market is determined by the following optimization problems:

$$\max \alpha = 0.67l_1 - 1.71x_2 - 2.89x_3 + 6.2l_2 x_2 - 1.65l_3 x_2$$

$$+5.48l_1l_3+1.37l_2l_3+8.84x_2x_3$$
$$s.t.\quad x_1+x_2+x_3=1,\ l_1+l_2+l_3=1$$

The optimal solutions to the above problems are $l_1=0$, $l_2=1$ and $l_3=0$; $x_1=0$, $x_2=87.85\%$ and $x_3=12.15\%$. From the optimal structure, we can see that when the value orientation of the market system only reflects the capital's interests. Although the market industrializes the economy through the adjustment of ownership structure and industrial structure. Considering the errors of empirical analysis, on the basis of such a system, the industrial structure regulated by the market should be less than 10% of the primary industry, 80% of the secondary industry, and 10% of the tertiary industry. It is obvious that such an industrial structure is not a reasonable one, which shows that the market system which only protects capital's interests will inevitably lead to an unreasonable economic structure. Therefore, in the long run, the market system itself should also protect the interests of workers. Now we analyze the optimal economic structure selected by the market in a market where the interests of labor are as im $s.t.$ portant as the interests of capital. This structure is the solution to the following problems:

$$\max\alpha=1.35l_1-1.78l_2+1.55l_3+1.71x_2-0.57x_3+6.2l_2x_2$$
$$-1.65l_3x_2+0.04l_1l_3+1.37l_2l_3+5.14x_2x_3$$
$$s.t.\quad x_1+x_2+x_3=1,\ l_1+l_2+l_3=1$$

The solution of the optimization problem is $l_1=0$, $l_2=0$ and $l_3=1$; $x_1=0$, $x_2=46.4\%$, and $x_3=53.6\%$. It shows that the interests of labor and capital is as important as the system of market environment, the market can industrialize the economy under the adjustment of the market through the adjustment of ownership. Considering the empirical analysis of error, and in such a system on the basis of market adjustment of industrial structure should be less than 10% of the first industry, secondary industry accounted for 40%, and the primary industry is 50%, slightly obviously this is a relatively reasonable industrial structure, it shows that whether the market system reflects the protection of workers' interests is related to whether the market can effectively regulate the industrial structure. However, from the perspective of ownership structure, when labor interests and capital interests are equally important, the ownership chosen by the market is the individual economic form of absolute privatization with a very low organizational level. Although the economy can achieve industrialization under such a market system, it is also industrialization with a very low degree of specialization and division of labor. Market system, therefore, must to protect the interests of the workers, but can't put the interests of labor and capital equal to or higher than the interests of capital, because in such a market system through market cannot form a high degree of organization of production form, this shows that in a market economy from the aspects of a capital dominated but must balance the interests of the labor. Below we analyze the economic structure that maximizes the size of the market. Such an economic structure is the solution to the following problems:

$$\max \gamma = 18.59x_2 + 10.78x_3 - 6.78l_1 + 14.1l_2 - 44.8l_2x_2$$
$$- 14.69l_3x_3 + 8.44l_1l_3 - 41.82x_2x_3$$
$$s.t.\ \ x_1 + x_2 + x_3 = 1,\ l_1 + l_2 + l_3 = 1$$

The solution of the problem is $l_1 = 65.5\%$, $l_2 = 0$ and $l_3 = 34.5\%$; $x_1 = 0$, $x_2 = 43.85\%$ and $x_3 = 56.15\%$. This shows that the industrial structure required to maximize the market scale is also that the secondary industry accounts for a little more than 40%, the tertiary industry accounts for a little more than 50%, and the primary industry is less than 10%. In other words, the expansion of the market scale requires the economy to be industrialized. However, the ownership structure that maximizes the market scale requires a large proportion of state-owned economy and nearly three levels of individual economy, which shows that state-owned economy plays an important role in increasing the market scale. It is not difficult to understand that the market scale measures the output efficiency of the market organization system. In the market organization system, both the state-owned economy and the individual economy will play an important role, in which the state-owned economy will take the dominant position.

As a result of this analysis, the economic structure is regulated by the market and eventually the economy will be industrialised. This means that the secondary industry accounts for a little over 40%, the primary industry for 50% and the primary industry for less than 10%. The ownership structure basic is private or individual economy, if the value orientation focus on labor market system, or the protection of the interests of the labor is greater than or equal to the benefit of the capital, the market will choose completely absolutely individual economy form of privatization, so in with market economic structure adjustment as the value orientation of the market system should focus on to protect the interests of the capital, but at the same time the profit of labor. At the same time, the state-owned economy plays a very important role in the construction of market organization system, so when adjusting the economic structure by market, we can use the state-owned economy construction to expand the market scale of the market organization system. In the market economy formed, the value orientation of the market system should focus on the interests of capital, but the interests of labor must be taken into account at the same time. In this way, through market regulation, the economy will realize industrialization and form a market-adapted industrial structure. At this time, the industrial structure accounts for 40% of the secondary industry, 50% of the tertiary industry and less than 10% of the primary industry.

10.4 Conclusion

Under the current conditions of production technology, the model empirically analyses the economic impact of the interaction between the industrial structure, ownership structure and industrial structure and ownership structure in the Chinese economy and optimises the impact of this interaction. We can discover that with the existing ownership structure intact, no matter under what kind of market system, China's economy can not realize industrialization through market regulation, nor can it expand the market scale; Under the condition that the existing industrial structure is unchanged, the market regulates the ownership structure. If the value orientation of the market system only protects the interests of capital, then the market will choose a larger share of non-state-owned economy. When the market system reflects the protection of labor interests, the share of state-owned economy selected by the market will exceed the share of non-state-owned economy. However, regardless of the value orientation of the market system is only to protect capital interests or to take into account labor interests at the same time, the economy can not make the total economic scale or market scale the largest through the ownership structure chosen by the market. At the same time, the analysis shows that under the condition that the existing industrial structure is unchanged, the increase of the private economy can increase the capital interests seven times more than the state-owned economy, but the increase of labor interests is only one-half of the state-owned economy, so the market system focuses on capital interests. And encourage capital to pursue profits in the market, then capital, whether state-owned capital or private capital, will choose the private sector from the perspective of its own interests. At this time, the mode of ownership adjustment chosen by the market is the private sector of state-owned capital, which has vigorously developed the private economy. At the same time, it also coordinated the development of the state-owned economy and increased the value of capital gains. However, this adjustment method will make the increase of labor factor income nearly double decrease, which is bound to increase the income gap between capital owners and labor owners. In short, the unilateral adjustment of the economic structure from the industrial structure or the ownership structure alone can not bring the economic structure to a reasonable state. Therefore, the adjustment of the economic structure needs to achieve a reasonable economic structure state through the coordinated adjustment of the ownership structure and the industrial structure.

When adjusting the economic structure through the market, the value orientation of the market system will play a key role. When the value orientation of the market system focuses on labor, or the protection of labor interests is greater than or equal to the interests of capital, then the ownership structure selected through the market is mainly the individual economy which is completely and absolutely privatized but has a low degree of organization. When the value orientation of the market system focuses on protecting the interests of capital while giving consideration to the interests of labor, the ownership structure selected through the market is mainly composed of the private economy with a certain degree of organization. That means simply from the perspective of elements of interest, the market will not choose the state-owned economy, but considering the size of the economy when the state-owned economic organization form in the market (including economic infrastructure) play a very important role in the construction of, so when adjusting ownership structure by market, we need to develop the role of the state-owned economy in the form of market organisation.

Chapter 11
Structural Efficiency and Technical Advance in China's Economic Growth

Since the reform and opening up, China's economy has maintained a sustained growth rate of more than 9% for 30 years from 1978 to 2008. Whether China's economy can maintain this sustained and high-speed growth trend in the future and how long this trend will last are worthy of our deep discussion. Krugman (1994) pointed out in his famous article "The Myth of Asia's Miracle" that the economic growth of most East Asian countries and regions mainly depends on the increase of factor input; technical advance has not played a significant role, so he believed that the economic growth of East Asia is unsustainable. Krugman's point of view aroused heated discussion in academic circles. Many scholars at home and abroad cited his point of view to prove the inevitability of the Asian financial crisis in 1997, and believed that the East Asian economy needs to adjust its growth path and promote economic growth by increasing factor productivity. Specifically, they believe that, from the perspective of neoclassical economics, a country's long-term economic growth can be divided into two aspects: one is the increase of factor input; the other is the increase of factor productivity,[1] that is, labor productivity or total factor productivity. The economic growth that depends solely on factor input at the cost of extensive consumption of factors and resources is unsustainable in the long run. Only by improving total factor productivity can the sustainability of economic growth be guaranteed. From the results of this chapter, we can see that the unsustainable growth model of East Asia pointed out by Krugman (1994) is comparatively similar to that of China before 1998. However, since 1998, China's economic growth model has increasingly demonstrated its own sustainability.

[1] In economics, people mainly studied single factor productivity in the early stage, which is labor productivity, while in the later stage, they mainly focused on total factor productivity.

The basic time frame for writing this chapter is 2008. The content of this chapter is based on the interim results of a project titled "Changes in Industrial Structure and Technological Progress in China's Economic Growth" by Liu Wei and Zhang Hui, which was published in the 11th issue of *Economic Research Journal* in 2008.

W. Liu, *Research on China's Market Economy Development*,
https://doi.org/10.1007/978-981-97-1398-1_11

Of course, many scholars also believe that total factor productivity is not equal to technological progress. It is only the residual in accounting. Moreover, it is a considerable misunderstanding to use total factor productivity to represent technological progress. More importantly, for developing countries like China, in the initial stage of reform and development, the contribution of pure technical advance to economic growth may be inferior to the contribution of industrial structure changes brought by marketization reform to economic growth. With the advancement of marketization reform, the benefits of reform may be gradually reduced, while the role of technical advance in economic growth will be gradually highlighted. This chapter is devoted to demonstrating these assumptions.

This chapter attempts to decompose technical advance and industrial structure change from factor productivity (labor productivity and total factor productivity), and make a horizontal and vertical comparative analysis of the impetus of industrial structure change and technological progress to economic growth. Through this analysis, this chapter hopes to study these questions: How much has the industrial structure change promoted the growth of China's economy in the past 30 years of the reform and opening up? How much share does it occupy compared with other factors such as technological progress? Or is it more important to promote marketization reform, or is it more important to promote technical advance? What is the fluctuating trend of the role of structural change in promoting the economy? Can we predict that China's future economic growth depends more on more profound marketization reform or technical advance?

11.1 Introduction

From the perspective of neoclassical production function, a country's long-term economic growth can be divided into two aspects: one is the increase of factor input; the other is the increase of labor productivity and total factor productivity.[2] As we all know, the economic growth that depends solely on factor input at the cost of extensive consumption of factors and resources is unsustainable in the long run. Total factor productivity is a more important factor in the long-term economic growth. And industrial structure change and technical advance are two important factors to promote labor productivity and total factor productivity respectively.

If we divide the improvement of labor productivity and total factor productivity into technical advance[3] and resource allocation efficiency, industrial structure change is to improve labor productivity and total factor productivity by improving

[2] In economics, people mainly studied single factor productivity in the early stage, which is labor productivity, while in the later stage, they mainly focused on total factor productivity.

[3] Total factor productivity can be decomposed into technical efficiency, technical advance and resource allocation efficiency. This book classifies the change of technical efficiency and technical advance as "technical advance." Production efficiency refers to the situation within the production possibility boundary, indicating the distance between the current output and the maximum possible output. Technical advance refers to the promotion of the production possibility boundary,

resource allocation efficiency. Together with technical advance, they have become two indispensable forces to promote long-term economic growth.

The reason for the change in industrial structure is that there is a persistent unbalance in economic development. The marginal reward of some industries is higher than that of other industries. Driven by the goal of maximizing benefits, factors such as labor and capital move from industries with lower marginal reward to industries with higher marginal reward. Therefore, the change of industrial structure shows the real existence of the "invisible hand" of the market. The impetus of industrial structure change to economic growth is actually the contribution of market system to economic growth. Technical advance depends more on the innovation ability of micro-enterprises themselves.

In the real economy, not only the changes in industrial structure and technical advance affect each other, but also their driving forces on economic growth are intertwined and overlapping. This chapter hopes to make a horizontal and vertical comparative analysis of the impetus of industrial structure change and technical advance to economic growth by decomposing labor productivity and total factor productivity. In short, this chapter mainly hopes to study these questions: How much has the industrial structure change promoted the growth of China's economy in the past 30 years of the reform and opening up? How much share does it occupy compared with other factors such as technical advance? Or is it more important to promote marketization reform, or is it more important to promote technical advance? What is the fluctuating trend of the role of structural change in promoting the economy? Can we predict that China's future economic growth depends more on more profound marketization reform or technical advance?

The impact of industrial structure changes on economic growth has been studied for a long time. It can be traced back to the 1930s, such as Clark (1940), Fisher (1931). However, Kuznets (1957) has earlier analyzed and measured the impact of three industries' output structure and labor structure on economic growth from an empirical perspective. The most famous contemporary research on the relationship between structural change and economic growth mainly came from the development economists, especially the structuralist schools such as Chenery and Syrquin (1977), Chenery and Elkington (1979), Chenery et al. (1986) and Syrquin (1984). Chenery and Syrquin constructed a standard model of economic structure change in the process of industrialization by using empirical econometric methods and input–output analysis methods, which provided a measurable scale for later researchers to analyze and measure the relationship between structural change and economic growth. In the 1970s and 1980s, they explored a lot of useful research on the relationship between economic structure and economic development from the history of industrialization and economic growth of developed countries; in the 1990s and early twenty-first century, the latest research mainly came from economists who are interested in the transition economy (China, Russia, Eastern Europe, etc.), emerging industrial countries (Singapore, Republic of Korea, etc.). For example, Fagerberg

---

and resource allocation efficiency refers to the improvement of resource efficiency caused by the redistribution of resources among departments.

(2000), Peneder (2003), Pilat (1993) and Timmer and Szirmai (2000) and have all tried to use new methods to measure the extent to which structural changes in the course of East Asian economic development have promoted factor productivity.

Relevant research literatures in China are quite abundant as well. These literatures mainly use input–output method and econometric method to study the impact of industrial structure on economic growth. The latest research mainly focuses on econometric method. Chen (2005), Liu and Li (2002), and Zhu and Han (2003) successively used static and dynamic econometric methods such as classical least square method, Granger causality test and co-integration test to study the impact of China's industrial structure on economic growth. Although the research methods are different, the conclusions are basically the same: the change of industrial structure really promotes economic growth. However, due to the limitations of measurement methods and data, the relative contribution of industrial structure changes has not been studied deeply in these literatures. Fan and Zhang (2002) were the first to quantitatively measure the relative contribution of industrial structure change to economic growth. By constructing a dynamic programming model (constraints are equal to the marginal output of each department), they solved an index with theoretical significance, that is, effective allocation of GDP. The ratio of real GDP to effective allocation of GDP can indicate the allocation efficiency improvement caused by industrial structure change.

This chapter uses the labor productivity decomposition and the total factor productivity decomposition to empirically measure the contribution of industrial structure change to China's economic growth, and compares it with the contribution of technological progress. The research shows that in the 30 years since the reform and opening up, the contribution of industrial structure change to China's economic growth has been remarkable for a time. However, with the improvement of the degree of marketization, the contribution of industrial structure change to economic growth has been declining, gradually giving way to technological progress. That is to say, the market force embodied in industrial structure change will gradually give way to the force of technological progress. In addition, the study also finds that the weakening effect of structural change does not mean that the benefits of marketization reform will disappear. Some developmental and institutional factors still hinder the further improvement of resource allocation efficiency. From this perspective, China still has a long way to go to improve the market mechanism.

11.2 Theoretical Assumption

Firstly, we should define the different roles and positions of industrial structure change and technological progress in economic transition theoretically. This section uses Fig. 11.1 to demonstrate the position of industrial structure change and technological progress in China's economic transformation. Figure 11.1 shows the production possibility boundary curve, commodity A represents agricultural products, commodity I represents industrial products, and we use commodity A and commodity

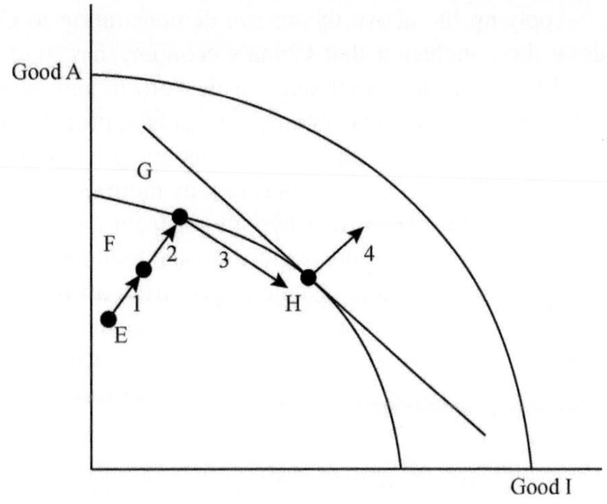

Fig. 11.1 The map to demonstrate the position of industrial structure change and technological progress

I to represent two industries respectively. Economic growth in the process of transition from planned economy to market economy can be divided into the following four steps.

Step 1: In Fig. 11.1, from point E to point F. It indicates that in the early stage of economic transition, the actual production point is closer to the production possibility boundary because of the utilization of idle factors in planned economy era, the improvement of production efficiency and the recovery of economic growth.

Step 2: From point F to point G. This indicates that the labor and capital factors are allocated according to the optimal market price ratio within the enterprise, instead of the distorted price allocation of resources under the economic system. This is shown in Fig. 11.1 as closer to the production possibility boundary.

Step 3: From point G to point H. This indicates the redistribution of resources among different industrial sectors. This step is the change of industrial structure. Under the guidance of the invisible hand of the market, resources are transferred from one industry to another, making production conform to the optimal conversion ratio.

Step 4: From point H to the upper right. This indicates that when the economy is above the optimal equilibrium point H, if the total factors and resources are fixed, the long-term economic growth can only rely on technological progress, that is, the production possibility boundary is pushed outward. If we assume that the total amount of resources is constantly growing, the increase of factor input and technological progress may simultaneously promote long-term economic growth.

In the neoclassical theoretical model, only when the economy is in an unbalanced state can resources be reallocated among different industries. If we call the gap between the existing and the best resource allocation efficiency as the gap of resource allocation efficiency, then the gap will shrink with the deepening of marketization reform.

Applying the above theoretical demonstration to China's reality, we can easily draw the conclusion that China's economy has gradually evolved from the non-equilibrium in the initial stage of the reform and opening up (Li 1998) to a more balanced state. As the economy gradually approaches equilibrium, the contribution of industrial structure changes to economic growth may be declining, and the future growth of China's economy may require more technological progress. The following will verify this theoretical hypothesis from an empirical point of view. We will use labor productivity decomposition and total factor productivity decomposition to separate the "structural change effect" from all the factors that promote economic growth, so as to analyze the relative contribution of industrial structure change to economic growth and compare it with the contribution of technological progress.

11.3 Contribution of Structural Transformation to Labor Productivity Growth in China (1978–2006)

11.3.1 Decomposition of Labor Productivity

This chapter will use the shift-share analysis method to decompose the effect of structural change from the growth of labor productivity. Recent studies on the effects of structural change in emerging industrial economies and transition economies are mainly conducted by Fagerberg (2000), Peneder (2003), and Timmer and Szirmai (2000).

Let LP^t represent the total labor productivity of the economy, in which LP_i^t represents the labor productivity of each industry sector, the upper bid t represents period, the lower bid i represents different industry sectors, $i = 1, 2, 3$, represents the primary industry, the secondary industry and the tertiary industry respectively. LP_i^t represents the labor productivity of industry i in period t, and S_i^t represents the labor share of industry i in period t.

Total labor productivity can be expressed as:

$$LP^t = \frac{Y^t}{L^t} = \sum_{i=1}^{n} \frac{Y_i^t L_i^T}{L_i^T L^T} = \sum_{i=1}^{n} LP_i^t S_i^t \tag{11.1}$$

According to Eq. (11.1), it can be inferred that the growth rate of total labor productivity in period t to period 0 is as follows:

$$\frac{LP^t - LP^0}{LP^0} = \frac{\sum_{i=1}^{n} (S_i^t - S_i^0) LP_i^0 + \sum_{i=1}^{n} (LP_i^t - LP_i^0)(S_i^t - S_i^0) + \sum_{i=1}^{n} (LP_i^t - LP_i^0) S_i^0}{LP^0} \tag{11.2}$$

Equation (11.2) is decomposed into the following three terms:

I: The first item on the right-hand side of Eq. (11.2) is called static structural change effect. It measures the net increase of total labor productivity caused by the shift of labor factors from industries with low labor productivity to industries with high labor productivity. If the labor factor flows to the industry i with higher relative labor productivity, the change value of the share of the industry in period t is greater than 0, and the weight we give to it is also greater, so the static structure change effect of industry i is greater.

II: The second item on the right-hand side of Eq. (11.2) is called dynamic structural change effect. It is different from the first item. It shows the dynamic effect caused by the movement of labor factors. It measures the net increase of total labor productivity caused by the shift from industries with slower labor productivity growth to industries with faster labor productivity growth. If the labor factor flows to the industry i with higher productivity, the change value of the share of the industry in the period t is greater than 0, and the weight we give to it is also greater, so the dynamic structural change effect of the industry i is also greater.

III: The third item on the right-hand side of Eq. (11.2) is called productivity growth effect. It is the increase of labor productivity in various industries caused by the change of technological efficiency and technological progress in each industry.

11.3.2 Calculation of Structural Transition Effect

According to Eq. (11.2), we calculate the static structural change effect, dynamic structural change effect and productivity growth effect of China's overall economy and three industries (see Table 11.1).

The numerical values in Table 11.1 only have relative meaning. It is easier to understand when we convert Table 11.1 into a percentage form (denominators are the overall labor productivity growth rate) (see Table 11.2).

Table 11.1 Structural change effect matrix using transfer share analysis

Year 1978–2006	Sum of column		I Static structural transition effect	II Dynamic structural transition effect	III Intra-industry growth effect
Sum of row	4.98	=	0.50	1.42	3.06
			=	=	=
Primary industry	0.42		−0.11	−0.35	0.88
Secondary industry	2.45		0.22	0.70	1.53
Tertiary industry	2.12		0.39	1.07	0.65

Table 11.2 Structural change effect matrix using transfer share analysis (percentage form)

Year 1978–2006	Sum of column		I Static structural transition effect	II Dynamic structural transition effect	III Intra-industry growth effect
Sum of row	100	=	10.0 (e_1)	28.5 (e_2)	61.5 (e_3)
			=	=	=
Primary industry	8.5 (p_1)		−2.2 (x_{11})	−7.0 (x_{12})	17.7 (x_{13})
Secondary industry	49.1 (p_2)		4.4 (x_{21})	14.0 (x_{22})	30.7 (x_{23})
Tertiary industry	42.5 (p_3)		7.8 (x_{31})	21.6 (x_{32})	13.1 (x_{33})

Note Variables in brackets after a numerical value are used to denote its matrix variables

The conclusion is obvious. From Table 11.2, we can see that the sum of structural change effects accounts for 38.5% of the total labor productivity growth rate, but from the perspective of three industries, they are diverse from each other.

The effect of the structural change of the primary industry is negative, because the rural labor force is constantly migrating from the agricultural sector, and the labor share shows a negative change. However, compared with the effect of structural change, the productivity growth effect of the primary industry is more significant ($x_{13} > |x_{11} + x_{12}|$). That is to say, the labor share of the primary industry has decreased by 1%, while the labor productivity of the whole economy has increased by more than 1%. This shows that the internal system reform and technological progress of the primary industry have jointly promoted the improvement of labor productivity.

The value of structural change effect of the secondary industry is positive, but lower than the productivity growth effect of the secondary industry ($x_{23} > x_{21} + x_{22}$). This shows that the labor productivity growth of the secondary industry depends more on factors such as changes in intra-industry technical efficiency and technological progress, rather than on the optimal allocation of inter-industry factors. In other words, for the secondary industry, the increase of labor productivity caused by technological efficiency changes and technological progress is greater than that caused by the improvement of resource allocation efficiency due to structural changes.

The structural change effect of tertiary industry is the most significant. Because the tertiary industry has absorbed a large number of surplus labors from rural and agricultural areas, from about 50 million employed people in 1978 to about 250 million employed people in 2006, while the share of the working population has also risen from 12 to 32%. The transfer of surplus rural labors from the agricultural sector with low labor productivity and low per capita output value to the tertiary industry in cities. This kind of labor migration between industries has greatly liberated the productivity. Compared with the surplus labor force staying in the countryside, the combination of rural surplus labor force and tertiary industry has greatly improved and optimized the efficiency of resource allocation in China, and the improvement of rural surplus labor force labor productivity has also caused the increase of total economic labor productivity. From the horizontal comparison of the three effects of the tertiary industry, the productivity growth effect is lower than the structural change effect, which indicates that in the course of the reform and opening up in the past 28 years (1978–2006), the labor productivity growth of the tertiary industry mainly depends on the improvement of resource allocation efficiency caused by the structural change effect, rather than on the technological efficiency change and technological progress of various industries.

11.3.3 Contribution Rate[4] of Structural Change Effect and Its Trend

In order to analyze the contribution rate of structural change effect, we need to smooth the fluctuation of structural change effect. The method we used is to divide 1978–2006 into six periods, 1978–1985, 1985–1988, 1988–1991, 1991–1998, 1998–2002 and 2002–2006.[5] These periods represent several economic fluctuation cycles. This paper calculates the contribution rate of effect of structural change in each economic fluctuation cycle. In the period of economic fluctuation, calculating the effect of structural change smooths the fluctuation of the effect of structural change, so that the contribution rate of the effect of structural change can be measured. We calculate not only the contribution rate of the structural change effect of the economy as a whole, but also the contribution rate of the primary industry, the secondary industry and the tertiary industry respectively.

11.3.3.1 The Contribution Rate of the Structural Change Effect of the Economy as a Whole and the Primary Industry

Figure 11.2 shows the fluctuation trend of contribution rate of economic overall structural change effect. Although the contribution rate of the structural change effect is obviously volatile due to the macroeconomic impact, in the long run, the contribution rate of the overall structural change effect of the economy shows a declining trend. Before 1990, the contribution rate of structural change effect was 35–50%, and after

[4] We define the contribution rate as the proportion of the structural change effect to the growth rate of labor productivity when both the structural change effect and labor productivity are positive. When the effect of structural change is negative, or contrary to the positive or negative sign of the growth rate of labor productivity, the ratio of the effect of structural change to the growth rate of labor productivity becomes meaningless. When the effect of structural change is significantly negative, we assume that the contribution rate of the effect of structural change is zero.

[5] The reason for dividing these six time intervals is based on our judgment of the cyclical fluctuations of the economy from 1978 to 2006. We try to include the economic cycle in these time intervals so that we can analyze the relative contribution rate of structural change effect and productivity growth effect.

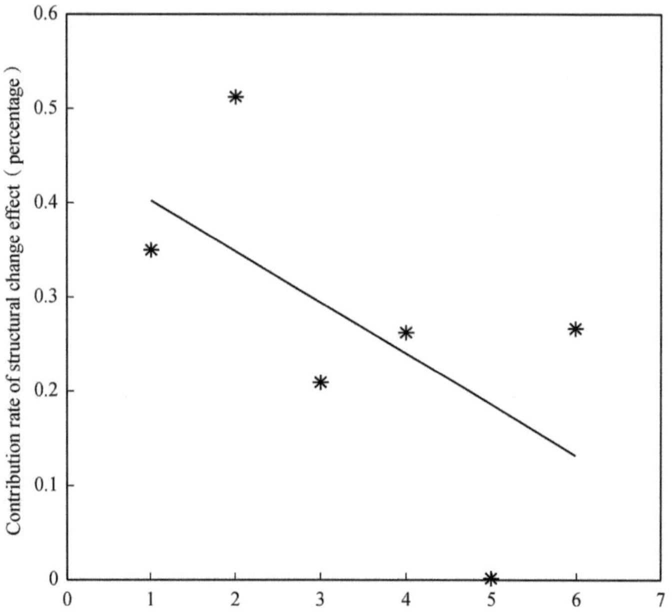

Fig. 11.2 Trends in the contribution rate of economic overall structural change effect

1990, the contribution rate of structural change effect was less than 30%. In the fifth period (1998–2002), the effect of structural change even tends to zero.

Table 11.3 shows the data of the structural change effect and productivity growth effect of the primary industry in six periods. Table 11.3 shows that in the 1980s, the growth of labor productivity in the primary industry was mainly due to the institutional change of agriculture (household contract responsibility system) from 1978 to 1985, which fully released the agricultural labor productivity in the fence of the original planned economic system, and the productivity growth effect reached 0.195. In 1985–1988 and 1988–1991, the labor productivity of the primary industry did not increase further on the basis of the growth caused by the reform in the original system. And the productivity growth effect was respectively only 0.010 and −0.020. Throughout the mid and late 1980s, the negative effect of the change in the first industrial structure indicates that in the process of industrialization, the employment share of the first industrial sector has decreased, and the surplus agricultural labor force has continuously shifted to the second and third industries.

During the economic downturn periods of 1988–1991 and 1998–2002, the effect of the primary industrial structure change is positive, indicating that the employment share of the primary industry has not declined, but is on the rise. Fortunately, after 1991, labor productivity in the primary industry has increased significantly. Especially in 1991–1998 and 2002–2006, the productivity growth effect of the primary industry basically reached or even exceeded the overall economic growth rate.

Table 11.3 The long-term trend of the structural change effect of primary industry

Cycle (years)	Labor productivity growth rate	Structural change effect	Productivity growth effect
1978–1985	0.140	−0.055	0.195
1985–1988	−0.004	−0.014	0.010
1988–1991	−0.019	0.001	−0.020
1991–1998	0.062	−0.061	0.123
1998–2002	0.014	0.001	0.013
2002–2006	0.047	−0.032	0.079

Because the positive and negative signs of the structural change effect and productivity growth effect of the primary industry are different, it is difficult to calculate the contribution rate of the structural change effect and productivity growth effect of the primary industry. In the case of normal economic growth (1978–1985, 1991–1998, 2002–2006), the growth rate of labor productivity in the primary industry is greater than zero, the effect of structural change is negative, and the effect of productivity growth is positive. This shows that for the primary industry, the increase of labor productivity caused by technological progress is greater than the decrease of labor productivity caused by structural change. Different from the secondary industry and the tertiary industry, if the labor productivity of the primary industry is greater than zero, it shows that the productivity growth effect is greater than the structural change effect, and it also shows that there are changes in technological progress and technological efficiency in the first industry.

11.3.3.2 The Trend of Contribution Rate of Structural Change Effect of Secondary Industry and Tertiary Industry

Similarly, we calculated the structural change effect and productivity growth effect of the secondary and tertiary industries in the six periods of 1978–1985, 1985–1988, 1988–1991, 1991–1998, 1998–2002 and 2002–2006, as well as their contribution rate to labor productivity growth, and plotted a histogram. Figure 11.3 is the contribution rate of the structural change effect of the secondary industry, and Fig. 11.4 is the contribution rate of the structural change effect of the tertiary industry.

Figures 11.3 and 11.4 show that during 1978–2006, the contribution rates of the structural change effect of the secondary and tertiary industries have gradually decreased.

Figure 11.3 shows the fluctuations of the contribution rate of the structural change effect of the secondary industry. If the contribution rate of the structural change effect of an industry is more than 50%, it shows that the increase of labor productivity in this industry is not mainly caused by technological progress and technological efficiency change in the industry, but mainly by the optimal allocation of resources. Before 1991 (1978–1985, 1985–1988, 1988–1991), the contribution rate of the structural

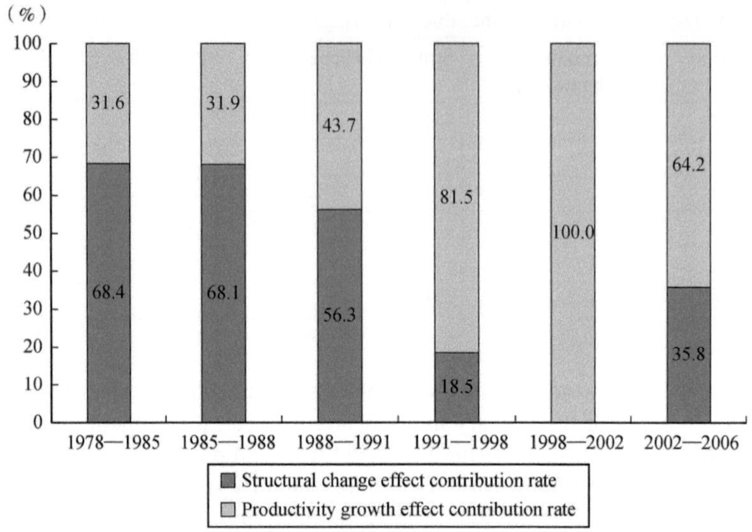

Fig. 11.3 Contribution rate of structural change effect of secondary industry. *Note* The sum of structural change effect (black column) and productivity growth effect (grey column) is the growth rate of labor productivity. The proportion of black column in the column indicates the relative importance of structural change effect

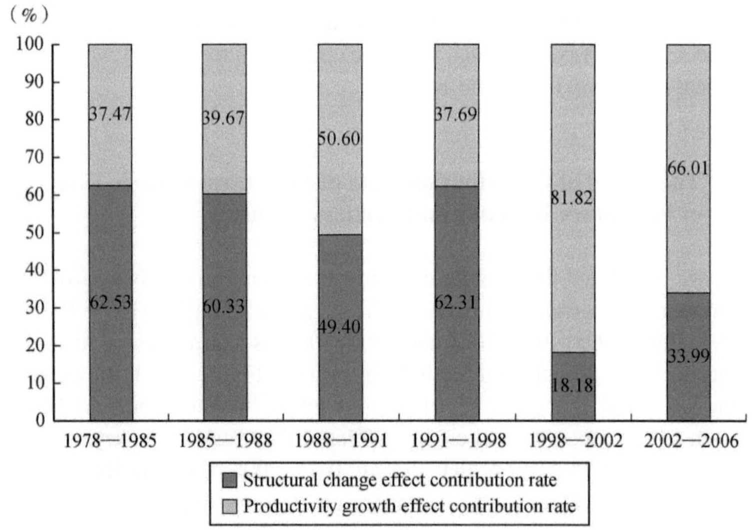

Fig. 11.4 Contribution rate of structural change effect of tertiary industry

change effect of the secondary industry was more than 50%. This shows that in the early period of the reform and opening up, because our market has just opened up, the labor productivity has increased rapidly due to the institutional change, and our country is in the era of shortage economy, so the economic growth at this time is basically a typical extensive growth driven by demand in shortage economy. When China's economy entered the 1990s, the contribution rate of the effect of structural change declined significantly, and the capital accumulation, technological research and development, and industrial upgrading of the secondary industry, especially industry, were put on the agenda. This is mainly due to the change in the economic situation in which supply exceeds demand. Finally, the demand was gradually met, while the market competition became more and more fierce. And this makes the enterprise no longer have broad profit space in the original completely extensive growth, and the enterprise has to find another development path. The most typical example of this situation is the deflation period from 1998 to 2002. The effect of structural change in the secondary industry is almost zero, while the effect of intra-industry productivity growth accounts for almost all of the share. This shows that during this period, the growth of labor productivity in the secondary industry is almost entirely dependent on the increase of intra-industry productivity, which is affected by the contraction of effective demand.

Compared with year 1991–1998 and year 2002–2006, the contribution rate of structural change effect is lower, which may not be consistent with our intuition. If they are not affected by economic cycles, the contribution rates of structural change effect should be descending. In this regard, we have two explanations: Firstly, year 1991–1998 is the basic period of capital accumulation and technological innovation in the secondary industry, especially in industry. And the marginal remuneration of capital accumulation and technological innovation is decreasing. Therefore, from 1991 to 1998, the contribution rate of productivity growth effect of secondary industry is 82%, while from 2002 to 2006, the contribution rate of productivity growth effect of secondary industry is 64%, the former is 18 percentage points higher than the latter. Secondly, the effect of structural change may be affected by the fluctuation of demand. The economic fluctuation between 1991 and 1998 is relatively large, such as inflation occurred in 1994 and signs of deflation began in 1998. While the economy from 2002 to 2006 is considered to be relatively stable and healthy growth. Therefore, the contribution rate of structural change effect from 2002 to 2006 is relatively high.

Figure 11.4 shows the fluctuations of the contribution rate of the change effect of the tertiary industrial structure. The fluctuations of the contribution rate of the structural change effect of the tertiary industry are similar to those of the secondary industry. Before 1991, except for the period of year 1988–1991, the effects of structural change and productivity growth were almost equal, the effects of structural change of tertiary industry were more than 60% in other periods. Unlike the secondary industry, the effect of structural change of the secondary industry is less than that of productivity growth, while that of the primary industry is greater than that of productivity growth in 1991–1998. We can infer that the transformation of the growth mode of the tertiary industry began in 1998. Before 1998, the tertiary industry was mainly

Table 11.4 Productivity growth effect and structural change effect of tertiary industry

Years	Labor productivity growth rate	Productivity growth effect	The structural change effect of tertiary industry
1978–1985	0.186	0.070	0.116
1985–1988	0.046	0.018	0.028
1988–1991	0.022	0.011	0.011
1991–1998	0.297	0.112	0.185
1998–2002	0.209	0.171	0.038
2002–2006	0.204	0.135	0.070

in the stage of extensive growth, and after 1998, it entered the stage of productivity growth.

From the situation during 1998–2002, the impact of deflation on economic growth is not always negative. The shrinkage of effective demand and the situation of over-supply make enterprises survive in the fierce market competition only by reducing production costs, improving technological efficiency and accelerating technological progress. Therefore, year 1998 may be the starting point for the tertiary industry to improve intra-industry technological efficiency, accelerate technological progress and change the mode of economic growth. Table 11.4 shows that the contribution rate of productivity growth effect of the tertiary industry is 82% in 1998–2002, which is the largest value of productivity growth effect in these six periods from 1978 to 2006. It shows that the time period which is from 1998 to 2002 is the period of the fastest growth of productivity in the tertiary industry during 28 years (1978–2006) (see Table 11.4).

11.4 Contribution of Structural Transformation to Total Factor Productivity Growth in China (1986–2002)

11.4.1 Decomposition Formula of Total Factor Productivity

In an unbalanced economy (unbalanced refers to the unequal marginal output of factors in different industrial sectors), the marginal productivity of factors in different industrial sectors is unequal. The flow of factors and resources between different sectors promotes the total factor productivity (TFP) of the economy as a whole. This is the role of industrial structural change in improving the efficiency of resource allocation and promoting economic growth. After deducting the growth of factor input, the total output growth of the economy can be divided into two parts: the growth of average total factor productivity of each industrial sector and the growth caused by structural changes.

Therefore, the basic method of calculating the effect of structural change is to compare the difference of TFP growth rate between aggregate level and sectoral level.[6] It is assumed that the production function is a differentiable function with constant returns to scale and neutral technological progress:

$$Y_i = f_i(K_i, L_i, t) \tag{11.3}$$

where, $i = 1, 2, 3$, means the first, second and third industries respectively, the growth rate of total output of each industry sector can be decomposed into:

$$G(Y_i) = \alpha_i G(K_i) + \beta_i G(L_i) + G(A_i) \tag{11.4}$$

where, $G(X) = (\mathrm{d}X/\mathrm{d}t)/X = \dot{X}/X$, $G(A_i)$ is the growth rate of TFP of i industry's total factor productivity, $\alpha_i = f(K_i)K_i/Y_i$ is the capital output elasticity of i industry, $\beta_i = f(L_i)L_i/Y_i$ is the labor output elasticity of i industry. Therefore, the total output growth rate $G(Y)$ expressed by sectoral variables is:

$$G(Y) = \frac{\mathrm{d}\left(\sum_i Y_i\right)}{Y} = \sum \rho_i G(Y_i) = \sum \rho_i \alpha_i G(K_i) + \sum \rho_i \beta_i G(L_i) + \sum \rho_i G(A_i) \tag{11.5}$$

where, $\rho_i = Y_i/Y$, which represents the share of the output value of each industry in the total output value. However, the growth rate of economic gross Y can also be expressed by economic gross variables:

$$G(Y) = \alpha G(K) + \beta G(L) + G(A) \tag{11.6}$$

where, $Y = \sum Y_i$, $K = \sum K_i$, $L = \sum L_i$, $\alpha = \sum \rho_i \alpha_i$, $\beta = \sum \rho_i \beta_i$, and $G(A)$ is the growth rate of TFP at the total level. The difference between the total TFP growth rate $G(A)$ and the sector TFP growth rate weighted average $\sum \rho_i G(A_i)$ is the contribution of structural change to economic growth, the effect of structural change. Therefore, the total structural effect (TSE) is equal to:

$$\mathrm{TSE} = G(A) - \sum \rho_i G(A_i) = \sum \rho_i \alpha_i G(k_i) + \sum \rho_i \beta_i G(l_i) \tag{11.7}$$

where, $k_i = K_i/K$, $l_i = L_i/L$ respectively indicate the share of capital and labor in the total capital and labor input of each industrial sector. The first term on the right-hand side of Eq. (11.5) shows the contribution of structural changes of labor factors to total factor productivity in various industrial sectors, and the second term shows the contribution of structural changes of capital factors to total factor productivity in various industrial sectors. In an unbalanced economy, the contribution of structural change to total factor productivity can be expressed as:

[6] Reference is made to the total factor productivity decomposition formula used by Syrquin (1984).

$$\text{TSE} = \frac{1}{Y}\sum \dot{K}_i[f(K_i) - f(K)] + \frac{1}{Y}\sum \dot{L}_i[f(L_i) - f(L)] = A(f_K) + A(f_L) \tag{11.8}$$

where, $f(K_i)$ and $f(L_i)$ respectively represent the marginal output of capital and labor in the i industrial sector, while $f(K)$ and $f(L)$ represent the marginal output of capital and labor in the overall economy.

$A(f_K)$ and $A(f_L)$ in Eq. (11.8) respectively represent the effect of industrial structure change in capital and labor factor markets, i.e., they represent the increase in total factor productivity caused by the flow of capital and labor between different sectors. The meaning of Eq. (11.8) is simple and clear: if the share of capital (labor) elements in industries that can achieve higher than average marginal remuneration ($f(K_i) - f(K) > 0$ or $f(L_i) - f(L) > 0$) increases rapidly, the structural change effect of capital (labor) is greater, whereas the share of capital (labor) elements in industries that achieve lower than average marginal remuneration ($f(K_i) - f(K) < 0$ or $f(L_i) - f(L) < 0$) is greater and the effect of capital (labor) structural change is small.

When the marginal output of capital and labor factors in different sectors of an economy tends to the same time, $A(f_K)$ and $A(f_L)$ tend to zero at the same time, and the total structural effect (TSE) will disappear. At this time, as shown in the Eqs. (11.3) and (11.4), the contribution of input from the perspective of aggregate and the weighted average contribution of input from different industrial sectors will be equal, while the TFP growth rate $G(A)$ from the perspective of aggregate and the weighted average value of TFP growth rate $\sum \rho_i G(A_i)$ from different industries will be equal.

When the marginal rewards of factors in different industries are not equal, those industries whose marginal rewards of factors are higher than the average level increase the share of capital (labor) factors, the contribution of total factor productivity of each industry will be underestimated by Eq. (11.3). The difference between Eqs. (11.4) and (11.3) is the structural change effect.

11.4.2 Data Description

In order to calculate the contribution rate of structural change effect in TFP growth rate, we need to calculate not only the numerical value of structural change effect, i.e., TSE based on Eq. (11.8), but also the TFP growth rate, i.e. $G(A)$ based on Eq. (11.6). The meanings of Eqs. (11.8) and (11.6) are simple and clear, but due to the limitations of data, it is not easy to calculate the contribution rate of structural change effect. The former requires us to know the stock variation of overall economy, capital, labor in various industries and their marginal remuneration, and the latter requires us to know the stock growth rate of overall economy, capital, labor in various industries and their output elasticity. So we face three tasks: First, calculating the marginal remuneration of overall economy, capital, labor in various industries; Second, calculating the output elasticity of overall economy, capital, labor in various industries; Third, calculating the stock and changes of overall economy, capital, labor in various industries. The output elasticity of capital and labor can be estimated directly by statistical regression method, and can also be calculated by the equation of output elasticity ($\alpha_i = f(K_i)K_i/Y_i$, is the output elasticity of capital, and $\beta_i = f(L_i)L_i/Y_i$ is the output elasticity of labor).[7] The two ways of calculating elasticity of factor output cut both ways. In order to maintain the consistency of the method and data, this paper uses elasticity equation to calculate the elasticity of factor output directly. Thus, three tasks become two: First, calculating the marginal remuneration of overall economy, capital, labor in various industries; Second, calculating the stock and changes of overall economy, capital, labor in various industries.

(1) We can find the remuneration of capital and labor in the gross domestic product income act. The "worker's remuneration" is the total remuneration of labor in the gross domestic product income approach, and the proportion of the "worker's remuneration" in the gross domestic product income approach is the output elasticity of labor; The sum of "net production tax", "operating surplus" and "depreciation of fixed assets" is the total capital income in the gross domestic product income approach. The proportion of the sum of "net production tax", "operating surplus" and "depreciation of fixed assets" in the gross domestic product income approach is the output elasticity of capital. It is noteworthy that in *China Statistical Yearbook*, there are only data tables of regional income approach of GDP, no tables of national income approach of GDP, and no national sub-industry income approach of GDP. The only data source is the national input–output table published by the National Bureau of Statistics (six tables in 1987, 1990, 1992, 1995, 1997 and 2002). We can find most of the data needed for analysis on these input–output tables.
(2) Two data are still missing in the analysis: the stock and increment of labor and the stock and increment of capital. Among them, the stock of labor, the increment of labor and the increment of capital (gross capital formation) can be easily found in *China Statistical Yearbook*, or can be obtained by simple calculus. However, the calculation of capital stock is a big problem. Here, we quote the conclusion of Xue (2007). This paper estimates the capital stock on the basis of the input–output table, which is consistent with the data used in this book.[8]

11.4.3 Solution and Analysis of Structural Transition Effect

In order to analyze the relative contribution of industrial structure change to economic growth, the Eq. (11.8) can be rephrased by combining Eqs. (11.4) and (11.5) as:

---

[7] If we know the marginal return $f(K_i)$ of capital and the capital stock K_i, we can calculate the output elasticity of capital.

[8] Xue (2007) estimated the capital stock to 2000. On his basis, we calculated the capital capital stock in 2001 and 2002 through the method of perpetual inventory method.

$$G(Y) = \alpha G(K) + \beta G(L) + \sum \rho_i G(A_i) + \text{TSE} \tag{11.9}$$

In Eq. (11.9), GDP growth is divided into four parts: (1) Contribution of capital input growth $\alpha G(K)$; ; (2) The contribution of labor input growth $\beta G(L)$; ; (3) The weighted average value of contribution of technical advance of various industries $\sum \rho_i G(A_i)$, which we call "net technical advance effect"; (4)The effect of industrial structure change. Total factor productivity is divided into two parts: the effect of technical advance and the effect of industrial structure change. There are four terms in the initial input table of the national input–output table: remuneration of workers, net production tax, business surplus and depreciation of fixed assets. The first one is the total remuneration of labor $f(L_i)L_i$, and then the sum of the three is the total remuneration of capital $f(K_i)K_i$. By introducing the data of capital stock Ki and labor stock Li, we can calculate the marginal remuneration of capital $f(K_i)$ and the marginal remuneration of labor $f(L_i)$. Using these data, the results as shown in Table 11.5 can be calculated.

Table 11.5 clearly shows the contribution of various factors of economic growth. As Krugman (1994) said in his article "The Myth of the Asian Miracle", the economic growth of most East Asian countries and regions mainly depends on increasing investment. Many scholars have questioned Krugman's research. We believe that in the cross-border data comparison, although the traditional total factor productivity calculation method cannot adequately measure the improvement of resource allocation efficiency and technological progress, it can still show the fluctuation law of the contribution share of factor input growth and total factor productivity growth to a country's economic growth in the comparison of time series data, and it also does not prevent us from explaining the impact law of industrial structure changes and technical advance to the economic growth. Liu and Cai (2008) studied the impact of technical advance and industrial structure on economic growth efficiency reflected

Table 11.5 Contribution rate of various factors to economic growth rate (percentages)

Year	Contribution rate of labor growth	Contribution rate of capital growth	Contribution rate of total factor productivity growth	Among	
				The effect of industrial structure change	Net technical advance effect
1986–1990[a]	10.7	84.2	5.1	–	–
1990–1992	9.1	79.5	11.4	58.2	41.8
1992–1995	5.9	80.4	13.7	42.3	57.7
1995–1997	5.6	74.3	20.1	34.9	65.1
1997–2002	3.5	68.0	28.5	11.3	88.7

Note [a]Due to lack of data, we did not use the input–output table of 1987 and only calculated the structural effects of 1990–2002. The result from 1986 to 1990, we borrowed the conclusion of Zhang (1991), was here as a reference. But Zhang Junkuan's article did not calculate the effect of industrial structure change and net technological progress effect by intermediate consumption rate from 1992 to 2005 through dynamic comparative analysis of direct consumption coefficient matrix in China's input–output table. The research conclusion shows that after the mid-1990s, the changes of industrial structure have not made a significant contribution to the economic growth efficiency reflected by the intermediate consumption rate. This also supports the point of view of this paper from another angle: many Asian emerging market countries, including China, are generally in the early stage of industrialization, which relies more on factor input and per capita capital stock growth; with the deepening of industrialization, China's economic growth will depend more on the improvement of total factor productivity. In Table 11.5, the dynamic change process, an overall downward trend of the contribution rate of labor and an overall upward trend of total factor productivity contribution rate in China's economic growth, shows the inner source of sustainable and high-speed economic growth in China. As long as we can seal a place in the fields of new technologies and industries in future economic growth, the economic growth of emerging market-oriented countries will remain sustainable.

From 1990 to 2002, we can see two trends: (1) The contribution rate of factor input growth and total factor productivity growth shows a trend of one falls another rises (although the contribution of capital input is not always rising); (2) Within the total factor productivity, the effects of industrial structure change and effects of net technical advance shows a trend of one falls another rises. The former is similar to Chenery's (1986) study of all industrialized countries; The latter draws a conclusion similar to that in the decomposition analysis of labor productivity, which is also the most important conclusion in this chapter: the contribution of market forces represented by industrial structure changes to China's long-term economic growth is gradually giving way to the power of technical advance.

11.5 Trend Analysis of the Contribution of Structural Efficiency to Economic Growth

Why is the promoting role of industrial structural change in economic growth weakening and why is the contribution rate of structural change effect declining? If we compare the effect of structural change to the potential energy formed by the gap[9] between inefficient allocation of resources and efficient allocation of resources, the main body of this potential energy is the "invisible hand" of the market. With the decreasing gap of resource allocation efficiency, the potential energy released in the process of industrial structural change (the effect of structural change) will gradually decrease.

The analysis below will show that the gap in resource allocation efficiency is indeed narrowing-the marginal returns of factors in different industries are

[9] Such a gap may be caused by institutional factors, such as the imbalance of the proportion of heavy and light industries in the planned economy, or by development factors, such as the gap between agricultural and industrial productivity before the industrial revolution in developed countries.

converging. However, due to some historical reasons, it is difficult to bridge the gap of factor allocation efficiency at some levels in a short period of time. Due to some institutional factors, factors appear the phenomenon of "anti-efficiency allocation": there is over-allocation of capital in the secondary industry, capital is "squeezing out" of labor, there is over-allocation of labor in the tertiary industry, and labor productivity is low. These anti-efficiency resource allocation methods not only make the existing gap of resource allocation efficiency not be well utilized, but also enlarge the gap of resource allocation efficiency.

This conclusion indicates, on the one hand, that the gap in resource allocation efficiency in China's economic reality has not disappeared, and the potential for future economic growth in China is still very huge. On the other hand, it also shows that the work to eliminate anti-market factors and improve market mechanisms is still arduous and far-reaching.

11.5.1 Development and Institutional Reasons for the Persistence of the Gap in Resource Allocation Efficiency

There are mainly developmental and institutional reasons why the gap in resource allocation efficiency will persist:

(1) The difference of urban–rural dual structure is an important reason for persistence of the gap in resource allocation efficiency. Due to the persistence of dual economic structure in urban and rural areas, on the one hand, the surplus rural labor force presents an "infinite supply" state, and the labor price remains at a relatively low level; on the other hand, the social demand is slowly growing due to the restriction of per capita income growth, so it still needs a long process to digest almost unlimited surplus rural labor force at a lower level of labor price. Therefore, this change in employment structure will persist, which is the same for all countries in the process of urbanization and industrialization.

(2) China's market-oriented reform is a gradual reform, which makes the market mechanism gradually release its enormous role. In the process of the reform and opening up, the product market is first liberalized, and then the factor market is liberalized, which makes the optimal allocation function of market mechanism play a role in stages and gradually. Even if the market is completely liberalized, the fully effective market only exists in theory. In reality, there are always various defects and obstacles in the market.

11.5.2 Counter-efficiency Allocation of Elements and Its Reasons

Using the input–output tables of 1992 and 2002, we calculate the share of capital and labor in each industry, the marginal remuneration of capital and labor in each industry, and the ratio of capital to labor and labor productivity in each industry. The results of Tables 11.6, 11.7 and 11.8 show roughly the state of resource anti-allocation efficiency in each industry. These anti-efficiency resource allocation not only makes the existing gap of resource allocation efficiency not well utilized, but also enlarges the gap of resource allocation efficiency.

Table 11.6 shows that, with the change in capital share, the capital share of primary industry and tertiary industry is declining, while the capital input share of secondary industry is on the rise (columns 3 and 4), which indicates that capital is concentrated in the secondary industry (mainly includes industry), new capital is mainly formed

Table 11.6 Structural change of capital

Item	Changes in capital input (RMB100 million)	Share of capital input in 1992 (%)	Share of capital input in 2002 (%)	Marginal return on capital in 1992 (RMB/1 capital)	Marginal return on capital in 2002 (RMB/1 capital)
Overall economy	91780.1	100	100	0.3359	0.2449
Primary industry	3073.4	5.1	3.9	0.4131	0.3309
Secondary industry	45215.0	38.9	46.1	0.4975	0.2753
Tertiary industry	43491.6	56.0	50.0	0.2166	0.2102

Table 11.7 Structural change of labor elements

Item	Changes in labor input (10,000 people)	Share of labor input in 1992 (%)	Share of labor input in 2002 (%)	Marginal remuneration for labor in 1992 (RMB/person)	Marginal remuneration for work in 2002 (RMB/person)
Economic overall	7588	100.0	100.0	1712	4127
Primary industry	−1829	58.5	50.0	1197	1865
Secondary industry	1425	21.7	21.4	2462	7367
Tertiary industry	7992	19.8	28.6	2412	5659

Table 11.8 Capital-labor ratio and labor productivity (RMB10,000/person)

Item	Capital-labor ratio		Labor productivity	
	Year		Year	
	1992	2002	1992	2002
Economic overall	0.62	1.80	3786	8532
Primary industry	0.05	0.14	1421	2329
Secondary industry	1.11	3.87	7964	18,027
Tertiary industry	1.74	3.15	6191	12,271

in the secondary industry, and even part of old capital is transferring to the secondary industry. In addition, the overall economy and the marginal return on capital of the three major industries are generally declining. Since the marginal return on capital here is close to the gross profit rate, it can be considered that the gross profit rate of capital is generally declining, which is consistent with the conclusion[10] of some studies. Among them, the gross profit margin in the secondary industry has fallen most rapidly. It fell from first to second place in terms of gross margin in 1992. The marginal return of capital in the primary industry also decreased significantly but at a relatively slower pace. Besides, gross profit margins in the primary industry have fallen the least, to almost the same level, but have been lower than those in the primary and secondary industry's.

From the perspective of the change of marginal return on capital, the deepening of capital in secondary industry, especially in industry, accelerates, and the ratio of capital output increases too fast, which leads to the decline of marginal return on capital too fast. This phenomenon leads to two results: (1) The marginal return of capital decreases too fast, which will slow down the growth of investment demand and may decrease the growth rate of output.[11] (2) If the capital of the industrial sector deepens too fast, each unit of capital can only drive less labor in the new additional output, which will lead to a continuous decline in the share of employment driven by the secondary industry (see Table 11.7).

Table 11.7 shows that the labor share of the primary industry has declined significantly, which indicates that the labor factors are flowing from rural areas to the secondary and tertiary industries in cities, which is naturally the result of China's urbanization and industrialization. However, the labor share of the secondary industry has declined slightly, which also confirms the conclusion of Table 11.7: the speed of absorbing labor in the secondary industry is declining, and capital may be squeezing out labor.

[10] Tang (1999) found that China's average profit margin growth rate is −0.5%, that is, the average profit margin of capital is declining. Tang (1999) calculated net profit margin, but depreciation rate and tax rate did not change significantly, gross profit margin also declined.

[11] Zhang (2002) believed that the rapid deepening of capital led to the acceleration of the decline of marginal return of capital, which was the main reason for the decline of GDP growth rate in the middle and late 1990s.

From the perspective of the marginal remuneration of labor, the gap of the marginal remuneration of labor in different industries is widening. The marginal remuneration of labor in the secondary industry has tripled, and the marginal remuneration of labor in the tertiary industry has doubled, while the increase of marginal labor remuneration in the primary industry is very small.

Table 11.8 shows that during 1992–2002, the capital-labor ratio of the tertiary industry increased significantly, from below the secondary industry to higher than the secondary industry, indicating that the tertiary industry has a strong ability to absorb labor. If the capital of the secondary industry squeezes out the labor, then the labor of the tertiary industry "squeezes out" the capital relatively. From 1992 to 2002, the employment elasticity of the tertiary industry was 0.278, while that of the secondary industry was 0.067. The ability of the tertiary industry to create employment was about four times that of the secondary industry.

In addition, Table 11.8 shows that the growth speed of productivity of labour in the tertiary industry is low, and its growth speed is only 2/3 of that in the secondary industry. Combining with the analysis of the third part, we can see that the growth of productivity of labor in the tertiary industry depends too much on scale expansion, and its technology and capital intensities need to be improved.

Of course, the reasons for the anti-efficiency allocation of elements of factors are very complex, mainly because the market system of China still needs to be improved. First of all, from the macro level, although the price of ordinary commodities can be freely priced, the free pricing of capital and labor factors is still subject to considerable restrictions. Secondly, from the micro level, property rights reform is still in the process of deepening.

11.6 Conclusion

This chapter uses the labor productivity decomposition and total factor productivity decomposition to measure the contribution of industrial structure change to economic growth, and compares it with the contribution of technological progress to economic growth. Research shows that since the reform and opening up, the impact of industrial structure changes on China's economic growth is very significant, but with the improvement of China's market-oriented degree, the role of industrial structure changes in facilitating economic growth is weakening. In the 1980s, the contribution rate of structural change effect was more than 50%. The contribution of industrial structure change to economic growth even exceeded that of technological progress. In the early and middle 1990s, the contribution to economic growth of industrial structure changes and technological progress was basically equal. Since 1998, the contribution of industrial structure changes to economic growth has become less and less significant, gradually giving way to technological progress, that is, the market forces represented by industrial structure changes have gradually given way to the forces of technological progress. Thus, Krugman's (1994) unsustainable growth model in East Asia is similar to that of China before 1998. However, in the process of China's economic growth after 1998, on the one hand, the contribution rate of factor input is gradually decreasing while the contribution rate of total factor productivity growth is constantly increasing; on the other hand, within the total factor productivity, the effect of industrial structure change and net technological progress also shows the ebb and flow of the relationship. Thus, after 1998, China's economic growth model has increasingly reflected its own sustainability. Of course, since 1998, implementing the scientific concept of development, transforming the mode of growth and enhancing the ability of technological innovation is not going to be a simple slogan for China anymore, but the only way to achieve the long-term sustained growth of China's economy.

This chapter also finds that the weakening of the contribution of industrial structure changes to China's economic growth does not mean that the benefits of market-oriented reform will return to zero. Several factors of development and system will also make it difficult for market mechanism to fully and effectively play its role. These factors of development and system not only show that the potential of China's economic growth in the future is still enormous, but also show that China's efforts to improve market mechanism will continue.

References

Bai X, Zhao S (1995) Brief discussion on measurement indicators of inter-regional industrial structure differences. Jiangsu Stat (12)

Bartlett B, Roth TP (1983) Introduction. In: Bartlett B, Roth TP (eds) The supply-side solution. MacMillan Publishers Ltd, London

Baxter M (1992) Fiscal policy, specialization, and trade in the two-sector model: the return of Ricardo?. J Polit Econ

Cai Z (2003) Connection between the national and regional data of expenditure approach of GDP. Econ Sci (4)

Chen L (1996) A review of the western traditional business cycle theory. Res Fin Econ Issues (6)

Chen J (2007) Report on the industrialization process of china: evaluation and research on industrialization level of Chinese provinces from 1995 to 2005. Social Sciences Academic Press (China), Beijing

Chen D et al (1981) History of political economy. Jilin People's Press, Changchun

Chenery HB, Syrquin M (1977) Patterns of development: 1955–1975. Oxford University Press

Chenery HB, Elkington H (1979) Structural change and development policy. Oxford University Press

Cheng R, Lu E (2001) Preliminary study on statistical indexes of industrial structure optimization and upgrading. China Stat (7)

Chenery HB, Robinson S, Syrquin M (1986) Industrialization and growth: a comparative study. Oxford University Press

China Center for National Accounting and Economic Growth (2003) Analysis of China's economic trend from 2003 to 2004. Econ Sci (6)

China Center for National Accounting and Economic Growth (2004a) China economic growth report 2004. China Economic Publishing House, Beijing

China Center for National Accounting and Economic Growth (2004b) China economic growth report 2004. China Financial & Economic Publishing House, Beijing

China Center for National Accounting and Economic Growth (2005) China economic growth report 2005. China Financial & Economic Publishing House, Beijing

China Center for National Accounting and Economic Growth (2006) China economic growth report 2006. China Economic Publishing House, Beijing

Dasgupta P, Stiglitz J (1980) Uncertainty, industrial structure and the speed of R&D. Bell J Econ

Fagerberg J (2000) Technological progress, structural change and productivity growth: a comparative study. Struct Chang Econ Dyn 11:393–411

Fan S, Zhang X (2002) China's economic growth and structural adjustment. China Econ Q (10)

Gang F et al (2001) Report on marketization process in various regions of China 2000. J Chin Acad Gov (3)

W. Liu, *Research on China's Market Economy Development*,
https://doi.org/10.1007/978-981-97-1398-1

Gong Y (2002) Industrial structure research. Shanghai University of Finance & Economics Press, Shanghai
Guo K (1990) On the content of industrial structure elevation. China Ind Econ (3)
Guo D (2001) How long will it take to catch up with that. In: Cao Z (ed) Resuscitation: China economic annual report. Lanzhou Univerisy Press, Lanzhou
International Statistical Information Centre of the National Bureau of Statistics (2001) International economic information, no 20
International Statistical Information Centre of the National Bureau of Statistics (2002). International economic information, no 3
Johansen L (1961) A method for separating the effects of capital accumulation and shifts in production functions upon growth in labor productivity. Econ J 71:775–782
Keynes JM (1983) The general theory of employment, interest and money. The Commercial Press, Beijing
Krugman P (1994) The myth of Asia's miracle: a cautionary fable. Foreign Aff 73:62–78
Kumar S, Russell R (2002) Technological change, technological catch-up and capital deepening: relative contributions to growth and convergence. Am Econ Rev 92(3):527–548
Kuznels S (1957) Quantitative aspects of the economic growth of nations: industrial distribution of national product and labor force. Econ Dev Cult Change 5(7), Supplement
Kwon JK, Paik H (1995) Factor price distortions, resource allocation, and growth: a computable general equilibrium analysis. Rev Econ Stat
Laffer AB (1983a) Foundations of supply-side economics: theory and evidence. Academic Press, New York
Laffer AB (1983b) Introduction. In: Canto VA, Joines DH, Laffer AB (eds) Foundations of supply-side economics: theory and evidence. Academic Press, New York
Li Y (1998) Unbalanced Chinese economy. Guangdong Economy Publishing House, Guangzhou
Li J (1999) The forecast and analysis of China's economic development in the 21st century (2000—2050). In: Zhang Z (ed) Expert discussion on economic issues in 21st century China. Henan People's Publishing House, Zhengzhou
Li X, et al (2003) China market economy development report. Foreign Economic and Trade Publishing House, Beijing
Li X, et al (2005) China market economy development report. Foreign Economic and Trade Publishing House, Beijing
Li X, et al (2008) China market economy development report. Foreign Economic and Trade Publishing House, Beijing
Lin JY (1999) Looking forward to the Chinese economy in the new millennium. In: Zhang Z (ed) Expert discussion on economic issues in 21st century China. Henan People's Publishing House, Zhengzhou
Liu W (1995a) Research on industrial structure in the process of industrialization. China Renmin University Press, Beijing
Liu W (1995b) Study on the industrial structure in the accelerated period of industrialization. China Renmin University Press, Beijing
Liu W (1999) Explanation of property right system of economic reform and development. Capital University of Economics and Business Press, Beijing
Liu W (2003) Why economics should study value?. Econ Theory Bus Manage (5)
Liu W (2006) What kind of historical value orientation should be used to understand and promote reform. Econ Perspect (5)
Liu W (2007a) New characteristics of macro-economic imbalance in China [J]. J Party Central Committee CPC (Chin Acad Gov) (1)
Liu W (2007b) The new characteristics of macro-economic imbalance in China. J Party School Central Committee CPC (Chin Acad Gov) (1)
Liu W, Cai Z (2004) Anti-cyclical force in the macro-control of macro-control. Econ Sci (2)
Liu W, Cai Z (2008) Technological progress, structural change and improvement of intermediate consumption in the national economy. Econ Res J (4)

Liu W, Li F (1998) General theory of property rights. Beijing Publishing Group, Beijing
Liu W, Li S (2001a) Change of ownership, economic equilibrium growth and factor efficiency improvement. Econ Res J (1)
Liu W, Li S (2001b) Ownership change and economic growth and factor efficiency improvement. Econ Res J (1)
Liu W, Li S (2002) Industrial structure and economic growth. China Ind Econ (5)
Liu W, Ping X (1990) Three theories of economic reform: property right theory, market theory, equilibrium theory. Peking University Press, Beijing
Liu W, Su J (2007) Supply management and macro-control at the present stage. Econ Res J (2)
Liu W, Zhang H (2008) Changes in industrial structure and technological progress in China's economic growth. Econ Res J (11)
Liu G et al (1998) Research on the model of China's economic system reform. Guangdong Economy Publishing House, Guangzhou
Liu W, Huang G, Li S (2002) Investigation on the history of ownership change in china during the transition period. J Peking Univ (Philos Soc Sci) (1)
Liu W, Li S, Huang G, Gai W (2003a) Economic analysis of the development of manufacturing industry in Beijing. China Ind Econ (3)
Liu W, Li S, Huang G, Gai W (2003b) Economic structure analysis of Beijing. China Ind Econ (1)
Liu W, Zhang H, Huang Z (2008) Investigation of the altitude of China's economic and industrial structure and the process of industrialization and regional differences. Econ Perspect (11)
Liu W, Xu X, Cai Z (2004) China's economic growth from the long-term development strategy. J Manage World (7)
Lun R (2005) Basic evaluation of industrial structure elevation. Jiangsu Soc Sci (2)
Luo R (2005) Looking at the income gap of residents from the Gini coefficient. Stat Obs (6)
Macro Group of China Center for Economic Research of Peking University (1989) Monetary policy? Fiscal policy?:Comments on China's macro-economic policy and suggestions for growth. Econ Res J (10). http://www.cenet.org.cn/cn/ReadNews.asp?NewsID=14516
Macro Group of China Center for Economic Research of Peking University (2005) Research on preventing deflation and maintaining rapid economic growth. Peking University Press, Beijing
Marx K (1970a) Das Kapital, vol 3. People's Publishing House, Beijing
Marx K (1970b) Das Kapital, vol 1. People's Publishing House, Beijing
Massel BF (1961) A disaggregated view of technical change. J Polit Econ 69:547–557
National Bureau of Statistcs (2004) China statistical yearbook. China Statistics Press, Beijing
National Bureau of Statistics. China statistical yearbook. China Statistics Press, Beijing, over the years
Paci R, Pigliaru F (1997) Structural change and convergence: an Italian regional perspective. Struct Chang Econ Dyn 8:297–318
Pan W, Chen S (1994) Quantitative measurement of industrial structure elevation and rationalization. Res Dev (1)
Peneder M (2003) Industrial structure and aggregate growth. Struct Chang Econ Dyn 14:427–448
Pilat D (1993) The sectoral productivity performance of Japan and the US: 1885–1990. Rev Income Wealth 39:357–375
Romer D (2000) Advanced macroeconomics. McGraw-Hill, Boston
Singh L (2004) Technological progress, structural change and productivity growth in manufacturing sector of South Korea. World Rev Sci Tech Sustain Dev 1:37–49
Solow RM (1957) Technical change and the aggregate production function. Rev Econ Stat 39
Song J (2000) On the measurement of the optimization and upgrading of industrial. Mod Econ Sci (5)
Sonobe T, Otsuka K (2001) A new decomposition approach to growth accounting: derivation of the formula and its application to prewar Japan. Japan World Econ 13:1–14
Su J (1998) Lowering interest rate helps to solve the problem of unemployment in China?. Econ Res J (10)

Syrquin M (1984) Resource allocation and productivity growth. In: Syrquin M, Taylor L, Westphal LE (eds) Economic structure performance essays in honor of Hollis B. Chenery. Academic Press, pp 75–101.

Syrquin M (1986) Productivity growth and factor reallocation, industrialization and growth a comparative study. Oxford University Press, pp 229–262

Tang Z (1999) Estimates of average profit margins in China. Econ Res J (5)

Tatom JA (1983) We are all supply-siders now. In: Bartlett B, Roth TP (eds) The supply-side solution. MacMillan Publishers Ltd., London

The World Bank (1989) World development report 1989. China Financial & Economic Publishing House, Beijing

Timmer PM, Szirmai A (2000) Productivity growth in Asian manufacturing: the structural bonus hypothesis examined. Struct Change Econ Dyn 2000(11):371–392

World Bank (1983) World development report. China Financial & Economic Publishing House, Beijing

World Bank (1985) World development report. China Financial & Economic Publishing House, Beijing

World Bank (2000) World development report for the 21st century: 1999/2000. China Financial & Economic Publishing House, Beijing

Wu J et al (1998) On competitive market system. Guangdong Economy Publishing House, Guangzhou

Xu X (1999) The World Bank's calculation method of per capita GNP. Econ Highlights

Xue J (2007) Accounting research on capital stock of 17 departments in China. Stat Res (7)

Yan Z (2001) A new exploration pf labor theory of value. Peking University Press, Beijing

Yin B, Hua G (1996) Supply-side school. Wuhan Publishing House, Wuhan

Zhang J (1991) Comprehensive analysis of economic benefits during the seventh five-year plan period: a calculation of the contribution rate of various factors to economic growth. Econ Res J (4)

Zhang J (2002) Growth, capital formation and technological choice: explaining the long-term factors of China's economic growth decline. China Econ Q (1)

Zhou C, Wei J (2007) Measurement model and empirical analysis of industrial structure level. Shanghai J Econ (6)

Zhou L, Yang Y, Liu W (1987) Promoting development and reform with industrial policy. Econ Res J (3)

Zhu Z (2004) The economic growth significantly weakened employment promotion. China Youth

MIX
Papier aus verantwortungsvollen Quellen
Paper from responsible sources
FSC® C105338
FSC
www.fsc.org

If you have any concerns about our products,
you can contact us on
ProductSafety@springernature.com

In case Publisher is established outside the EU,
the EU authorized representative is:
Springer Nature Customer Service Center GmbH
Europaplatz 3, 69115 Heidelberg, Germany

Printed by Libri Plureos GmbH
in Hamburg, Germany